Penguin Plays
Classic Irish Drama

William Butler Yeats, the Irish dramatist, poet,
autobiographer, critic and occult philosopher, was born in
1865. At the age of nineteen he attended an art school in
Dublin, but already his central interest was in writing.
In 1899, under the patronage of Lady Gregory he founded
the Irish Literary Theatre with Edward Martyn. In 1904
this became the famous Abbey Theatre. His *Collected Plays*
were published posthumously in 1953, and only *Cathleen ni
Houlihan* was popular in Ireland. Towards the end of his
life he enjoyed many honours, including the Nobel Prize and
membership of the Irish Senate. He died in France in 1939.

John Millington Synge was born in 1871 of an old
Anglo-Irish family. Due to ill-health he was educated mainly
by private tutors before going to Trinity College, Dublin. In
1895 he went to Paris and in the following year met W. B.
Yeats and consequently joined the Irish League. He was
first a literary adviser and then a director of the Abbey
Theatre, and his own plays appeared in repertory. Among
these are *In the Shadow of the Glen*, *Riders to the Sea* and
The Well of Saints. He died after a long illness in 1909.

Sean O'Casey was born in Dublin in 1880 of a poor
Protestant family and was thus largely self-educated. In
1926 he moved to England, where he lived in exile. He
discouraged any professional performances of his plays in
Ireland after the Archbishop of Dublin refused to inaugurate
the Dublin festival if O'Casey's play *The Drums of Father
Ned* was included (1958). His attempts at experimental
drama were not well received in Ireland. Among these are
The Flying Wasp, *The Bishop's Bonfire* and *Juno and the
Paycock*. He died in 1964.

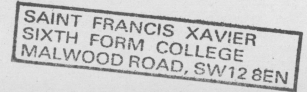

Classic Irish Drama

Introduced by W. A. Armstrong

The Countess Cathleen
W. B. Yeats

The Playboy of the
Western World
J. M. Synge

Cock-a-doodle Dandy
Sean O'Casey

 Penguin Books

Penguin Books Ltd, Harmondsworth, Middlesex, England
Penguin Books, 40 West 23rd Street, New York, New York 10010, U.S.A.
Penguin Books Australia Ltd, Ringwood, Victoria, Australia
Penguin Books Canada Ltd, 2801 John Street, Markham, Ontario, Canada L3R 1B4
Penguin Books (N.Z.) Ltd, 182–190 Wairau Road, Auckland 10, New Zealand

The Countess Cathleen. First published by T. Fisher Unwin 1892.
Reprinted in this edition from *The Collected Plays of W. B. Yeats*
by permission of Mrs W. B. Yeats and Macmillan & Co. Ltd

The Playboy of the Western World. First published by
Maunsel & Co., Dublin, 1907

Cock-a-Doodle Dandy. First published by Macmillan 1949.
Reprinted in this edition from *The Collected Plays of Sean O'Casey*, Vol. 4,
by permission of the author and Macmillan & Co. Ltd

This selection first published in Penguin Books 1964
Reprinted 1967, 1970, 1971, 1973, 1975, 1977, 1978, 1979, 1981, 1984

Made and printed in Singapore by Richard Clay (SE Asia) Pte Ltd
Set in Monotype Scotch Roman

Contents

Acknowledgements

I am very grateful to Professor W. S. Maguinness and Dr A. J. Gossage of King's College, London, and to Messrs R. B. D. French and B. Kennelly of Trinity College, Dublin, who have kindly helped me to elucidate some of the more difficult passages and allusions in *Cock-a-doodle Dandy*.

W.A.A.

The Irish Dramatic Movement

Deep in the Celtic soul is the image of a hero who seems to be defeated but is not defeated. In a favourite Irish myth, the mortally-wounded Cuchulain ties himself to a rock to die standing, and, laughing at a raven slipping in the blood from his wounds, triumphs over death. Charles Stewart Parnell became a hero of the same archetypal kind. His party crumbled beneath him when he was on the verge of winning Home Rule for Ireland in 1890; a few months later, he was dead. Yet Parnell lived on as a hero in the minds of the younger generation of Irishmen and the lull in political activity which followed his death gave them the time and the opportunity to imagine and strive for a completer natural unity than any known in Ireland before or after Strongbow's invasion in 1169 began the long centuries of English domination.

One way of working for unity was to revive the ancient Irish language and publish translations of its myths, legends, and folk-lore. Douglas Hyde founded the Gaelic League for this purpose in 1893, and in the same year he published *Love-Songs of Connacht*, a work which revealed the distinctive qualities not only of Gaelic poetry but of the Irish English into which he had translated it, and encouraged Lady Augusta Gregory and J. M. Synge to use the English spoken in the west of Ireland as a medium for drama. To W. B. Yeats, the prime founder of the Irish Dramatic Movement, the cultural unity of his nation was especially to be created by dramatizing Irish myths and legends and by their performance awakening heroic passions dormant in the racial memory. The thesis of this brief essay is that the finest plays of the Irish Dramatic Movement have remained true to this desire to reveal to Ireland her better or inner self, and that they have done so either by making ancient myths strike chords in the modern

consciousness, or by transmuting the historical or the local
or the topical into the archetypal by the use of significant
characters, allusions, or symbols.

In 1898, Yeats, Edward Martyn, George Moore, and
Lady Gregory founded the Irish Literary Theatre, and in
1899 its work began with a performance of Yeats's *The
Countess Cathleen* on 9 May and Martyn's *The Heather
Field* on 10 May. Both were acted by English players because no suitable Irish company was available. In 1900
and 1901, English players were again imported to give a
few performances. In 1902, however, an important development took place when a company of gifted Irish amateur
actors, headed by Frank and William G. Fay, joined forces
with Yeats and Lady Gregory to form the Irish National
Theatre Society. In 1903 the Society presented some of
its plays in London. These performances were greatly
admired, particularly by a wealthy English Quaker, Miss
A. F. Horniman, who bought the Mechanics' Institute in
Dublin in 1904, converted it into the Abbey Theatre, and
gave the Society the free use of it, together with an annual
subsidy.

Despite its growing fame, the Society encountered
various types of opposition and difficulty. In 1907, there
were riots at four performances of Synge's masterpiece,
The Playboy of the Western World, because some patriots
regarded certain lines in it as an insult to Irish woman-
hood. In 1908, the Fay brothers quarrelled with Yeats,
Synge, and Lady Gregory about the management of the
theatre and left the company. In 1910, Miss Horniman
withdrew after another disagreement, and Yeats and Lady
Gregory became the patentees of the theatre. By that time,
however, the Abbey Theatre was world-famous.

The prestige of the Abbey Company owed much to its
distinctive style of acting. William Fay was a talented
comic actor and Frank Fay was a fine verse-speaker. Dis-
satisfied with the pantomimic movement and obtrusive
stage business of Beerbohm Tree's romantic acting and
with the understated naturalism of Hawtrey and Gerald
du Maurier, they collaborated with Yeats in the creation of

a new histrionic style. In the portrayal of heroes of myth
and legend, they taught their company to move with a
measured dignity like that of classical French actors, to
speak the poetry in a kind of chant, and to sing the songs
in the plays without any unnatural prolonging of the vowel
sounds. In plays of peasant life, their actors sometimes
walked with a clumsiness appropriate to their roles, but
they used action and stage business very sparingly; they
usually stood still and listened, the speaker of the moment
being the only person on the stage to use gestures. In
refreshing contrast to this repose and economy of bodily
movement was the lilt of their diction, delivered in rich
Irish accents with compelling pace and continuity. This
was the art which the Fay brothers, Sara Allgood, Maire
O'Neill, Arthur Sinclair, and Barry Fitzgerald bequeathed
to F. J. McCormick, Maureen Delany, Eileen Crowe, and
Cyril Cusack.

Yeats did his utmost to concentrate attention on the
words of the Abbey plays. Instead of the elaborately
realistic scenery favoured by contemporary actor-
managers, he used curtains or backgrounds of subdued
colours for exteriors and settings with a bare minimum of
properties for interiors. The observations which he published under the title *The Irish Dramatic Movement* show
that he believed that two types of drama should be culti-
vated; the play of peasant life and the poetic play drawing
upon national myths and symbols. Most of his early plays
are of the latter kind and are shaped by the theory of
tragedy which he expounds in his essays *Estrangement* and
The Tragic Theatre. Yeats believed in an *anima mundi*, an
ideal world of heroic passions. The tragic character, as he
conceives it, is imbued with a passion so pure and intense
that it achieves contact with this ideal world. The tragic
experience may involve renunciation but ecstasy is its distinctive characteristic.

The Countess Cathleen shows Yeats working towards the
embodiment of these ideas. They are particularly well
exemplified by *Cathleen ni Houlihan* and *The Shadowy
Waters. Cathleen ni Houlihan* is one of the finest short plays

ever written. Its historical setting is the year 1798, when French troops landed in Mayo and were joined by many peasants in an abortive attempt to establish an Irish republic. The play shows an old woman coming to the cottage of a Mayo peasant and talking of the four green fields* that have been taken from her and of the friends who are gathering to help her. Recognizing her as Cathleen ni Houlihan, the legendary incarnation of Ireland, the peasant's son throws aside his wedding garments and goes to join the insurgents. *The Shadowy Waters* is set in the mythical past and ends with the poet Forgael and Dectora sailing alone into the sunset, impelled by their ideal passion to risk death in quest of a region where love is eternal. Both plays use myth and symbol to express themes of renunciation and ecstatic aspiration, but *The Shadowy Waters* is much the more characteristic of the 'remote, spiritual, and ideal' drama to which Yeats was dedicated.

In 1894 Yeats had met J. M. Synge in Paris and had urged him to give up his cosmopolitan existence, to go to the Aran Islands, and to focus his imagination on Irish life. Synge did so and became the greatest of the Irish dramatists of peasant life, though not in the heroic vein which Yeats had probably hoped for. Synge's view of life was tragi-satiric, and during his lifetime many of his fellow-countrymen disliked his work because they saw only the satiric aspect. Synge had a deep affection for the peasant communities that he knew, but in his plays he satirizes their credulity, violence, and parochialism. In each of his plays, moreover, a central character is exiled or set apart from a community because he or she has finer perceptions than it is capable of. Christy Mahon's situation at the end of *The Playboy of the Western World* is a pre-eminent example of this alienation. In *The Shadow of the Glen* and *The Well of the Saints*, Nora Burke and the Daols gladly give up peasant life to become tramps, finding happiness in a more primitive contact with nature. Only in *Riders to the Sea* is there a reconciliation between the

* An Irish audience recognizes at once the reference to Ulster, Munster, Leinster, and Connaught.

imaginative character and the community, though there
is a characteristic tragic irony in the circumstances which
bring it about, for it is only when old Maurya's premoni-
tions are fulfilled by the death of her last son that the other
characters unite with her in a ritual of grief. In his last
play, *Deirdre of the Sorrows*, Synge turned to ancient myth,
but his concentrated plots and exquisite modulation of
peasant idioms in *Riders to the Sea* and *The Playboy of the
Western World* make the imaginative stoicism of Maurya
and the rebellious youth of Christy Mahon as archetypal
as the profound fatalism of Deirdre.

During the first decade of the Irish Dramatic Movement,
William Boyle, Padraic Colum, and Lady Gregory likewise wrote plays of peasant and country life. There was
salt as well as sweetness in their treatment of peasant
humours; Boyle's *The Building Fund* explores the avarice
of an old woman, Colum's *The Land* is an early dramatization of the Irish impulse to emigrate, and in Lady Gregory's
The Workhouse Ward the paupers prefer quarrelling to
solitude. During its second decade, the Movement was in
danger of splitting into two schools, the one specializing
in harsh realism, the other in a stylized mythopoeic drama.
The realistic phase was initiated by three dramatists from
County Cork – Lennox Robinson, T. C. Murray, and R. J.
Ray – and extended by the Ulster playwrights Rutherford
Mayne and St John Ervine. All were influenced to some
degree by Ibsen's naturalistic plays and the recent work of
the Manchester realists in England. Their plays portray the
darker side of peasant life, religious bigotry, and current
political and industrial problems. In Murray's *Birthright*,
a young peasant kills his brother for the sake of land; in
Robinson's *Patriots*, a political agitator loses faith in the
nationalism which has led him to commit murder and wreck
his marriage; in Ervine's *Mixed Marriage*, a Catholic girl
is killed by soldiers during riots stirred up by a strike-
leader, a Protestant who opposed her marriage to his son.

Shortly after these developments took place, Yeats came
under the influence of the Noh plays of Japan and wrote
Four Plays for Dancers, which were designed for drawing-

room performances against purely symbolic backgrounds
with masked actors employing a set of conventionalized
movements and dances to the accompaniment of a drum,
a gong, and a zither.

Two things prevented Irish drama from bifurcating into
realism and exoticism: the Easter Rising of 1916 and the
genius of Sean O'Casey. In Yeats's famous phrase, 'a
terrible beauty' was born in Easter Week. It transfigured
Irish drama as well as Irish life. The insurrection against
English rule at Easter, 1916, is an outstanding instance of
that Celtic paradox, the physical defeat from whose ashes
spiritual victory rises like a phoenix. The insurgents were
defeated but the subsequent execution of Pearse, Connolly,
and their other leaders horrified Ireland and made the Sinn
Féin movement strong enough to resist English troops
during the troubles of 1920–21 and to exact the treaty
which set up the Irish Free State in 1921. Unhappily, the
achievement of independence was followed by the civil war
of 1922–23 between the Free Staters and the Diehard
Republicans who believed that the ideals of Sinn Féin had
been betrayed by the acceptance of a treaty which separated Ulster from the rest of Ireland.

Theatrical activity was at a low ebb in Ireland during
these embattled years, but they stirred the conscience and
stimulated the imagination of the nation even more deeply
than the death of Parnell, and they found their profoundest
interpreter in a dramatist from the slums of Dublin, Sean
O'Casey. Portraying the violent disruption of personal and
political relationships during the Easter Rising and the
Troubles of 1921 in *The Shadow of a Gunman*, *Juno and the
Paycock*, and *The Plough and the Stars*, O'Casey is as topical
as the realists, as tragi-satiric as Synge, and as mythopoeic
in essence as Yeats is in *Cathleen ni Houlihan*. The same
mother-symbol of Ireland's sufferings emerges from the
contrast between feminine altruism and masculine selfish-
ness in all three plays. It is one of the many ironies of *The
Shadow of a Gunman* that the self-centred Shields never
realizes that his catch-phrase – 'Oh, Cathleen ni Houlihan,
your way's a thorny way' – applies to Minnie Powell, who

gives her life to save Davoren, a poet masquerading as a
patriotic gunman. In *Juno and the Paycock*, Juno Boyle
has the wisdom and sympathy of her classical namesake,
but she speaks and acts like a Cathleen ni Houlihan as she
leads her pregnant daughter out of the chaos precipitated
by her feckless husband and the Civil War. In *The Plough
and the Stars*, the only truly heroic characters are the
women who suffer madness and death during the Easter
Rising. There were riots when this play was performed at
the Abbey Theatre in 1926.

Soon afterwards, O'Casey left Ireland to become a per-
manent resident in England. In 1928, the Abbey Theatre
rejected his play about the First World War, *The Silver
Tassie*, as 'too abstract'. Nevertheless, O'Casey had
revived the great tradition of Synge by creating myths
which combined a heroic idealism with a tragi-satiric com-
mentary on some aspects of the national character. In the
nineteen-twenties, Lady Gregory and Yeats contributed to
this revival by essaying new themes and techniques. In
The Story Brought by Brigit, Lady Gregory offers Biblical
parallels to various Irish characters and attitudes at the
time of the Easter Rising. In *The Cat and the Moon*, Yeats
relaxes the conventions which he had adapted from the
Noh play and represents the Irish peasant and the Irish
aristocrat in the persons of a Blind Beggar and a Lame
Beggar, whose dialogues and pantomimic actions in front
of a tree anticipate the tragi-comic symbolism of Samuel
Beckett's *Waiting for Godot*.

After the establishment of the Free State, the material
fortunes of the Irish theatre improved. In 1924, Yeats and
Lady Gregory offered the Abbey Theatre to the government as the nucleus of a National Theatre. The offer
was not accepted, but the government showed its apprecia-
tion of the achievements of the Abbey Theatre by voting
it an annual subsidy of £850, so making it the first state-
subsidized theatre in the English-speaking world. Another
important development began in 1928, when the Dublin
Gate Theatre Company was founded by Micheál Mac
Liammóir and Hilton Edwards. Its policy was to encourage

Irish dramatists to experiment by presenting a cosmopolitan repertoire and to stimulate the visual sensibility of a nation 'whose ears had always been its strongest point of aesthetic perception' by setting new standards in lighting, scenery, and costumes.

It was more successful in the latter than in the former aim, though it discovered in Denis Johnston a resourceful and highly experimental playwright. His first play, *The Old Lady Says 'No'*, is an audacious expressionist comedy in which he subjects Robert Emmet, Cathleen ni Houlihan, and patriotic songs and slogans to anti-romantic treatment. In *The Scythe and the Stars*, he deflates heroic interpretations of the Easter Rising. In his best play, *The Moon in the Yellow River*, he shows the bewilderment of a German engineer, representative of industrial democracy, when he is confronted by the nihilism of a cultured Irishman, the violence of Free Stater and Republican, and the inconsequentiality of other Irish temperaments.

Like Johnston, the best Irish playwrights of the past thirty years have been concerned with the problems which have faced Eire since 1921, but whereas he remains quizzical and detached, they suggest positive attitudes by means of myths or archetypal characters who serve as touchstones. In *The White Steed*, a play rejected by the Abbey Theatre, Paul Vincent Carroll relates modern instance to ancient myth when his heroine defies a despotic priest, proudly declaring herself a descendant of Aideen, Cuchulain, and Oisin, the legendary poet who spent 300 years in the Land of Youth, then rode back on a white steed and found Ireland swarming with alien priests and little black men. Similarly, in *The Quare Fellow* and *The Hostage*, Brendan Behan judges his characters according to their reactions to that archetypal figure, the scapegoat, represented in the former play by a condemned murderer, and in the latter by an English soldier who is about to be killed as a reprisal by stupid members of the Irish Republican Army.

In his latest work, O'Casey has likewise used mirth, myth, and symbol to incite the youth of Ireland to free themselves from various kinds of hypocrisy and repression.

Thus the strikers in *Red Roses for Me* nerve themselves to face their oppressors by recalling the deeds of such legendary champions of Ireland as Finn Mac Cool, Goll, and Oscar, and the young men and women in *The Drums of Father Ned* liberate themselves from the puritanism of Father Fillifogue, the money-grubbing of businessmen, and the shibboleths of Free Staters and diehard Republicans, uniting in a Dionysian ritual of joy under the guidance of Father Ned, who is more Celtic sprite than Catholic clergyman. Similar methods are used to express similar themes in *Cock-a-doodle Dandy*. During the past sixty-five years, Irish drama has developed concentrically, like a banyan tree; its first stem sprang from the rich soil of national myth and legend, and the branches which it has since put forth have regularly dropped roots to draw sustenance from the same vital source.

The recent history of the Irish theatre has been chequered. In 1951 a fire put the Abbey Theatre out of action and the company has since been obliged to perform at the Queen's Theatre, a mediocre playhouse ill-suited to the economy of movement and vocal sublety of the Abbey style. Regrettably, the production of verse plays has been suspended. In 1958, *The Drums of Father Ned* was withdrawn from the Dublin Theatre Festival because the Archbishop of Dublin disliked what he had heard about the play. As a reprisal, O'Casey prohibited the performance of any of his plays in his native land, so that for the first time in its history the twentieth-century Irish theatre had no living Irish writer of undoubted genius at its disposal.

There are some hopeful signs, however. The Dublin Theatre Festivals give more opportunities to little-known dramatists than any others in the British Isles. A new Abbey Theatre of modern design will be opened in 1964 and will have a small studio stage for experimental work in its basement. The genial humanism of the late Pope John XXIII and his disciples may produce a climate of Catholic opinion more favourable to the phenomenal dramatic and histrionic gifts of the Irish nation than any that it has known in the past.

The Countess Cathleen

An old legend, the deeds of a beautiful patriot, his frustrated love for her, and his own inventiveness provided W. B. Yeats with the themes of *The Countess Cathleen*. The old legend was *The Countess Kathleen O'Shea* which he had published in his *Fairy and Folk Tales of the Irish Peasantry** in 1888. The beautiful patriot was Maud Gonne, whom Yeats first met in 1889 and with whom he quickly fell in love. Her fine presence and ability as an actress quickened his desire to dramatize the legend and to have her play the title-role. He began work on the first version of *The Countess Cathleen* within a few weeks of meeting her. Both Yeats and Maud Gonne were devoted to the rehabilitation of Ireland, but whereas he sought it through a revival of national culture in the form of a mythopoeic poetry and drama, she sought it through incessant political agitation and rejected his proposals of marriage. The version of the play published in 1892 was followed by major revisions published in 1895, 1901, 1912, and 1923. In every version Yeats strove to fuse legendary with personal material and to stage it in accordance with his developing aesthetic ideals. The final version is his longest and one of his most deeply-pondered plays.

Yeats regarded the legend of *The Countess Kathleen O'Shea* as 'one of the supreme parables of the world'. From it he took over the story of how two wealthy merchants suddenly appeared in Ireland and trafficked for souls, giving the highest prices for the least spotted. He also took over the details of how the Countess tried to stop this infamous trade by selling her jewels and estates to help the poor, of how the demon-merchants stole her gold, of how she died of grief, and of how God nullified the sale of her soul because of her boundless charity. This legend of

* See pp. 60–62.

self-sacrifice resembles the Greek myth concerning Alcestis,
which was dramatized by Euripides.

Whereas the legend has a city setting and only hints at
conditions of famine, Yeats places his action in a peasant
community and attributes the selling of souls to blighted
crops. An Irish audience inevitably associates the play with
the terrible famine of 1847. Some details of the relationship
between the Countess and the peasants in the play closely
parallel that between Maud Gonne and the peasants of
Kerry and Donegal. During the 1897 famine in Kerry, Maud
helped to draft a leaflet which quoted St Thomas Aquinas
to prove that a starving man could justifiably take food
without the owner's permission. This advice is re-echoed in
Scene 3 of the play when the Countess declares that

> A learned theologian has laid down
> That starving men may take what's necessary
> And yet be sinless.

During the evictions in Donegal in 1890 Maud became a
legendary figure of deliverance among the peasants, but
her labours induced an attack of tuberculosis which im-
perilled her life.

The turbulence and dangers of Maud Gonne's chosen
way of life distressed Yeats, and some of his personal feelings are expressed by the poet Aleel, the most important
of the characters in the play invented entirely by the
dramatist. But these feelings fit into the pattern of the
play, which shows characters symbolic of Ireland – peasant
and poet – progressing from division to unity of feeling
through the transcendent power of Cathleen's altruism. A
division among the peasants is at once apparent in the first
scene, in which Shemus and Teigue scorn the faith in God,
the loyalty to the Countess, and the abhorrence of diabolical agents expressed by Mary Rua. In the second and third
scenes, Oona, Aleel, and the Countess are likewise at
variance. Aleel, the unchristened lover of pagan myth and
solitude, tries to divert the Countess from 'the evil of the
times', urging her to withdraw to the hills in accordance
with the advice given him by Aengus, the love-god, in a

dream. But the Countess is a Christian committed to saving
the people and she sadly renounces Aleel and his visions.
Symbolically, the fourth scene sets peasant and poet side
by side, the one rhapsodizing over gold, the other lament-
ing his lost love.

A profound change comes in the fifth scene. Through the
intensity of his imaginative sympathy Aleel has become so
completely identified with the Countess that the merchants
cannot take his soul when he offers it for nothing; it is
hers. When the Countess signs away her soul and falls
dying a peasant woman is moved to pray that 'us and ours
be lost so she be shriven'. Transcending their previous
selves, poet and peasant are now ecstatically united in an
altruistic passion comparable to that of the Countess
herself. 'A poet creates tragedy,' wrote Yeats in *Estrangement* (Section 24), 'from . . . that soul which is like in all
men. It has not joy, as we understand that word, but
ecstasy, which is from the contemplation of things vaster
than the individual and imperfectly seen, perhaps, by all
those that still live.'

If the Countess is purely and simply an incarnation of
pity in that feminine form so common in Irish literature,
it is because Yeats believed that lyric passion rather than
intricate characterization was the true province of tragedy.
A movement from diversity to unity is reflected in the
imagery as well as the action of the play. At first Aleel's
eyes are focused solely on the pagan past, but in his final
visions of the victory of the angels, pagan and Christian
lore are harmonized. Biting images of earth, animal, and
peasant life give a stark realism to the early scenes of
famine, but in Oona's final speech they are universalized
into symbols of the predestined triumph of time:

> The years like great black oxen tread the world,
> And God the herdsman goads them on behind,
> And I am broken by their passing feet.

W.A.A.

The Countess Cathleen

W. B. Yeats

'The sorrowful are dumb for thee'
Lament of Morian Shehone
for Miss Mary Bourke

To Maud Gonne

Characters

SHEMUS RUA, *a Peasant*
MARY, *his wife*
TEIGUE, *his son*
ALEEL, *a Poet*
THE COUNTESS CATHLEEN
OONA, *her foster-mother*
Two Demons disguised as Merchants
Peasants, Servants, Angelical Beings

The Scene is laid in Ireland and in old times.

The Countess Cathleen was first performed at the Abbey Theatre, Dublin, on 8 May 1899, with the following cast:

FIRST MERCHANT	Marcus St John
SECOND MERCHANT	Trevor Lowe
SHEMUS RUA	Valentine Grace
TEIGUE RUA	Charles Sefton
MARY RUA	Madame San Carolo
ALEEL	Florence Farr
OONA	Anna Mather
THE COUNTESS CATHLEEN	May Whitty

Peasants, Servants, and others played by C. Holmes, J. Wilcox, D. Paget, M. Kelly, and F. E. Wilkinson.

Scene One

A room with lighted fire, and a door into the open air, through which one sees, perhaps, the trees of a wood, and these trees should be painted in flat colour upon a gold or diapered sky. The walls are of one colour. The scene should have the effect of missal painting. MARY, *a woman of forty years or so, is grinding a quern.*

MARY: What can have made the grey hen flutter so?
> [TEIGUE, *a boy of fourteen, is coming in with turf, which he lays beside the hearth.*]

TEIGUE: They say that now the land is famine-struck
  The graves are walking.

MARY: What can the hen have heard?

TEIGUE: And that is not the worst; at Tubber-vanach
  A woman met a man with ears spread out,
  And they moved up and down like a bat's wing.

MARY: What can have kept your father all this while?

TEIGUE: Two nights ago, at Carrick-orus churchyard,
  A herdsman met a man who had no mouth,
  Nor eyes, nor ears; his face a wall of flesh;
  He saw him plainly by the light of the moon.

MARY: Look out, and tell me if your father's coming.
> [TEIGUE *goes to door.*]

TEIGUE: Mother!

MARY: What is it?

TEIGUE: In the bush beyond,
  There are two birds – if you can call them birds –
  I could not see them rightly for the leaves –
  But they've the shape and colour of horned owls,
  And I'm half certain they've a human face.

MARY: Mother of God, defend us!

TEIGUE: They're looking at me.
  What is the good of praying? father says.

God and the Mother of God have dropped asleep.
What do they care, he says, though the whole land
Squeal like a rabbit under a weasel's tooth?
MARY: You'll bring misfortune with your blasphemies
Upon your father, or yourself, or me.
Would God that he were home – ah, there he is.
    [SHEMUS *comes in.*]
What was it kept you in the wood? You know
I cannot get all sorts of accidents
Out of my mind till you are home again.
SHEMUS: I'm in no mood to listen to your clatter.
Although I tramped the woods for half a day,
I've taken nothing, for the very rats,
Badgers, and hedgehogs seem to have died of drought,
And there was scarce a wind in the parched leaves.
TEIGUE: Then you have brought no dinner.
SHEMUS: After that
I sat among the beggars at the cross-roads,
And held a hollow hand among the others.
MARY: What, did you beg?
SHEMUS: I had no chance to beg,
For when the beggars saw me they cried out
They would not have another share their alms,
And hunted me away with sticks and stones.
TEIGUE: You said that you would bring us food or money.
SHEMUS: What's in the house?
TEIGUE: A bit of mouldy bread.
MARY: There's flour enough to make another loaf.
TEIGUE: And when that's gone?
MARY: There is the hen in the coop.
SHEMUS: My curse upon the beggars, my curse upon
    them!
TEIGUE: And the last penny gone.
SHEMUS: When the hen's gone,
What can we do but live on sorrel and dock,
And dandelion, till our mouths are green?
MARY: God, that to this hour has found bit and sup,
Will cater for us still.
SHEMUS: His kitchen's bare.

There were five doors that I looked through this day
And saw the dead and not a soul to wake them.
MARY: Maybe He'd have us die because He knows,
When the ear is stopped and when the eye is stopped,
That every wicked sight is hid from the eye,
And all fool talk from the ear!
[*A stringed instrument without.*]
SHEMUS: Who's passing there?
And mocking us with music?
TEIGUE: A young man plays it.
There's an old woman and a lady with him.
SHEMUS: What is the trouble of the poor to her?
Nothing at all or a harsh radishy sauce
For the day's meat.
MARY: God's pity on the rich!
Had we been through as many doors, and seen
The dishes standing on the polished wood
In the wax candle light, we'd be as hard,
And there's the needle's eye at the end of all.
SHEMUS: My curse upon the rich!
TEIGUE: They're coming here.
SHEMUS: Then down upon that stool, down quick, I say,
And call up a whey face and a whining voice,
And let your head be bowed upon your knees.
MARY: Had I but time to put the place to rights!
[CATHLEEN, OONA, *and* ALEEL *enter.*]
CATHLEEN: God save all here. There is a certain house,
An old grey castle with a kitchen garden,
A cider orchard and a plot for flowers,
Somewhere among these woods.
MARY: We know it, lady.
A place that's set among impassable walls
As though world's trouble could not find it out.
CATHLEEN: It may be that we are that trouble, for we —
Although we've wandered in the wood this hour —
Have lost it too, yet I should know my way,
For I lived all my childhood in that house.
MARY: Then you are Countess Cathleen?
CATHLEEN: And this woman,

Oona, my nurse, should have remembered it,
For we were happy for a long time there.
OONA: The paths are overgrown with thickets now,
Or else some change has come upon my sight.
CATHLEEN: And this young man, that should have known
    the woods –
Because we met him on their border but now,
Wandering and singing like a wave of the sea –
Is so wrapped up in dreams of terrors to come
That he can give no help.
MARY: You have still some way,
But I can put you on the trodden path
Your servants take when they are marketing.
But first sit down and rest yourself awhile,
For my old fathers served your fathers, lady,
Longer than books can tell – and it were strange
If you and yours should not be welcome here.
CATHLEEN: And it were stranger still were I ungrateful
For such kind welcome – but I must be gone,
For the night's gathering in.
SHEMUS: It is a long while
Since I've set eyes on bread or on what buys it.
CATHLEEN: So you are starving even in this wood,
Where I had thought I would find nothing changed.
But that's a dream, for the old worm o' the world
Can eat its way into what place it pleases.
    [*She gives money.*]
TEIGUE: Beautiful lady, give me something too;
I fell but now, being weak with hunger and thirst,
And lay upon the threshold like a log.
CATHLEEN: I gave for all and that was all I had.
But look, my purse is empty. I have passed
By starving men and women all this day,
And they have had the rest; but take the purse,
The silver clasps on't may be worth a trifle.
And if you'll come tomorrow to my house
You shall have twice the sum.
    [ALEEL *begins to play.*]
SHEMUS [*muttering*]:   What, music, music!

CATHLEEN: Ah, do not blame the finger on the string;
   The doctors bid me fly the unlucky times
   And find distraction for my thoughts, or else
   Pine to my grave.
SHEMUS: I have said nothing, lady.
   Why should the like of us complain?
OONA: Have done.
   Sorrows that she's but read of in a book
   Weigh on her mind as if they had been her own.
     [OONA, MARY, *and* CATHLEEN *go out.* ALEEL *looks
     defiantly at Shemus.*]
ALEEL [*singing*]: Were I but crazy for love's sake
                 I know who'd measure out his length,
                 I know the heads that I should break,
                 For crazy men have double strength.
                 I know – all's out to leave or take,
                 Who mocks at music mocks at love;
                 Were I but crazy for love's sake,
                 No need to pick and choose.
   [*Snapping his fingers in Shemus' face*]
                        Enough!
            I know the heads that I should break.
   [*He takes a step towards the door and then turns again.*]
   Shut to the door before the night has fallen,
   For who can say what walks, or in what shape
   Some devilish creature flies in the air; but now
   Two grey horned owls hooted above our heads.
   [*He goes out, his singing dies away.* MARY *comes in.*
   SHEMUS *has been counting the money.*]
SHEMUS: So that fool's gone.
TEIGUE: He's seen the horned owls too.
   There's no good luck in owls, but it may be
   That the ill luck's to fall upon his head.
MARY: You never thanked her ladyship.
SHEMUS: Thank her
   For seven halfpence and a silver bit?
TEIGUE: But for this empty purse?
SHEMUS: What's that for thanks,
   Or what's the double of it that she promised,

With bread and flesh and every sort of food
Up to a price no man has heard the like of
And rising every day?

MARY: We have all she had;
She emptied out the purse before our eyes.

SHEMUS [*to Mary, who has gone to close the door*]: Leave that
     door open.

MARY: When those that have read books,
And seen the seven wonders of the world,
Fear what's above or what's below the ground,
It's time that poverty should bolt the door.

SHEMUS: I'll have no bolts, for there is not a thing
That walks above the ground or under it
I had not rather welcome to this house
Than any more of mankind, rich or poor.

TEIGUE: So that they brought us money.

SHEMUS: I heard say
There's something that appears like a white bird,
A pigeon or a seagull or the like,
But if you hit it with a stone or a stick
It clangs as though it had been made of brass,
And that if you dig down where it was scratching
You'll find a crock of gold.

TEIGUE: But dream of gold
For three nights running, and there's always gold.

SHEMUS: You might be starved before you've dug it out.

TEIGUE: But maybe if you called, something would come.
They have been seen of late.

MARY: Is it call devils?
Call devils from the wood, call them in here?

SHEMUS: So you'd stand up against me, and you'd say
Who or what I am to welcome here.
     [*He hits her.*]
That is to show who's master.

TEIGUE: Call them in.

MARY: God help us all!

SHEMUS: Pray, if you have a mind to.
It's little that the sleepy ears above
Care for your words; but I'll call what I please.

TEIGUE: There is many a one, they say, had money from
    them.
SHEMUS [*at door*]: Whatever you are that walk the woods
    at night,
So be it that you have not shouldered up
Out of a grave – for I'll have nothing human –
And have free hands, a friendly trick of speech,
I welcome you. Come, sit beside the fire.
What matter if your head's below your arms
Or you've a horse's tail to whip your flank,
Feathers instead of hair, that's all but nothing.
Come, share what bread and meat is in the house,
And stretch your heels and warm them in the ashes.
And after that, let's share and share alike
And curse all men and women. Come in, come in.
What, is there no one there?
    [*Turning from door*]
                            And yet they say
They are as common as the grass, and ride
.Even upon the book in the priest's hand.
    [TEIGUE *lifts one arm slowly and points towards the door
    and begins moving backward.* SHEMUS *turns, he also sees
    something and begins moving backward.* MARY *does the
    same. A man dressed as an Eastern merchant comes in
    carrying a small carpet. He unrolls it and sits cross-
    legged at one end of it. Another man dressed in the same
    way follows, and sits at the other end. This is done
    slowly and deliberately. When they are seated they take
    money out of embroidered purses at their girdles and
    begin arranging it on the carpet.*]
TEIGUE: You speak to them.
SHEMUS: No, you.
TEIGUE: 'Twas you that called them.
SHEMUS [*coming nearer*]: I'd make so bold, if you would
    pardon it,
To ask if there's a thing you'd have of us.
Although we are but poor people, if there is,
Why, if there is —
FIRST MERCHANT: We've travelled a long road,

For we are merchants that must tramp the world,
And now we look for supper and a fire
And a safe corner to count money in.
SHEMUS: I thought you were . . . but that's no matter
  now —
There had been words between my wife and me
Because I said I would be master here,
And ask in what I pleased or who I pleased,
And so . . . but that is nothing to the point,
Because it's certain that you are but merchants.
FIRST MERCHANT: We travel for the Master of all mer-
  chants.
SHEMUS: Yet if you were that I had thought but now
I'd welcome you no less. Be what you please
And you'll have supper at the market rate.
That means that what was sold for but a penny
Is now worth fifty.
FIRST MERCHANT [arranging money]: Our Master bids us pay
So good a price that all who deal with us
Shall eat, drink, and be merry.
SHEMUS [to Mary]:   Bestir yourself,
Go kill and draw the fowl, while Teigue and I
Lay out the plates and make a better fire.
MARY: I will not cook for you.
SHEMUS: Not cook! not cook!
Do not be angry. She wants to pay me back
Because I struck her in that argument.
But she'll get sense again. Since the dearth came
We rattle one on another as though we were
Knives thrown into a basket to be cleaned.
MARY: I will not cook for you, because I know
In what unlucky shape you sat but now
Outside this door.
TEIGUE: It's this, your honours:
Because of some wild words my father said
She thinks you are not of those who cast a shadow.
SHEMUS: I said I'd make the devils of the wood
Welcome, if they'd a mind to eat and drink;
But it is certain that you are men like us.

FIRST MERCHANT: It's strange that she should think we
    cast no shadow,
  For there is nothing on the ridge of the world
  That's more substantial than the merchants are
  That buy and sell you.
MARY: If you are not demons,
  And seeing what great wealth is spread out there,
  Give food or money to the starving poor.
FIRST MERCHANT: If we knew how to find deserving poor
  We'd do our share.
MARY: But seek them patiently.
FIRST MERCHANT: We know the evils of mere charity.
MARY: Those scruples may befit a common time.
  I had thought there was a pushing to and fro,
  At times like this, that overset the scale
  And trampled measure down.
FIRST MERCHANT: But if already
  We'd thought of a more prudent way than that?
SECOND MERCHANT: If each one brings a bit of merchan-
    dise,
  We'll give him such a price he never dreamt of.
MARY: Where shall the starving come at merchandise?
FIRST MERCHANT: We will ask nothing but what all men
    have.
MARY: Their swine and cattle, fields and implements
  Are sold and gone.
FIRST MERCHANT: They have not sold all yet.
  For there's a vaporous thing – that may be nothing,
  But that's the buyer's risk – a second self,
  They call immortal for a story's sake.
SHEMUS: They come to buy our souls?
TEIGUE: I'll barter mine.
  Why should we starve for what may be but nothing?
MARY: Teigue and Shemus –
SHEMUS: What can it be but nothing?
  What has God poured out of His bag but famine?
  Satan gives money.
TEIGUE: Yet no thunder stirs.
FIRST MERCHANT: There is a heap for each.

[SHEMUS *goes to take money.*]

But, no, not yet,
For there's work I have to set you to.

SHEMUS: So, then, you're as deceitful as the rest,
And all that talk of buying what's but a vapour
Is fancy bread. I might have known as much,
Because that's how the trick-o'-the-loop man talks.

FIRST MERCHANT: That's for the work, each has its
separate price;
But neither price is paid till the work's done.

TEIGUE: The same for me.

MARY: O God, why are You still?

FIRST MERCHANT: You've but to cry aloud at every cross-
road,
At every house door, that we buy men's souls
And give so good a price that all may live
In mirth and comfort till the famine's done,
Because we are Christian men.

SHEMUS: Come, let's away.

TEIGUE: I shall keep running till I've earned the price.

SECOND MERCHANT [*who has risen and gone towards fire*]:
Stop; you must have proof behind the words,
So here's your entertainment on the road.

[*He throws a bag of money on the ground.*]

Live as you please; our Master's generous.

[TEIGUE *and* SHEMUS *have stopped.* TEIGUE *takes
the money. They go out.*]

MARY: Destroyers of souls, God will destroy you quickly.
You shall at last dry like dry leaves and hang
Nailed like dead vermin to the doors of God.

SECOND MERCHANT: Curse to your fill, for saints will have
their dreams.

FIRST MERCHANT: Though we're but vermin that our
Master sent
To overrun the world, he at the end
Shall pull apart the pale ribs of the moon
And quench the stars in the ancestral night.

MARY: God is all-powerful.

SECOND MERCHANT: Pray, you shall need Him.

You shall eat dock and grass, and dandelion,
Till that low threshold there becomes a wall,
And when your hands can scarcely drag your body
We shall be near you.

    [MARY *faints.*]

    [*The* FIRST MERCHANT *takes up the carpet, spreads it before the fire and stands in front of it warming his hands.*]

FIRST MERCHANT: Our faces go unscratched.
Wring the neck o' that fowl, scatter the flour,
And look if there is bread upon the shelves.
We'll turn the fowl upon the spit and roast it,
And eat the supper we were bidden to,
Now that the house is quiet, praise our Master,
And stretch and warm our heels among the ashes.

Scene Two

FRONT SCENE. — *A wood with perhaps distant view of turreted house at one side, but all in flat colour, without light and shade and against a diapered or gold background.*

    [*Countess* CATHLEEN *comes in leaning upon* ALEEL'S *arm.* OONA *follows them.*]

CATHLEEN [*stopping*]: Surely this leafy corner, where one smells
    The wild bee's honey, has a story too?

OONA: There is the house at last.

ALEEL: A man, they say,
Loved Maeve the Queen of all the invisible host,
And died of his love nine centuries ago.
And now, when the moon's riding at the full,
She leaves her dancers lonely and lies there
Upon that level place, and for three days
Stretches and sighs and wets her long pale cheeks.

CATHLEEN: So she loves truly.

ALEEL: No, but wets her cheeks,
  Lady, because she has forgot his name.
CATHLEEN: She'd sleep that trouble away – though it must
  be
  A heavy trouble to forget his name –
  If she had better sense.
OONA: Your own house, lady.
ALEEL: She sleeps high up on wintry Knocknarea
  In an old cairn of stones; while her poor women
  Must lie and jog in the wave if they would sleep –
  Being water-born – yet if she cry their names
  They run up on the land and dance in the moon
  Till they are giddy and would love as men do,
  And be as patient and as pitiful.
  But there is nothing that will stop in their heads,
  They've such poor memories, though they weep for it.
  O yes, they weep; that's when the moon is full.
CATHLEEN: Is it because they have short memories
  They live so long?
ALEEL: What's memory but the ash
  That chokes our fires that have begun to sink?
  And they've a dizzy, everlasting fire.
OONA: There is your own house, lady.
CATHLEEN: Why, that's true,
  And we'd have passed it without noticing.
ALEEL: A curse upon it for a meddlesome house!
  Had it but stayed away I would have known
  What Queen Maeve thinks on when the moon is pinched;
  And whether now – as in the old days – the dancers
  Set their brief love on men.
OONA: Rest on my arm.
  These are no thoughts for any Christian ear.
ALEEL: I am younger, she would be too heavy for you.
  [*He begins taking his lute out of the bag.* CATHLEEN *who
  has turned towards Oona, turns back to him.*]
  This hollow box remembers every foot
  That danced upon the level grass of the world,
  And will tell secrets if I whisper to it.
  [*Sings*]

> Lift up the white knee;
> Hear what they sing,
> Those young dancers
> That in a ring
> Raved but now
> Of the hearts that broke
> Long, long ago
> For their sake.

OONA: New friends are sweet.

ALEEL: But the dance changes,
> Lift up the gown,
> All that sorrow
> Is trodden down.

OONA: The empty rattle-pate! Lean on this arm,
That I can tell you is a christened arm,
And not like some, if we are to judge by speech.
But as you please. It is time I was forgot.
Maybe it is not on this arm you slumbered
When you were as helpless as a worm.

ALEEL: Stay with me till we come to your own house.

CATHLEEN [*sitting down*]: When I am rested I will need no
    help.

ALEEL: I thought to have kept her from remembering
The evil of the times for full ten minutes;
But now when seven are out you come between.

OONA: Talk on; what does it matter what you say,
For you have not been christened?

ALEEL: Old woman, old woman,
You robbed her of three minutes' peace of mind,
And though you live unto a hundred years,
And wash the feet of beggars and give alms,
And climb Cro-Patrick, you shall not be pardoned.

OONA: How does a man who never was baptized
Know what Heaven pardons?

ALEEL: You are a sinful woman.

OONA: I care no more than if a pig had grunted.
    [*Enter Cathleen's* STEWARD]

STEWARD: I am not to blame, for I had locked the gate.
The forester's to blame. The men climbed in

At the east corner where the elm-tree is.

CATHLEEN: I do not understand you. Who has climbed?

STEWARD: Then God be thanked, I am the first to tell you.
I was afraid some other of the servants –
Though I've been on the watch – had been the first,
And mixed up truth and lies, your ladyship.

CATHLEEN [*rising*]: Has some misfortune happened?

STEWARD: Yes, indeed.
The forester that let the branches lie
Against the wall's to blame for everything,
For that is how the rogues got into the garden.

CATHLEEN: I thought to have escaped misfortune here.
Has anyone been killed?

STEWARD: O no, not killed.
They have stolen half a cart-load of green cabbage.

CATHLEEN: But maybe they were starving.

STEWARD: That is certain.
To rob or starve, that was the choice they had.

CATHLEEN: A learned theologian has laid down
That starving men may take what's necessary,
And yet be sinless.

OONA: Sinless and a thief!
There should be broken bottles on the wall.

CATHLEEN: And if it be a sin, while faith's unbroken
God cannot help but pardon. There is no soul
But it's unlike all others in the world,
Nor one but lifts a strangeness to God's love
Till that's grown infinite, and therefore none
Whose loss were less than irremediable
Although it were the wickedest in the world.

     [*Enter* TEIGUE *and* SHEMUS]

STEWARD: What are you running for? Pull off your cap.
Do you not see who's there?

SHEMUS: I cannot wait.
I am running to the world with the best news
That has been brought it for a thousand years.

STEWARD: Then get your breath and speak.

SHEMUS: If you'd my news
You'd run as fast and be as out of breath.

TEIGUE: Such news, we shall be carried on men's shoulders.

SHEMUS: There's something every man has carried with him
And thought no more about than if it were
A mouthful of the wind; and now it's grown
A marketable thing!

TEIGUE: And yet it seemed
As useless as the paring of one's nails.

SHEMUS: What sets me laughing when I think of it,
Is that a rogue who's lain in lousy straw,
If he but sell it, may set up his coach.

TEIGUE [*laughing*]: There are two gentlemen who buy
    men's souls.

CATHLEEN: O God!

TEIGUE: And maybe there's no soul at all.

STEWARD: They're drunk or mad.

TEIGUE: Look at the price they give. [*Showing money.*]

SHEMUS [*tossing up money*]: 'Go cry it all about the
    world', they said.
'"Money for souls, good money for a soul."'

CATHLEEN: Give twice and thrice and twenty times their
    money,
And get your souls again. I will pay all.

SHEMUS: Not we! not we! For souls – if there are souls –
But keep the flesh out of its merriment.
I shall be drunk and merry.

TEIGUE: Come, let's away. [*He goes.*]

CATHLEEN: But there's a world to come.

SHEMUS: And if there is,
I'd rather trust myself into the hands
That can pay money down than to the hands
That have but shaken famine from the bag.
    [*He goes out* R. *lilting*]
'There's money for a soul, sweet yellow money.
There's money for men's souls, good money, money.'

CATHLEEN [*to Aleel*]: Go call them here again, bring them
    by force,
Beseech them, bribe, do anything you like;
    [ALEEL *goes.*]
And you too follow, add your prayers to his.

[OONA, *who has been praying, goes out.*]
Steward, you know the secrets of my house.
How much have I?
STEWARD: A hundred kegs of gold.
CATHLEEN: How much have I in castles?
STEWARD: As much more.
CATHLEEN: How much have I in pasture?
STEWARD: As much more.
CATHLEEN: How much have I in forests?
STEWARD: As much more.
CATHLEEN: Keeping this house alone, sell all I have,
   Go barter where you please, but come again
   With herds of cattle and with ships of meal.
STEWARD: God's blessing light upon your ladyship.
   You will have saved the land.
CATHLEEN: Make no delay. [STEWARD *goes* L.]
   [ALEEL *and* OONA *return.*]
CATHLEEN: They have not come; speak quickly.
ALEEL: One drew his knife
   And said that he would kill the man or woman
   That stopped his way; and when I would have stopped
      him
   He made this stroke at me; but it is nothing.
CATHLEEN: You shall be tended. From this day for ever
   I'll have no joy or sorrow of my own.
OONA: Their eyes shone like the eyes of birds of prey.
CATHLEEN: Come, follow me, for the earth burns my feet
   Till I have changed my house to such a refuge
   That the old and ailing, and all weak of heart,
   May escape from beak and claw; all, all, shall come
   Till the walls burst and the roof fall on us.
   From this day out I have nothing of my own.
   [*She goes.*]
OONA [*taking Aleel by the arm and as she speaks bandaging
   his wound*]: She has found something now to put her
      hand to,
   And you and I are of no more account
   Than flies upon a window-pane in the winter.
   [*They go out.*]

Scene Three

Hall in the house of Countess Cathleen. At the left an oratory with steps leading up to it. At the right a tapestried wall, more or less repeating the form of the oratory, and a great chair with its back against the wall. In the centre are two or more arches through which one can see dimly the trees of the garden. CATHLEEN *is kneeling in front of the altar in the oratory; there is a hanging lighted lamp over the altar.* ALEEL *enters.*

ALEEL: I have come to bid you leave this castle and fly
  Out of these woods.
      [CATHLEEN *rises from the altar and comes in to the hall.*]
CATHLEEN: What evil is there here
  That is not everywhere from this to the sea?
ALEEL: They who have sent me walk invisible.
CATHLEEN: So it is true what I have heard men say,
  That you have seen and heard what others cannot.
ALEEL: I was asleep in my bed, and while I slept
  My dream became a fire; and in the fire
  One walked and he had birds about his head.
CATHLEEN: I have heard that one of the old gods walked
      so.
ALEEL: It may be that he is angelical;
  And, lady, he bids me call you from these woods.
  And you must bring but your old foster-mother,
  And some few serving-men, and live in the hills,
  Among the sounds of music and the light
  Of waters, till the evil days are done.
  For here some terrible death is waiting you,
  Some unimagined evil, some great darkness
  That fable has not dreamt of, nor sun nor moon
  Scattered.
CATHLEEN: No, not angelical.
ALEEL: This house

You are to leave with some old trusty man,
And bid him shelter all that starve or wander
While there is food and house-room.
CATHLEEN: He bids me go
Where none of mortal creatures but the swan
Dabbles, and there you would pluck the harp, when the
    trees
Had made a heavy shadow about our door,
And talk among the rustling of the reeds,
When night hunted the foolish sun away
With stillness and pale tapers. No – no – no!
I cannot. Although I weep, I do not weep
Because that life would be most happy, and here
I find no way, no end. Nor do I weep
Because I had longed to look upon your face,
But that a night of prayer has made me weary.
ALEEL [*prostrating himself before her*]: Let Him that made
      mankind, the angels and devils
And dearth and plenty, mend what He has made,
For when we labour in vain and eye still sees,
Heart breaks in vain.
CATHLEEN: How would that quiet end?
ALEEL: How but in healing?
CATHLEEN: You have seen my tears,
And I can see your hand shake on the floor.
ALEEL [*faltering*]: I thought but of healing. He was
      angelical.
CATHLEEN [*turning away from him*]: No, not angelical, but
      of the old gods,
Who wander about the world to waken the heart –
The passionate, proud heart – that all the angels,
Leaving nine heavens empty, would rock to sleep.
    [*She goes to the oratory door;* ALEEL *holds his clasped
    hands towards her for a moment hesitatingly, and then
    lets them fall beside him.*]
CATHLEEN: Do not hold out to me beseeching hands.
This heart shall never waken on earth. I have sworn,
By her whose heart the seven sorrows have pierced,
To pray before this altar until my heart

Has grown to Heaven like a tree, and there
Rustled its leaves, till Heaven has saved my people.

ALEEL [*who has risen*]: When one so great has spoken of
    love to one
So little as I, though to deny him love,
What can he but hold out beseeching hands,
Then let them fall beside him, knowing how greatly
They have overdared?

> [*He goes towards the door of the hall. The Countess*
> CATHLEEN *takes a few steps towards him.*]

CATHLEEN: If the old tales are true,
    Queens have wed shepherds and kings beggar-maids;
    God's procreant waters flowing about your mind
    Have made you more than kings or queens; and not
      you
    But I am the empty pitcher.

ALEEL: Being silent,
    I have said all, yet let me stay beside you.

CATHLEEN: No, no, not while my heart is shaken. No,
    But you shall hear wind cry and water cry,
    And curlew cry, and have the peace I longed for.

ALEEL: Give me your hand to kiss.

CATHLEEN: I kiss your forehead.
    And yet I send you from me. Do not speak;
    There have been women that bid men to rob
    Crowns from the Country-under-Wave or apples
    Upon a dragon-guarded hill, and all
    That they might sift the hearts and wills of men,
    And trembled as they bid it, as I tremble
    That lay a hard task on you, that you go,
    And silently, and do not turn your head.
    Good-bye; but do not turn your head and look;
    Above all else, I would not have you look.

> [ALEEL *goes.*]

I never spoke to him of his wounded hand,
And now he is gone. [*She looks out.*]
I cannot see him, for all is dark outside.
Would my imagination and my heart
Were as little shaken as this holy flame!

[*She goes slowly into the oratory. The distant sound of an
alarm bell.* THE TWO MERCHANTS *enter hurriedly.*]

SECOND MERCHANT: They are ringing the alarm, and in a
　　　moment
They'll be upon us.

FIRST MERCHANT [*going to a door at the side*]: Here is the
　　　Treasury.
You'd my commands to put them all to sleep.

SECOND MERCHANT: Some angel or else her prayers pro-
　　　tected them.
[*Goes into the Treasury and returns with bags of
treasure.* FIRST MERCHANT *has been listening at the
oratory door.*]

FIRST MERCHANT: She has fallen asleep.
[SECOND MERCHANT *goes out through one of the arches
at the back and stands listening. The bags are at his feet.*]

SECOND MERCHANT:　　　　We've all the treasure now,
So let's away before they've tracked us out.

FIRST MERCHANT: I have a plan to win her.

SECOND MERCHANT:　　　　You have time enough
If you would kill her and bear off her soul
Before they are upon us with their prayers;
They search the Western Tower.

FIRST MERCHANT:　　　　That may not be.
We cannot face the heavenly host in arms.
Her soul must come to us of its own will;
But being of the ninth and mightiest Hell,
Where all are kings, I have a plan to win it.
Lady, we've news that's crying out for speech.
[CATHLEEN *wakes and comes to door of oratory.*]

CATHLEEN: Who calls?

FIRST MERCHANT:　　　Lady, we have brought news.

CATHLEEN:　　　　　　　　　What are you?

FIRST MERCHANT: We are merchants, and we know the
　　　book of the world
Because we have walked upon its leaves; and there
Have read of late matters that much concern you;
And noticing the castle door stand open,
Came in to find an ear.

CATHLEEN: The door stands open
That no one who is famished or afraid
Despair of help or of a welcome with it.
But you have news, you say.

FIRST MERCHANT: We saw a man
Heavy with sickness in the bog of Allen,
Whom you had bid buy cattle. Near Fair Head
We saw your grain ships lying all becalmed
In the dark night; and not less still than they,
Burned all their mirrored lanthorns in the sea.

CATHLEEN: Thanks be to God there's money in the house
That can buy grain from those who have stored it up
To prosper on the hunger of the poor.
But you've been far and know the signs of things,
When will this famine end?

FIRST MERCHANT: Day copies day,
And there's no sign of change, nor can it change,
With the wheat withered and the cattle dead.

CATHLEEN: And heard you of the demons who buy souls?

FIRST MERCHANT: There are some men who hold they
    have wolves' heads,
And say their limbs – dried by the infinite flame –
Have all the speed of storms; others, again,
Say they are gross and little; while a few
Will have it they seem much as mortals are,
But tall and brown and travelled – like us, lady –
Yet all agree a power is in their looks
That makes men bow, and flings a casting-net
About their souls, and that all men would go
And barter those poor vapours, were it not
You bribe them with the safety of your gold.

CATHLEEN: Praise God that I am wealthy! Why do they
    sell?

FIRST MERCHANT: As we came in at the great door we saw
Your porter sleeping in his niche – a soul
Too little to be worth a hundred pence,
And yet they buy it for a hundred crowns.
But for a soul like yours, I heard them say,
They would give five hundred thousand crowns and more.

CATHLEEN: How can a heap of crowns pay for a soul?
Is the green grave so terrible a thing?

FIRST MERCHANT: Some sell because the money gleams, and some
Because they are in terror of the grave,
And some because their neighbours sold before,
And some because there is a kind of joy
In casting hope away, in losing joy,
In ceasing all resistance, in at last
Opening one's arms to the eternal flames,
In casting all sails out upon the wind:
To this – full of the gaiety of the lost –
Would all folk hurry if your gold were gone.

CATHLEEN: There is a something, Merchant, in your voice
That makes me fear. When you were telling how
A man may lose his soul and lose his God
Your eyes were lighted up, and when you told
How my poor money serves the people, both –
Merchants, forgive me – seemed to smile.

FIRST MERCHANT: I laugh
To think that all these people should be swung
As on a lady's shoe-string, – under them
The glowing leagues of never-ending flame.

CATHLEEN: There is a something in you that I fear;
A something not of us; were you not born
In some most distant corner of the world?

[*The* SECOND MERCHANT, *who has been listening at the door, comes forward, and as he comes a sound of voices and feet is heard.*]

SECOND MERCHANT: Away now – they are in the passage
– hurry,
For they will know us, and freeze up our hearts
With Ave Marys, and burn all our skin
With holy water.

FIRST MERCHANT: Farewell; for we must ride
Many a mile before the morning come;
Our horses beat the ground impatiently.

[*They go out. A number of* PEASANTS *enter by other door.*]

FIRST PEASANT: Forgive us, lady, but we heard a noise.

SECOND PEASANT: We sat by the fireside telling vanities.

FIRST PEASANT: We heard a noise, but though we have
    searched the house
We have found nobody.

CATHLEEN: You are too timid,
For now you are safe from all the evil times,
There is no evil that can find you here.

OONA [*entering hurriedly*]: Ochone! The treasure-room is
    broken in.
The door stands open, and the gold is gone.
    [PEASANTS *raise a lamentable cry.*]

CATHLEEN: Be silent. [*The cry ceases.*] Have you seen
    nobody?

OONA: Ochone!
That my good mistress should lose all this money!

CATHLEEN: Let those among you not too old to ride
Get horses and search all the country round.
I'll give a farm to him who finds the thieves.
    [*A* MAN *with keys at his girdle has come in while she
    speaks. There is a general murmur of* 'The porter! the
    porter!'*]

PORTER: Demons were here. I sat beside the door
In my stone niche, and two owls passed me by,
Whispering with human voices.

OLD PEASANT: God forsakes us.

CATHLEEN: Old man, old man, He never closed a door
Unless one opened. I am desolate
Because of a strange thought that's in my heart;
But I have still my faith; therefore be silent;
For surely He does not forsake the world,
But stands before it modelling in the clay
And moulding there His image. Age by age
The clay wars with His fingers and pleads hard
For its old, heavy, dull and shapeless ease;
But sometimes – though His hand is on it still –
It moves awry and demon hordes are born.
    [PEASANTS *cross themselves.*]
Yet leave me now, for I am desolate.

I hear a whisper from beyond the thunder.
[*She comes from the oratory door.*]
Yet stay an instant. When we meet again
I may have grown forgetful. Oona, take
These two – the larder and the dairy keys.
[*To the Porter.*]
But take you this. It opens the small room
Of herbs for medicine, every kind of herb.
The book of cures is on the upper shelf.
PORTER: Why do you do this, lady; did you see
Your coffin in a dream?
CATHLEEN: Ah, no, not that.
But I have come to a strange thought. I have heard
A sound of wailing in unnumbered hovels,
And I must go down, down – I know not where –
Pray for all men and women mad from famine;
Pray, you good neighbours.
[*The Peasants all kneel. Countess* CATHLEEN *ascends
the steps to the door of the oratory, and turning round
stands there motionless for a little, and then cries in a
loud voice*]
                        Mary, Queen of angels,
And all you clouds on clouds of saints, farewell!

Scene Four

FRONT SCENE. – *A wood near the Castle, as in Scene Two.
A group of* PEASANTS *pass.*

FIRST PEASANT: I have seen silver and copper, but not
    gold.
SECOND PEASANT: It's yellow and it shines.
FIRST PEASANT: It's beautiful.
    The most beautiful thing under the sun,
    That's what I've heard.
THIRD PEASANT: I have seen gold enough.

FOURTH PEASANT: I would not say that it's so beautiful.
FIRST PEASANT: But doesn't a gold piece glitter like the
    sun?
  That's what my father, who'd seen better days,
  Told me when I was but a little boy –
  So high – so high, it's shining like the sun,
  Round and shining, that is what he said.
SECOND PEASANT: There's nothing in the world it cannot
    buy.
FIRST PEASANT: They've bags and bags of it.
    [*They go out. The* TWO MERCHANTS *follow silently.*
    Then ALEEL *passes over the stage singing.*]
ALEEL: Impetuous heart be still, be still,
  Your sorrowful love can never be told,
  Cover it up with a lonely tune.
  He who could bend all things to His will
  Has covered the door of the infinite fold
  With the pale stars and the wandering moon.

Scene Five

*The house of Shemus Rua. There is an alcove at the back with
curtains; in it a bed, and on the bed is the body of Mary with
candles round it. The* TWO MERCHANTS *while they speak put
a large book upon a table, arrange money, and so on.*

FIRST MERCHANT: Thanks to that lie I told about her ships
  And that about the herdsman lying sick,
  We shall be too much thronged with souls tomorrow.
SECOND MERCHANT: What has she in her coffers now but
    mice?
FIRST MERCHANT: When the night fell and I had shaped
    myself
  Into the image of the man-headed owl,
  I hurried to the cliffs of Donegal,
  And saw with all their canvas full of wind

And rushing through the parti-coloured sea
Those ships that bring the woman grain and meal.
They're but three days from us.
SECOND MERCHANT: When the dew rose
I hurried in like feathers to the east,
And saw nine hundred oxen driven through Meath
With goads of iron. They're but three days from us.
FIRST MERCHANT: Three days for traffic.
    [PEASANTS *crowd in with* TEIGUE *and* SHEMUS.]
SHEMUS: Come in, come in, you are welcome.
That is my wife. She mocked at my great masters,
And would not deal with them. Now there she is;
She does not even know she was a fool,
So great a fool she was.
TEIGUE: She would not eat
One crumb of bread bought with our masters' money,
But lived on nettles, dock, and dandelion.
SHEMUS: There's nobody could put into her head
That death is the worst thing can happen us,
Though that sounds simple, for her tongue grew rank
With all the lies that she had heard in chapel.
Draw to the curtain. [TEIGUE *draws it.*] You'll not play
    the fool
While these good gentlemen are there to save you.
SECOND MERCHANT: Since the drought came they drift
    about in a throng.
Like autumn leaves blown by the dreary winds.
Come, deal – come, deal.
FIRST MERCHANT: Who will come deal with us?
SHEMUS: They are out of spirit, sir, with lack of food,
Save four or five. Here, sir, is one of these;
The others will gain courage in good time.
MIDDLE-AGED MAN: I come to deal – if you give honest
    price.
FIRST MERCHANT [*reading in a book*]: 'John Maher, a man
    of substance, with dull mind,
And quiet senses and unventurous heart.
The angels think him safe.' Two hundred crowns,
All for a soul, a little breath of wind.

MIDDLE-AGED MAN: I ask three hundred crowns. You have
    read there
That no mere lapse of days can make me yours.
FIRST MERCHANT: There is something more writ here –
    'Often at night
He is wakeful from a dread of growing poor,
And thereon wonders if there's any man
That he could rob in safety.'
A PEASANT: Who'd have thought it?
And I was once alone with him at midnight.
ANOTHER PEASANT: I will not trust my mother after this.
FIRST MERCHANT: There is this crack in you – two hundred
    crowns.
A PEASANT: That's plenty for a rogue.
ANOTHER PEASANT: I'd give him nothing.
SHEMUS: You'll get no more – so take what's offered you.
    [*A general murmur, during which the* MIDDLE-AGED
    MAN *takes money, and slips into background, where he
    sinks on to a seat.*]
FIRST MERCHANT: Has no one got a better soul than that?
If only for the credit of your parishes,
Traffic with us.
A WOMAN: What will you give for mine?
FIRST MERCHANT [*reading in book*]: 'Soft, handsome and
    still young' – not much, I think.
'It's certain that the man she's married to
Knows nothing of what's hidden in the jar
Between the hour-glass and the pepper-pot.'
THE WOMAN: The scandalous book!
FIRST MERCHANT: 'Nor how when he's away
At the horse-fair the hand that wrote what's hid
    Will tap three times upon the window-pane.'
THE WOMAN: And if there is a letter, that is no reason
Why I should have less money than the others.
FIRST MERCHANT: You're almost safe. I give you fifty
    crowns.
    [*She turns to go.*]
A hundred, then.
SHEMUS: Woman, have sense – come, come.

Is this a time to haggle at the price?
There, take it up. There, take it up. That's right.
[*She takes them and goes into the crowd.*]
FIRST MERCHANT: Come, deal, deal, deal. It is but for
   charity
We buy such souls at all; a thousand sins
Made them our Master's long before we came.
   [ALEEL *enters.*]
ALEEL: Here, take my soul, for I am tired of it.
I do not ask a price.
SHEMUS: Not ask a price?
How can you sell your soul without a price?
I would not listen to his broken wits.
His love for Countess Cathleen has so crazed him
He hardly understands what he is saying.
ALEEL: The trouble that has come on Countess Cathleen,
The sorrow that is in her wasted face,
The burden in her eyes, have broke my wits,
And yet I know I'd have you take my soul.
FIRST MERCHANT: We cannot take your soul, for it is hers.
ALEEL: No, but you must. Seeing it cannot help her
I have grown tired of it.
FIRST MERCHANT: Begone from me,
I may not touch it.
ALEEL: Is your power so small?
And must I bear it with me all my days?
May you be scorned and mocked!
FIRST MERCHANT: Drag him away.
He troubles me.
   [TEIGUE *and* SHEMUS *lead Aleel into the crowd.*]
SECOND MERCHANT: His gaze has filled me, brother,
With shaking and a dreadful fear.
FIRST MERCHANT: Lean forward
And kiss the circlet where my Master's lips
Were pressed upon it when he sent us hither;
You shall have peace once more.
   [SECOND MERCHANT *kisses the gold circlet that is about
   the head of the First Merchant.*]
                              I, too, grow weary,

But there is something moving in my heart
Whereby I know that what we seek the most
Is drawing near – our labour will soon end.
Come, deal, deal, deal, deal, deal; are you all dumb?
What, will you keep me from our ancient home,
And from the eternal revelry?

SECOND MERCHANT: Deal, deal.

SHEMUS: They say you beat the woman down too low.

FIRST MERCHANT: I offer this great price: a thousand
    crowns
For an old woman who was always ugly.
    [*An old* PEASANT WOMAN *comes forward, and he takes
    up a book and reads:*]
There is but little set down here against her.
'She has stolen eggs and fowl when times were bad,
But when the times grew better has confessed it;
She never missed her chapel of a Sunday
And when she could, paid dues.' Take up your money.

OLD WOMAN: God bless you, sir. [*She screams.*] O, sir, a
    pain went through me!

FIRST MERCHANT: That name is like a fire to all damned
    souls.
    [*Murmur among the* PEASANTS, *who shrink back from
    her as she goes out.*]

A PEASANT: How she screamed out!

SECOND PEASANT: And maybe we shall scream so.

THIRD PEASANT: I tell you there is no such place as Hell.

FIRST MERCHANT: Can such a trifle turn you from your
    profit?
Come, deal; come, deal.

MIDDLE-AGED MAN: Master, I am afraid.

FIRST MERCHANT: I bought your soul, and there's no sense
    in fear
Now the soul's gone.

MIDDLE-AGED MAN: Give me my soul again.

WOMAN [*going on her knees and clinging to Merchant*]: And
    take this money too, and give me mine.

SECOND MERCHANT: Bear bastards, drink or follow some
    wild fancy;

For cryings out and sighs are the soul's work,
And you have none. [*Throws the Woman off.*]

PEASANT: Come, let's away.

ANOTHER PEASANT: Yes, yes.

ANOTHER PEASANT: Come quickly; if that woman had not
    screamed
I would have lost my soul.

ANOTHER PEASANT: Come, come away.
    [*They turn to door, but are stopped by shouts of* 'Countess
    Cathleen! Countess Cathleen!']

CATHLEEN [*entering*]: And so you trade once more?

FIRST MERCHANT: In spite of you.
What brings you here, saint with the sapphire eyes?

CATHLEEN: I come to barter a soul for a great price.

SECOND MERCHANT: What matter, if the soul be worth the
    price?

CATHLEEN: The people starve, therefore the people go
Thronging to you. I hear a cry come from them
And it is in my ears by night and day,
And I would have five hundred thousand crowns
That I may feed them till the dearth go by.

FIRST MERCHANT: It may be the soul's worth it.

CATHLEEN: There is more:
The souls that you have bought must be set free.

FIRST MERCHANT: We know of but one soul that's worth
    the price.

CATHLEEN: Being my own it seems a priceless thing.

SECOND MERCHANT: You offer us –

CATHLEEN: I offer my own soul.

A PEASANT: Do not, do not, for souls the like of ours
Are not precious to God as your soul is.
O, what would Heaven do without you, lady?

ANOTHER PEASANT: Look how their claws clutch in their
    leathern gloves.

FIRST MERCHANT: Five hundred thousand crowns; we
    give the price.
The gold is here; the souls even while you speak
Have slipped out of our bond, because your face
Has shed a light on them and filled their hearts.

But you must sign, for we omit no form
In buying a soul like yours.
SECOND MERCHANT: Sign with this quill.
   It was a feather growing on the cock
   That crowed when Peter dared deny his Master,
   And all who use it have great honour in Hell.
      [CATHLEEN *leans forward to sign*.]
ALEEL [*rushing forward and snatching the pen from her*]:
   Leave all things to the Builder of the Heavens.
CATHLEEN: I have no thoughts; I hear a cry – a cry.
ALEEL [*casting the pen on the ground*]: I have seen a vision
         under a green hedge,
   A hedge of hips and haws – men yet shall hear
   The archangels rolling Satan's empty skull
   Over the mountain-tops.
FIRST MERCHANT: Take him away.
      [TEIGUE *and* SHEMUS *drag him roughly away so that he
      falls upon the floor among the Peasants.* CATHLEEN
      *picks up the parchment and signs, then turns towards
      the Peasants.*]
CATHLEEN: Take up the money, and now come with me;
   When we are far from this polluted place
   I will give everybody money enough.
      [*She goes out, the* PEASANTS *crowding round her and
      kissing her dress. Aleel and the two Merchants are left
      alone.*]
SECOND MERCHANT: We must away and wait until she dies,
   Sitting above her tower as two grey owls,
   Waiting as many years as may be, guarding
   Our precious jewel; waiting to seize her soul.
FIRST MERCHANT: We need but hover over her head in the
         air,
   For she has only minutes. When she signed
   Her heart began to break. Hush, hush, I hear
   The brazen door of Hell move on its hinges,
   And the eternal revelry float hither
   To hearten us.
SECOND MERCHANT: Leap feathered on the air
   And meet them with her soul caught in your claws.

[*They rush out.* ALEEL *crawls into the middle of the
room. The twilight has fallen and gradually darkens as
the scene goes on. There is a distant muttering of thunder
and a sound of rising storm.*]

ALEEL: The brazen door stands wide, and Balor comes
    Borne in his heavy car, and demons have lifted
    The age-weary eyelids from the eyes that of old
    Turned gods to stone; Barach, the traitor, comes
    And the lascivious race, Cailitin,
    That cast a Druid weakness and decay
    Over Sualtim's and old Dectora's child;
    And that great king Hell first took hold upon
    When he killed Naoise and broke Deirdre's heart;
    And all their heads are twisted to one side,
    For when they lived they warred on beauty and peace
    With obstinate, crafty, sidelong bitterness.
        [OONA *enters.*]
    Crouch down, old heron, out of the blind storm.

OONA: Where is the Countess Cathleen? All this day
    Her eyes were full of tears, and when for a moment
    Her hand was laid upon my hand it trembled,
    And now I do not know where she is gone.

ALEEL: Cathleen has chosen other friends than us,
    And they are rising through the hollow world.
    Demons are out, old heron.

OONA: God guard her soul!

ALEEL: She's bartered it away this very hour,
    As though we two were never in the world.
        [*He points downward.*]
    First, Orchil, her pale, beautiful head alive,
    Her body shadowy as vapour drifting
    Under the dawn, for she who awoke desire
    Has but a heart of blood when others die;
    About her is a vapoury multitude
    Of women alluring devils with soft laughter;
    Behind her a host heat of the blood made sin,
    But all the little pink-white nails have grown
    To be great talons.
        [*He seizes Oona and drags her into the middle of the room*

*and points downward with vehement gestures. The wind
roars.*]
> They begin a song
And there is still some music on their tongues.
OONA [*casting herself face downwards on the floor*]: O Maker
   of all, protect her from the demons,
And if a soul must needs be lost, take mine.
   [ALEEL *kneels beside her, but does not seem to hear her
   words. The* PEASANTS *return. They carry the Countess
   Cathleen and lay her upon the ground before Oona and
   Aleel. She lies there as if dead.*]
OONA: O that so many pitchers of rough clay
Should prosper and the porcelain break in two!
   [*She kisses the hands of Cathleen.*]
A PEASANT: We were under the tree where the path
   turns,
When she grew pale as death and fainted away.
And while we bore her hither cloudy gusts
Blackened the world and shook us on our feet.
Draw the great bolt, for no man has beheld
So black, bitter, blinding, and sudden a storm.
   [*One who is near the door draws the bolt.*]
CATHLEEN: O, hold me, and hold me tightly, for the storm
   Is dragging me away.
   [OONA *takes her in her arms. A* WOMAN *begins to wail.*]
PEASANTS: Hush!
OTHER PEASANTS: Hush!
PEASANT WOMEN: Hush!
OTHER PEASANT WOMEN: Hush!
CATHLEEN [*half rising*]: Lay all the bags of money in a
   heap,
And when I am gone, old Oona, share them out
To every man and woman: judge, and give
According to their needs.
A PEASANT WOMAN: And will she give
Enough to keep my children through the dearth?
ANOTHER PEASANT WOMAN: O Queen of Heaven, and all
   you blessed saints,
Let us and ours be lost so she be shriven.

CATHLEEN: Bend down your faces, Oona and Aleel;
   I gaze upon them as the swallow gazes
   Upon the nest under the eave, before
   She wander the loud waters. Do not weep
   Too great a while, for there is many a candle
   On the High Altar though one fall. Aleel,
   Who sang about the dancers of the woods
   That know not the hard burden of the world,
   Having but breath in their kind bodies, farewell!
   And farewell, Oona, you who played with me,
   And bore me in your arms about the house
   When I was but a child and therefore happy,
   Therefore happy, even like those that dance.
   The storm is in my hair and I must go. [*She dies.*]
OONA: Bring me the looking-glass.
      [*A* WOMAN *brings it to her out of the inner room.*
      OONA *holds it over the lips of Cathleen. All is silent for a
      moment. And then she speaks in a half scream*]
                                    O, she is dead!
A PEASANT: She was the great white lily of the world.
ANOTHER PEASANT: She was more beautiful than the pale
      stars.
AN OLD PEASANT WOMAN: The little plant I loved is
      broken in two.
      [ALEEL *takes looking-glass from Oona and flings it upon
      the floor so that it is broken in many pieces.*]
ALEEL: I shatter you in fragments, for the face
   That brimmed you up with beauty is no more:
   And die, dull heart, for she whose mournful words
   Made you a living spirit has passed away
   And left you but a ball of passionate dust.
   And you, proud earth and plumy sea, fade out!
   For you may hear no more her faltering feet,
   But are left lonely amid the clamorous war
   Of angels upon devils.
      [*He stands up; almost everyone is kneeling, but it has
      grown so dark that only confused forms can be seen.*]
                                    And I who weep
   Call curses on you, Time and Fate and Change,

And have no excellent hope but the great hour
When you shall plunge headlong through bottomless
   space.
   [*A flash of lightning followed immediately by thunder.*]
A PEASANT WOMAN: Pull him upon his knees before his
   curses
Have plucked thunder and lightning on our heads.
ALEEL: Angels and devils clash in the middle air,
And brazen swords clang upon brazen helms.
   [*A flash of lightning followed immediately by thunder.*]
Yonder a bright spear, cast out of a sling,
Has torn through Balor's eye, and the dark clans
Fly screaming as they fled Moytura of old.
   [*Everything is lost in darkness.*]
AN OLD MAN: The Almighty wrath at our great weakness
   and sin
Has blotted out the world and we must die.
   [*The darkness is broken by a visionary light. The
   PEASANTS seem to be kneeling upon the rocky slope of a
   mountain, and vapour full of storm and ever-changing
   light is sweeping above them and behind them. Half in
   the light, half in the shadow, stand armed angels. Their
   armour is old and worn, and their drawn swords dim
   and dinted. They stand as if upon the air in formation
   of battle and look downward with stern faces. The
   PEASANTS cast themselves on the ground.*]
ALEEL: Look no more on the half-closed gates of Hell,
But speak to me, whose mind is smitten of God,
That it may be no more with mortal things,
And tell of her who lies there.
   [*He seizes one of the angels.*]
                                   Till you speak
You shall not drift into eternity.
THE ANGEL: The light beats down; the gates of pearl are
   wide;
And she is passing to the floor of peace,
And Mary of the seven times wounded heart
Has kissed her lips, and the long blessed hair
Has fallen on her face; The Light of Lights

Looks always on the motive, not the deed,
The Shadow of Shadows on the deed alone.
[ALEEL *releases the Angel and kneels.*]
OONA: Tell them who walk upon the floor of peace
That I would die and go to her I love;
The years like great black oxen tread the world,
And God the herdsman goads them on behind,
And I am broken by their passing feet.
[*A sound of far-off horns seems to come from the heart of the light. The vision melts away, and the forms of the kneeling* PEASANTS *appear faintly in the darkness.*]

CURTAIN

Notes

Source Material: The play is partly based on the following story in Yeats's compilation: *Fairy, and Folk Tales of the Irish Peasantry* (London, 1888), pp. 232–5 [reprinted by kind permission of Mrs W. B. Yeats]:

The Countess Kathleen O'Shea*

A very long time ago, there suddenly appeared in old Ireland two unknown merchants of whom nobody had ever heard, and who nevertheless spoke the language of the country with the greatest perfection. Their locks were black, and bound round with gold, and their garments were of rare magnificence.

Both seemed of like age; they appeared to be men of fifty, for their foreheads were wrinkled and their beards tinged with grey.

In the hostelry where the pompous traders alighted it was sought to penetrate their designs; but in vain—they led a silent and retired life. And whilst they stopped there, they did nothing but count over and over again out of their money-bags pieces of gold, whose yellow brightness could be seen through the windows of their lodging.

'Gentlemen,' said the landlady one day, 'how is it that you are so rich, and that, being able to succour the public misery, you do no good works?'

'Fair hostess,' replied one of them, 'we didn't like to present alms to the honest poor, in dread we might be deceived by make-believe paupers. Let want knock at our door, we shall open it.'

The following day, when the rumour spread that two rich strangers had come, ready to lavish their gold, a crowd besieged their dwelling; but the figures of those who came out were widely different. Some carried pride in their mien; others were shame-faced.

* *This was quoted in a London-Irish newspaper. I am unable to find out the original source. (Yeats's note.) The story is a fairly close translation of 'Les Marchands d'Ames' in Léo Léspès, Les Matinées de Timothé Trimm (Paris, n.d.). Ed.*

The two chapmen traded in souls for the demon. The souls of the aged was worth twenty pieces of gold, not a penny more; for Satan had had time to make his valuation. The soul of a matron was valued at fifty, when she was handsome, and a hundred when she was ugly. The soul of a young maiden fetched an extravagant sum: the freshest and purest flowers are the dearest.

At that time there lived in the city an angel of beauty, the Countess Kathleen O'Shea. She was the idol of the people and the providence of the indigent. As soon as she learned that these miscreants profited to the public misery to steal away hearts from God, she called to her butler.

'Patrick,' said she to him, 'how many pieces of gold in my coffers?'

'A hundred thousand.'

'How many jewels?'

'The money's worth of the gold.'

'How much property in castles, forests, and lands?'

'Double the rest.'

'Very well, Patrick; sell all that is not gold; and bring me the account. I only wish to keep this mansion and the demesne that surrounds it.'

Two days afterwards the orders of the pious Kathleen were executed, and the treasure was distributed to the poor in proportion to their wants. This, says the tradition, did not suit the purposes of the Evil Spirit, who found no more souls to purchase. Aided by an infamous servant, they penetrated into the retreat of the noble dame, and purloined from her the rest of her treasure. In vain she struggled with all her strength to save the contents of her coffers; the diabolical thieves were the stronger. If Kathleen had been able to make the sign of the Cross, adds the legend, she would have put them to flight, but her hands were captive. The larceny was effected.

Then the poor called for aid to the plundered Kathleen, alas, to no good: she was able to succour their misery no longer; she had to abandon them to the temptation.

Meanwhile, but eight days had to pass before the grain and provender would arrive in abundance from the western lands. Eight such days were an age. Eight days required an immense sum to relieve the exigencies of the dearth, and the poor should either perish in the agonies of hunger, or, denying the holy maxims of the Gospel, vend, for base lucre, their souls, the richest gift from the bounteous hand of the Almighty. And

Kathleen hadn't anything, for she had given up her mansion
to the unhappy. She passed twelve hours in tears and mourning,
rending her sun-tinted hair, and bruising her breast, of the
whiteness of the lily; afterwards she stood up, resolute, ani-
mated by a vivid sentiment of despair.

She went to the traders in souls.

'What do you want?' they said.

'You buy souls?'

'Yes, a few still, in spite of you. Isn't that so, saint, with the
eyes of sapphire?'

'To-day I am come to offer you a bargain,' replied she.

'What?'

'I have a soul to sell, but it is costly.'

'What does that signify if it is precious? The soul, like the
diamond, is appraised by its transparency.'

'It is mine.'

The two emissaries of Satan started. Their claws were clutched
under their gloves of leather; their grey eyes sparkled; the soul,
pure, spotless, virginal of Kathleen – it was a priceless ac-
quisition!

'Beauteous lady, how much do you ask?'

'A hundred and fifty thousand pieces of gold.'

'It's at your service,' replied the traders, and they tendered
Kathleen a parchment sealed with black, which she signed
with a shudder.

The sum was counted out to her.

As soon as she got home she said to the butler, 'Here, dis-
tribute this: with this money that I give you the poor can tide
over the eight days that remain, and not one of their souls will
be delivered to the demon.'

Afterwards she shut herself up in her room, and gave orders
that none should disturb her.

Three days passed: she called nobody, she did not come out.

When the door was opened, they found her cold and stiff;
she was dead of grief.

But the sale of this soul, so adorable in its charity, was
declared null by the Lord: for she had saved her fellow-citizens
from eternal death.

After the eight days had passed, numerous vessels brought
into famished Ireland immense provisions in grain. Hunger was
no longer possible. As to the traders, they disappeared from
their hotel without anyone knowing what became of them.
But the fishermen of the Blackwater pretend that they are

enchained in a subterranean prison by order of Lucifer, until
they shall be able to render up the soul of Kathleen, which
escaped from them.

Scene One

25 *needle's eye*: 'It is easier for a camel to go through the eye
    of a needle than for a rich man to enter into the Kingdom
    of God' (Matthew xix, 24).
26 *the old worm o' the world*: Satan, evil.
32 *the trick-o'-the-loop-man*: the man in charge of the hoop-la
    sideshow at a fair.

Scene Two

33 *Maeve the queen of all the invisible host*: Maeve, the warlike
    queen of Connaught in Irish myths, was also reputed to
    be queen of the elfin people, as here.
34 *Knocknarea*: 'mountain of the Ring', is in Sligo. Its summit
    is supposed to be the site of Maeve's cairn.
35 *Cro-Patrick*: Croagh Patrick, a mountain in south-western
    Mayo, is dedicated to St Patrick and is a centre for
    pilgrimages.
36 *a learned theologian*: St Thomas Aquinas (see introduction
    to this play).

Scene Three

39 *he had birds about his head*: Aengus, the Celtic love-god,
    whose kisses were transformed to birds.
40 *her whose heart the seven sorrows have pierced*: the Blessed
    Virgin Mary whose seven sorrows were the prophecy of
    Simeon (Luke xi, 15), the flight into Egypt, the three
    days' disappearance of Jesus, his painful journey to
    Calvary, his crucifixion, the removal of his body from
    the Cross, and its entombment.
41 *the Country-under-Wave*: one of the other-worlds of Celtic
    mythology.
41 *apples Upon a dragon-guarded hill*: according to Greek
    mythology, the golden apples which Ge gave to Hera

when she married Zeus were guarded by the nymphs
called Hesperides and by the dragon named Ladon.

42 *ninth and mightiest Hell*: the ninth and lowest circle of Hell
in Dante's *Inferno* is allocated to the sin of fraud, which
the First Merchant now practises on the Countess.

43 *the bog of Allen*: in County Kildare.

43 *Fair Head*: on the northern coast of County Antrim.

45 *telling vanities*: telling trivial tales.

45 *Ochone!*: alas!

Scene Five

54 *Balor*: one of the Celtic gods of darkness, whose gaze
destroyed anyone on whom it fell.

54 *Barach*: a lord who helped the mythical king Conchubar to
revenge himself on Naisi, who had eloped with Deirdre,
whom Conchubar loved.

54 *the lascivious race, Cailitin . . . Dectora's child*: Calatin, a
wizard employed by Queen Maeve, was slain in battle by
Cuchulain, the son of Sualtim and Dectora. Calatin's
three sons and three daughters helped to bring about
Cuchulain's death by weakening one of his arms with a
spell and by afflicting his mind with hallucinations.

54 *that great king . . . broke Deirdre's heart*: Conchubar, King
of Ulster; see above.

54 *their heads are twisted to one side*: in Canto xx of his *Inferno*,
Dante describes the sorcerers in the eighth circle of Hell,
whose heads are twisted so that they can only look
behind them.

54 *Orchil*: a queen of the Celtic underworld.

57 *Yonder a bright spear . . . Moytura of old*: according to Irish
mythology, the gods of light defeated the gods of darkness at the second battle of Moytura, in which Lugh, the
sun-god, put out Balor's death-dealing eye.

The Playboy of the
Western World

Lady Gregory once spoke, more proudly than apologetically,
of 'the incorrigible Irish genius for myth-making'. J. M.
Synge's *The Playboy of the Western World* both satirizes
and exemplifies this national proclivity. During his first
visit to the Aran Islands in 1898, Synge heard the story of
how a Connemara man killed his father with a spade in a
fit of temper and was concealed by the islanders of Inishmaan because they associated the police with the hated
English jurisdiction. Six years later, Synge visited the
north-western part of County Mayo, a lonely, barren region
with strong traditions of violence and resistance to English
rule, where he noticed that 'in spite of the beauty of the
scenery the people in it are debased and nearly demoralized
by bad housing and lodging and the endless misery of the
rain. . . .' From these expeditions came the theme and the
setting of *The Playboy of the Western World*, which he
published in 1907.

In his adaptation of the story of parricide, Synge makes
Christy Mahon a man of Kerry, not Connemara. He strikes
his father because he has ordered him to marry an ugly,
middle-aged widow. Christy is thus a rebel against the
peasant custom of the arranged marriage as well as a
breaker of the English law. In the play, the father is only
stunned by the blow, but Christy thinks he has killed him,
and when he describes his exploit at the shebeen into which
he stumbles after wandering for eleven days, he is lionized
by his hearers. The shebeen is not in the Aran Islands but
on the north-western coast of Mayo. In one of his letters,
Synge remarked that the plot of *The Playboy*, even if it
had not a basis in fact, was probable, 'given the pyschic
state of the locality' represented in the play. The 'psychic
state' produced by its remoteness, and lawlessness is early
indicated by Pegeen Mike's wistful recollections of a dead

villager who 'got six months for maiming ewes' and was
so accomplished a story-teller that he could make old
women weep. The community is thus avid for the Prome-
thean myth of poetry, violence, and liberation which
Christy brings to it. He is urged to stay at the shebeen,
young women of the village bring him gifts, and his favours
are sought by Widow Quin and Pegeen Mike.

At the beginning of the play, Pegeen Mike is preparing to
marry Shawn Keogh, the antithesis of all that Christy
represents. Timid, inhibited, and puritanical, he submits
his life to the rulings of Father Reilly, the parish priest.
Pegeen and her father are on the point of rejecting Shawn
in favour of Christy when his father appears. Enraged by
the loss of their myth, the villagers revile their former hero.
But when Christy fells his father with a spade, they cannot
bear the reality of the myth; they have more in common
with Shawn Keogh than they realized. They tie Christy's
arms with a rope and Pegeen burns him with hot turf.
When Old Mahon crawls in, Christy establishes a new
relationship with him and they contemptuously shake the
dust of the village from their feet. Pegeen's final predica-
ment is tragi-comic. She strikes Keogh a box on the ear,
for she now realizes that Christy had a heroic strain in him
and that she has lost him for ever.

Except for Keogh, all the characters in the play have
abounding eloquence and animal spirits, but none of them
seems capable of moral idealism, and only Pegeen and
Christy achieve an awareness of beauty and a degree of
self-knowledge. Christy acquires these virtues gradually.
To begin with he is abject and timid, but once he has confessed his supposed parricide, the admiration of the villagers stimulates his imagination, which sets in motion a
development of character which eventually makes him
equal to the myth he has created. 'It's the poets are your
like,' Pegeen assures him, 'fine, fiery fellows with great
rages when their temper's roused,' and in the process of
magnifying his act of violence Christy's imagination
enables him to discern the meanness of his previous
existence. It also enables him to express his feelings for

Pegeen poetically, with an awareness of the sweetness of nature which contrasts powerfully with the cruelty so often suggested by the random references of other characters to birds and beasts. His development is complete at the end of the play when he departs with his father; Christy is now the dominant personality, and he shows a shrewd awareness of the process which has changed his character when he ironically blesses the villagers for having turned him into 'a likely gaffer in the end of all, the way I'll go romancing through a romping lifetime from this hour to the dawning of the judgement day'.

This last speech of Christy's exemplifies the knowledge of reality and the joy in words which Synge's preface to the play finds indispensable to the highest drama. In the preface he also acknowledges his indebtedness to the folk imagination of various regions of Ireland. Some of the most memorable passages in the play were transcribed without alteration from the notebooks of local idioms which he compiled during his travels. For instance, Christy's picturesque description of his father in Act One as 'naked as an ash tree in the moon of May' contains a simile which Synge had heard in Kerry. The preface, however, does less than justice to the art with which the dramatist blended the dialects of different regions and the fine discrimination with which he selected idioms from his notebooks, using them with unfailing dramatic propriety and making them an organic part of an exquisitely sustained rhythm. Synge revised some parts of *The Playboy* no fewer than thirteen times.

W.A.A.

The Playboy of the
Western World

John Millington Synge

Characters

CHRISTOPHER MAHON
OLD MAHON, *his father, a squatter*
MICHAEL JAMES FLAHERTY (called MICHAEL JAMES),
   a publican
MARGARET FLAHERTY (called PEGEEN MIKE), *his daughter*
WIDOW QUIN, *a woman of about thirty*
SHAWN KEOGH, *her cousin, a young farmer*
PHILLY CULLEN and JIMMY FARRELL, *small farmers*
SARA TANSEY, SUSAN BRADY and HONOR BLAKE, *village girls*
A BELLMAN
SOME PEASANTS

*The action takes place near a village, on a wild coast of Mayo.
The first Act passes on an evening of autumn, the other two Acts
on the following day.*

The Playboy of the Western World *was first performed at the
Abbey Theatre, Dublin, on 26 January 1907, with the following
cast:*

CHRISTOPHER MAHON	W. G. Fay
OLD MAHON	A. Power
MICHAEL JAMES FLAHERTY	Arthur Sinclair
PEGEEN MIKE	Maire O'Neill
SHAWN KEOGH	F. J. Fay
PHILLY CULLEN	J. A. O'Rourke
JIMMY FARRELL	J. M. Kerrigan
WIDOW QUIN	Sara Allgood
SARA TANSEY	Brigit O'Dempsey
SUSAN BRADY	Alice O'Sullivan
HONOR BLAKE	May Craig
PEASANTS	U. Wright, Harry Young

Preface

In writing *The Playboy of the Western World*, as in my other plays, I have used one or two words only that I have not heard among the country people of Ireland, or spoken in my own nursery before I could read the newspapers. A certain number of the phrases I employ I have heard also from herds and fishermen along the coast from Kerry to Mayo or from beggar-women and ballad-singers nearer Dublin; and I am glad to acknowledge how much I owe to the folk-imagination of these fine people. Anyone who has lived in real intimacy with the Irish peasantry will know that the wildest sayings and ideas in this play are tame indeed, compared with the fancies one may hear in any little hill-side cabin in Geesala, or Carraroe, or Dingle Bay. All art is a collaboration; and there is little doubt that in the happy ages of literature, striking and beautiful phrases were as ready to the story-teller's or the playwright's hand, as the rich cloaks and dresses of his time. It is probable that when the Elizabethan dramatist took his ink-horn and sat down to his work he used many phrases that he had just heard, as he sat at dinner, from his mother or his children. In Ireland, those of us who know the people have the same privilege. When I was writing *The Shadow of the Glen*, some years ago, I got more aid than any learning could have given me from a chink in the floor of the old Wicklow house where I was staying, that let me hear what was being said by the servant girls in the kitchen. This matter, I think, is of importance, for in countries where the imagination of the people, and the language they use, is rich and living, it is possible for a writer to be rich and copious in his words, and at the same time to give the reality, which is the root of all poetry, in a comprehensive and natural form. In the modern literature of towns, however, richness is found only in sonnets, or prose poems, or in one or two elaborate books that are far away from the profound and common interests of life. One has, on one side, Mallarmé and Huysmans producing this literature; and on the other, Ibsen and Zola dealing with the reality of life in joyless and pallid words. On the stage one must have reality, and one must have joy; and that is why the intellectual modern drama has failed, and people have grown sick of the false joy of the musical comedy, that has been given them in place of the rich joy found only in what is superb and wild in reality. In a good play every speech should be as fully flavoured as a nut or apple, and such speeches cannot be written by anyone who works among people who have shut their lips on poetry. In Ireland, for a few years more, we have a popular imagination that is fiery, and magnificent, and tender; so that those of us who wish to write start with a chance that is not given to writers in places where the springtime of the local life has been forgotten, and the harvest is a memory only, and the straw has been turned into bricks.

J.M.S.

21 January 1907

> *The following letter was written to a young man at the time of the first production of* The Playboy of the Western World *and gives a further idea of Synge's views on the play.*

19 February 1907

Dear Sir,

I must ask you to excuse me for delaying so long before returning your interesting essay and thanking you for it. During the week of the play I had influenza rather severely, and as soon as it was over, I had to take to my bed where I have been ever since, otherwise you should have heard from me long ago.

With a great deal of what you say I am most heartily in agreement – as where you see that I wrote the *Playboy* directly, as a piece of life, without thinking, or caring to

think, whether it was a comedy, tragedy, or extravaganza,
or whether it would be held to have, or not to have a purpose – also where you speak very accurately and rightly
about Shakespeare's 'mirror'. In the same way, you see,
what it seems so impossible to get our Dublin people to see,
obvious as it is – that the wildness, and if you will, vices of
the Irish peasantry are due, like their extraordinary good
points of all kinds, to the *richness* of their nature – a thing
that is priceless beyond words.

I fancy when you read the play – or see it performed in
more possible conditions – you will find Christy Mahon
more interesting than you are inclined to do now. Remember on the first production of a play the most subtle characters always tend to come out less strongly than the
simple characters, because those who act the more subtle
parts can do no more than feel their way until they have
acted the whole play a number of times.

Whether or not I agree with your final interpretation of
the whole play is my secret. I follow Goethe's rule, to tell
no one what one means in one's writings. I am sure you
will agree that the rule is a good one.

J. M. SYNGE

Act One

*Country public-house or shebeen, very rough and untidy.
There is a sort of counter on the right with shelves, holding
many bottles and jugs, just seen above it. Empty barrels stand
near the counter. At back, a little to left of counter, there is a
loor into the open air, then, more to the left, there is a settle
with shelves above it, with more jugs, and a table beneath a
window. At the left there is a large open fireplace, with turf
fire, and a small door into inner room.*

[PEGEEN, *a wild-looking but fine girl, of about twenty, is
writing at table. She is dressed in the usual peasant dress.*]

PEGEEN [*slowly as she writes*]: Six yards of stuff for to make
a yellow gown. A pair of lace boots with lengthy heels on
them and brassy eyes. A hat is suited for a wedding-day.
A fine-tooth comb. To be sent with three barrels of
porter in Jimmy Farrell's creel cart on the evening of the
coming Fair to Mister Michael James Flaherty. With the
best compliments of this season. Margaret Flaherty.

SHAWN KEOGH [*a fat and fair young man comes in as she
signs, looks round awkwardly, when he sees she is alone*]:
Where's himself?

PEGEEN [*without looking at him*]: He's coming. [*She directs
letter.*] To Mister Sheamus Mulroy, Wine and Spirit
Dealer, Castlebar.

SHAWN [*uneasily*]: I didn't see him on the road.

PEGEEN: How would you see him [*licks stamp and puts it
on letter*] and it dark night this half-hour gone by?

SHAWN [*turning towards door again*]: I stood a while outside
wondering would I have a right to pass on or to walk in
and see you, Pegeen Mike [*comes to fire*], and I could hear
the cows breathing and sighing in the stillness of the air,
and not a step moving any place from this gate to the
bridge.

PEGEEN [*putting letter in envelope*]: It's above at the cross-roads he is, meeting Philly Cullen and a couple more are going along with him to Kate Cassidy's wake.

SHAWN [*looking at her blankly*]: And he's going that length in the dark night.

PEGEEN [*impatiently*]: He is surely, and leaving me lonesome on the scruff of the hill. [*She gets up and puts envelope on dresser, then winds clock.*] Isn't it long the nights are now, Shawn Keogh, to be leaving a poor girl with her own self counting the hours to the dawn of day?

SHAWN [*with awkward humour*]: If it is, when we're wedded in a short while you'll have no call to complain, for I've little will to be walking off to wakes or weddings in the darkness of the night.

PEGEEN [*with rather scornful good-humour*]: You're making mighty certain, Shaneen, that I'll wed you now.

SHAWN: Aren't we after making a good bargain, the way we're only waiting these days on Father Reilly's dispensation from the bishops, or the Court of Rome.

PEGEEN [*looking at him teasingly, washing up at dresser*]: It's a wonder, Shaneen, the Holy Father'd be taking notice of the likes of you; for if I was him I wouldn't bother with this place where you'll meet none but Red Linahan, has a squint in his eye, and Patcheen is lame in his heel, or the mad Mulrannies were driven from California and they lost in their wits. We're a queer lot these times to go troubling the Holy Father on his sacred seat.

SHAWN [*scandalized*]: If we are, we're as good this place as another, maybe, and as good these times as we were for ever.

PEGEEN [*with scorn*]: As good, is it? Where now will you meet the like of Daneen Sullivan knocked the eye from a peeler; or Marcus Quin, God rest him, got six months for maiming ewes, and he a great warrant to tell stories of holy Ireland till he'd have the old women shedding down tears about their feet. Where will you find the like of them, I'm saying?

SHAWN [*timidly*]: If you don't, it's a good job, maybe; for [*with peculiar emphasis on the words*] Father Reilly has small conceit to have that kind walking around and talking to the girls.

PEGEEN [*impatiently throwing water from basin out of the door*]: Stop tormenting me with Father Reilly [*imitating his voice*] when I'm asking only what way I'll pass these twelve hours of dark, and not take my death with the fear. [*Looking out of the door.*]

SHAWN [*timidly*]: Would I fetch you the Widow Quin, maybe?

PEGEEN: Is it the like of that murderer? You'll not, surely.

SHAWN [*going to her, soothingly*]: Then I'm thinking himself will stop along with you when he sees you taking on; for it'll be a long night-time with great darkness, and I'm after feeling a kind of fellow above in the furzy ditch, groaning wicked like a maddening dog, the way it's good cause you have, maybe, to be fearing now.

PEGEEN [*turning on him sharply*]: What's that? Is it a man you seen?

SHAWN [*retreating*]: I couldn't see him at all; but I heard him groaning out, and breaking his heart. It should have been a young man from his words speaking.

PEGEEN [*going after him*]: And you never went near to see was he hurted or what ailed him at all?

SHAWN: I did not, Pegeen Mike. It was a dark, lonesome place to be hearing the like of him.

PEGEEN: Well, you're a daring fellow, and if they find his corpse stretched above in the dews of dawn, what'll you say then to the peelers, or the Justice of the Peace?

SHAWN [*thunderstruck*]: I wasn't thinking of that. For the love of God, Pegeen Mike, don't let on I was speaking of him. Don't tell your father and the men is coming above; for if they heard that story they'd have great blabbing this night at the wake.

PEGEEN: I'll maybe tell them, and I'll maybe not.

SHAWN: They are coming at the door. Will you wisht, I'm saying?

PEGEEN: Wisht yourself.

[*She goes behind counter.* MICHAEL JAMES, *fat, jovial*

publican, comes in followed by PHILLY CULLEN, *who is
thin and mistrusting, and* JIMMY FARRELL, *who is fat
and amorous, about forty-five.*]

MEN [*together*]: God bless you! The blessing of God on this
place!

PEGEEN: God bless you kindly.

MICHAEL [*to men, who go to the counter*]: Sit down now, and
take your rest. [*Crosses to Shawn at the fire.*] And how is
it you are, Shawn Keogh? Are you coming over the sands
to Kate Cassidy's wake?

SHAWN: I am not, Michael James. I'm going home the
short cut to my bed.

PEGEEN [*speaking across the counter*]: He's right, too, and
have you no shame, Michael James, to be quitting off for
the whole night, and leaving myself lonesome in the
shop?

MICHAEL [*good-humouredly*]: Isn't it the same whether I
go for the whole night or a part only? and I'm thinking
it's a queer daughter you are if you'd have me crossing
backward through the Stooks of the Dead Women, with
a drop taken.

PEGEEN: If I am a queer daughter, it's a queer father'd be
leaving me lonesome these twelve hours of dark, and I
piling the turf with the dogs barking, and the calves
mooing, and my own teeth rattling with the fear.

JIMMY [*flatteringly*]: What is there to hurt you, and you
a fine, hardy girl would knock the head of any two men
in the place?

PEGEEN [*working herself up*]: Isn't there the harvest boys
with their tongues red for drink, and the ten tinkers is
camped in the east glen, and the thousand militia – bad
cess to them! – walking idle through the land. There's
lots surely to hurt me, and I won't stop alone in it, let
himself do what he will.

MICHAEL: If you're that afeard, let Shawn Keogh stop
along with you. It's the will of God, I'm thinking, himself should be seeing to you now.

[*They all turn on Shawn.*]

SHAWN [*in horrified confusion*]: I would and welcome,

Michael James, but I'm afeard of Father Reilly; and
what at all would the Holy Father and the Cardinals of
Rome be saying if they heard I did the like of that?

MICHAEL [*with contempt*]: God help you! Can't you sit in
by the hearth with the light lit and herself beyond in the
room? You'll do that surely, for I've heard tell there's a
queer fellow above, going mad or getting his death, maybe, in the gripe of the ditch, so she'd be safer this night
with a person here.

SHAWN [*with plaintive despair*]: I'm afeard of Father
Reilly, I'm saying. Let you not be tempting me, and we
near married itself.

PHILLY [*with cold contempt*]: Lock him in the west room.
He'll stay then and have no sin to be telling to the
priest.

MICHAEL [*to Shawn, getting between him and the door*]: Go
up now.

SHAWN [*at the top of his voice*]: Don't stop me, Michael
James. Let me out of the door, I'm saying, for the love
of the Almighty God. Let me out [*trying to dodge past
him*]. Let me out of it, and may God grant you His indul-
gence in the hour of need.

MICHAEL [*loudly*]: Stop your noising, and sit down by the
hearth.

[*Gives him a push and goes to counter laughing.*]

SHAWN [*turning back, wringing his hands*]: Oh, Father
Reilly, and the saints of God, where will I hide myself
today? Oh, St Joseph and St Patrick and St Brigid and
St James, have mercy on me now!

[SHAWN *turns round, sees door clear, and makes a rush
for it.*]

MICHAEL [*catching him by the coat-tail*]: You'd be going, is
it?

SHAWN [*screaming*]: Leave me go, Michael James, leave
me go, you old Pagan, leave me go, or I'll get the curse
of the priests on you, and of the scarlet-coated bishops
of the Courts of Rome. [*With a sudden movement he pulls
himself out of his coat, and disappears out of the door,
leaving his coat in Michael's hands.*]

MICHAEL [*turning round, and holding up coat*]: Well, there's the coat of a Christian man. Oh, there's sainted glory this day in the lonesome west; and by the will of God I've got you a decent man, Pegeen, you'll have no call to be spying after if you've a score of young girls, maybe, weeding in your fields.

PEGEEN [*taking up the defence of her property*]: What right have you to be making game of a poor fellow for minding the priest, when it's your own the fault is, not paying a penny pot-boy to stand along with me and give me courage in the doing of my work? [*She snaps the coat away from him, and goes behind counter with it.*]

MICHAEL [*taken aback*]: Where would I get a pot-boy? Would you have me send the bellman screaming in the streets of Castlebar?

SHAWN [*opening the door a chink and putting in his head, in a small voice*]: Michael James!

MICHAEL [*imitating him*]: What ails you?

SHAWN: The queer dying fellow's beyond looking over the ditch. He's come up, I'm thinking, stealing your hens. [*Looks over his shoulder.*] God help me, he's following me now [*he runs into room*], and if he's heard what I said, he'll be having my life, and I going home lonesome in the darkness of the night.

[*For a perceptible moment they watch the door with curiosity. Someone coughs outside. Then* CHRISTY MAHON, *a slight young man, comes in very tired and frightened and dirty.*]

CHRISTY [*in a small voice*]: God save all here!

MEN: God save you kindly!

CHRISTY [*going to the counter*]: I'd trouble you for a glass of porter, woman of the house.

[*He puts down a coin.*]

PEGEEN [*serving him*]: You're one of the tinkers, young fellow, is beyond camped in the glen?

CHRISTY: I am not; but I'm destroyed walking.

MICHAEL [*patronizingly*]: Let you come up then to the fire. You're looking famished with the cold.

CHRISTY: God reward you. [*He takes up his glass and goes*

a little way across to the left, then stops and looks about him.] Is it often the polis do be coming into this place, master of the house?

MICHAEL: If you'd come in better hours, you'd have seen 'Licensed for the Sale of Beer and Spirits, to be Consumed on the Premises', written in white letters above the door, and what would the polis want spying on me, and not a decent house within four miles, the way every living Christian is a bona fide, saving one widow alone?

CHRISTY [*with relief*]: It's a safe house, so. [*He goes over to the fire, sighing and moaning. Then he sits down, putting his glass beside him, and begins gnawing a turnip, too miserable to feel the others staring at him with curiosity.*]

MICHAEL [*going after him*]: Is it yourself is fearing the polis? You're wanting, maybe?

CHRISTY: There's many wanting.

MICHAEL: Many, surely, with the broken harvest and the ended wars. [*He picks up some stockings, etc., that are near the fire, and carries them away furtively.*] It should be larceny, I'm thinking?

CHRISTY [*dolefully*]: I had it in my mind it was a different word and a bigger.

PEGEEN: There's a queer lad. Were you never slapped in school, young fellow, that you don't know the name of your deed?

CHRISTY [*bashfully*]: I'm slow at learning, a middling scholar only.

MICHAEL: If you're a dunce itself, you'd have a right to know that larceny's robbing and stealing. Is it for the like of that you're wanting?

CHRISTY [*with a flash of family pride*]: And I the son of a strong farmer [*with a sudden qualm*], God rest his soul, could have bought up the whole of your old house a while since, from the butt of his tail-pocket, and not have missed the weight of it gone.

MICHAEL [*impressed*]: If it's not stealing, it's maybe something big.

CHRISTY [*flattered*]: Ay; it's maybe something big.

JIMMY: He's a wicked-looking young fellow. Maybe he followed after a young woman on a lonesome night.

CHRISTY [*shocked*]: Oh, the saints forbid, mister; I was all times a decent lad.

PHILLY [*turning on Jimmy*]: You're a silly man, Jimmy Farrell. He said his father was a farmer a while since, and there's himself now in a poor state. Maybe the land was grabbed from him, and he did what any decent man would do.

MICHAEL [*to Christy, mysteriously*]: Was it bailiffs?

CHRISTY: The divil a one.

MICHAEL: Agents?

CHRISTY: The divil a one.

MICHAEL: Landlords?

CHRISTY [*peevishly*]: Ah, not at all, I'm saying. You'd see the like of them stories on any little paper of a Munster town. But I'm not calling to mind any person, gentle, simple, judge or jury, did the like of me.

[*They all draw nearer with delighted curiosity.*]

PHILLY: Well, that lad's a puzzle-the-world.

JIMMY: He'd beat Dan Davies' circus, or the holy missioners making sermons on the villainy of man. Try him again, Philly.

PHILLY: Did you strike golden guineas out of solder, young fellow, or shilling coins itself?

CHRISTY: I did not, mister, not sixpence nor a farthing coin.

JIMMY: Did you marry three wives maybe? I'm told there's a sprinkling have done that among the holy Luthers of the preaching north.

CHRISTY [*shyly*]: I never married with one, let alone with a couple or three.

PHILLY: Maybe he went fighting for the Boers, the like of the man beyond, was judged to be hanged, quartered, and drawn. Were you off east, young fellow, fighting bloody wars for Kruger and the freedom of the Boers?

CHRISTY: I never left my own parish till Tuesday was a week.

PEGEEN [*coming from counter*]: He's done nothing, so. [*To

Christy] If you didn't commit murder or a bad, nasty thing; or false coining, or robbery, or butchery, or the like of them, there isn't anything that would be worth your troubling for to run from now. You did nothing at all.

CHRISTY [*his feelings hurt*]: That's an unkindly thing to be saying to a poor orphaned traveller, has a prison behind him, and hanging before, and hell's gap gaping below.

PEGEEN [*with a sign to the men to be quiet*]: You're only saying it. You did nothing at all. A soft lad the like of you wouldn't slit the windpipe of a screeching sow.

CHRISTY [*offended*]: You're not speaking the truth.

PEGEEN [*in mock rage*]: Not speaking the truth, is it? Would you have me knock the head of you with the butt of the broom?

CHRISTY [*twisting round on her with a sharp cry of horror*]: Don't strike me. I killed my poor father, Tuesday was a week, for doing the like of that.

PEGEEN [*with blank amazement*]: Is it killed your father?

CHRISTY [*subsiding*]: With the help of God I did, surely, and that the Holy Immaculate Mother may intercede for his soul.

PHILLY [*retreating with* JIMMY]: There's a daring fellow.

JIMMY: Oh, glory be to God!

MICHAEL [*with great respect*]: That was a hanging crime, mister honey. You should have had good reason for doing the like of that.

CHRISTY [*in a very reasonable tone*]: He was a dirty man, God forgive him, and he getting old and crusty, the way I couldn't put up with him at all.

PEGEEN: And you shot him dead?

CHRISTY [*shaking his head*]: I never used weapons. I've no licence, and I'm a law-fearing man.

MICHAEL: It was with a hilted knife maybe? I'm told, in the big world, it's bloody knives they use.

CHRISTY [*loudly, scandalized*]: Do you take me for a slaughter-boy?

PEGEEN: You never hanged him, the way Jimmy Farrell hanged his dog from the licence, and had it screeching and wriggling three hours at the butt of a string, and himself swearing it was a dead dog, and the peelers swearing it had life?

CHRISTY: I did not, then. I just riz the loy and let fall the edge of it on the ridge of his skull, and he went down at my feet like an empty sack, and never let a grunt or groan from him at all.

MICHAEL [*making a sign to Pegeen to fill Christy's glass*]: And what way weren't you hanged, mister? Did you bury him then?

CHRISTY [*considering*]: Aye. I buried him then. Wasn't I digging spuds in the field?

MICHAEL: And the peelers never followed after you the eleven days that you're out?

CHRISTY [*shaking his head*]: Never a one of them, and I walking forward facing hog, dog, or divil on the highway of the road.

PHILLY [*nodding wisely*]: It's only with a common week-day kind of a murderer them lads would be trusting their carcase, and that man should be a great terror when his temper's roused.

MICHAEL: He should then. [*To Christy*] And where was it, mister honey, that you did the deed?

CHRISTY [*looking at him with suspicion*]: Oh, a distant place, master of the house, a windy corner of high, distant hills.

PHILLY [*nodding with approval*]: He's a close man, and he's right, surely.

PEGEEN: That'd be a lad with the sense of Solomon to have for a pot-boy, Michael James, if it's the truth you're seeking one at all.

PHILLY: The peelers is fearing him, and if you'd that lad in the house there isn't one of them would come smelling around if the dogs itself were lapping poteen from the dungpit of the yard.

JIMMY: Bravery's a treasure in a lonesome place, and a lad would kill his father, I'm thinking, would face a foxy divil with a pitchpike on the flags of hell.

PEGEEN: It's the truth they're saying, and if I'd that lad

in the house, I wouldn't be fearing the looséd khaki cut-
throats, or the walking dead.

CHRISTY [*swelling with surprise and triumph*]: Well, glory
be to God!

MICHAEL [*with deference*]: Would you think well to stop
here and be pot-boy, mister honey, if we gave you good
wages, and didn't destroy you with the weight of work?

SHAWN [*coming forward uneasily*]: That'd be a queer kind
to bring into a decent, quiet household with the like of
Pegeen Mike.

PEGEEN [*very sharply*]: Will you wisht? Who's speaking
to you?

SHAWN [*retreating*]: A bloody-handed murderer the like
of . . .

PEGEEN [*snapping at him*]: Whisht, I am saying; we'll take
no fooling from your like at all. [*To Christy with a
honeyed voice*] And you, young fellow, you'd have a
right to stop, I'm thinking, for we'd do our all and utmost to content your needs.

CHRISTY [*overcome with wonder*]: And I'd be safe this place
from the searching law?

MICHAEL: You would, surely. If they're not fearing you,
itself, the peelers in this place is decent, drouthy poor
fellows, wouldn't touch a cur dog and not give warning
in the dead of night.

PEGEEN [*very kindly and persuasively*]: Let you stop a short
while anyhow. Aren't you destroyed walking with your
feet in bleeding blisters, and your whole skin needing
washing like a Wicklow sheep.

CHRISTY [*looking round with satisfaction*]: It's a nice room,
and if it's not humbugging me you are, I'm thinking that
I'll surely stay.

JIMMY [*jumps up*]: Now, by the grace of God, herself will
be safe this night, with a man killed his father holding
danger from the door, and let you come on, Michael
James, or they'll have the best stuff drunk at the wake.

MICHAEL [*going to the door with men*]: And begging your
pardon, mister, what name will we call you, for we'd like
to know?

CHRISTY: Christopher Mahon.

MICHAEL: Well, God bless you, Christy, and a good rest till we meet again when the sun'll be rising to the noon of day.

CHRISTY: God bless you all.

MEN: God bless you.

[*They go out, except* SHAWN, *who lingers at the door.*]

SHAWN [*to Pegeen*]: Are you wanting me to stop along with you and keep you from harm?

PEGEEN [*gruffly*]: Didn't you say you were fearing Father Reilly?

SHAWN: There'd be no harm staying now, I'm thinking, and himself in it too.

PEGEEN: You wouldn't stay when there was need for you, and let you step off nimble this time when there's none.

SHAWN: Didn't I say it was Father Reilly . . .

PEGEEN: Go on, then, to Father Reilly [*in a jeering tone*], and let him put you in the holy brotherhoods, and leave that lad to me.

SHAWN: If I meet the Widow Quin . . .

PEGEEN: Go on, I'm saying, and don't be waking this place with your noise. [*She hustles him out out and bolts door.*] That lad would wear the spirits from the saints of peace. [*Bustles about, then takes off her apron and pins it up in the window as a blind,* CHRISTY *watching her timidly. Then she comes to him and speaks with bland good-humour.*] Let you stretch out now by the fire, young fellow. You should be destroyed travelling.

CHRISTY [*shyly again, drawing off his boots*]: I'm tired surely, walking wild eleven days, and waking fearful in the night. [*He holds up one of his feet, feeling his blisters, and looking at them with compassion.*]

PEGEEN [*standing beside him, watching him with delight*]: You should have had great people in your family, I'm thinking, with the little, small feet you have, and you with a kind of a quality name, the like of what you'd find on the great powers and potentates of France and Spain.

CHRISTY [*with pride*]: We were great, surely, with wide
and windy acres of rich Munster land.

PEGEEN: Wasn't I telling you, and you a fine, handsome
young fellow with a noble brow?

CHRISTY [*with a flash of delighted surprise*]: Is it me?

PEGEEN: Aye. Did you never hear that from the young
girls where you come from in the west or south?

CHRISTY [*with venom*]: I did not, then. Oh, they're bloody
liars in the naked parish where I grew a man.

PEGEEN: If they are itself, you've heard it these days, I'm
thinking, and you walking the world telling out your
story to young girls or old.

CHRISTY: I've told my story no place till this night,
Pegeen Mike, and it's foolish I was here, maybe, to be
talking free; but you're decent people, I'm thinking, and
yourself a kindly woman, the way I wasn't fearing you
at all.

PEGEEN [*filling a sack with straw*]: You've said the like of
that, maybe, in every cot and cabin where you've met
a young girl on your way.

CHRISTY [*going over to her, gradually raising his voice*]: I've
said it nowhere till this night, I'm telling you; for I've
seen none the like of you the eleven long days I am walking the world, looking over a low ditch or a high ditch
on my north or south, into stony, scattered fields, or
scribes of bog, where you'd see young, limber girls, and
fine, prancing women making laughter with the men.

PEGEEN: If you weren't destroyed travelling, you'd have
as much talk and streeleen, I'm thinking, as Owen Roe
O'Sullivan or the poets of the Dingle Bay; and I've heard
all times it's the poets are your like – fine, fiery fellows
with great rages when their temper's roused.

CHRISTY [*drawing a little nearer to her*]: You've a power of
rings, God bless you, and would there be any offence if I
was asking are you single now?

PEGEEN: What would I want wedding so young?

CHRISTY [*with relief*]: We're alike, so.

PEGEEN [*she puts sack on settle and beats it up*]: I never
killed my father. I'd be afeard to do that, except I was

the like of yourself with blind rages tearing me within,
for I'm thinking you should have had great tussling
when the end was come.

CHRISTY [*expanding with delight at the first confidential
talk he has ever had with a woman*]: We had not then. It
was a hard woman was come over the hill; and if he
was always a crusty kind when he'd a hard woman
setting him on, not the divil himself or his four fathers
could put up with him at all.

PEGEEN [*with curiosity*]: And isn't it a great wonder that
one wasn't fearing you?

CHRISTY [*very confidentially*]: Up to the day I killed my
father, there wasn't a person in Ireland knew the kind
I was, and I there drinking, waking, eating, sleeping, a
quiet, simple poor fellow with no man giving me heed.

PEGEEN [*getting a quilt out of cupboard and putting it on the
sack*]. It was the girls were giving you heed, maybe, and
I'm thinking it's most conceit you'd have to be gaming
with their like.

CHRISTY [*shaking his head, with simplicity*]: Not the girls
itself, and I won't tell you a lie. There wasn't anyone
heeding me in that place saving only the dumb beasts
of the field. [*He sits down at fire.*]

PEGEEN [*with disappointment*]: And I thinking you should
have been living the like of a king of Norway or the
eastern world. [*She comes and sits beside him after placing
bread and mug of milk on the table.*]

CHRISTY [*laughing piteously*]: The like of a king, is it? And
I after toiling, moiling, digging, dodging from the dawn
till dusk; with never a sight of joy or sport saving only
when I'd be abroad in the dark night poaching rabbits
on hills, for I was a divil to poach, God forgive me, [*very
naïvely*] and I near got six months for going with a dung
fork and stabbing a fish.

PEGEEN: And it's that you'd call sport, is it, to be abroad
in the darkness with yourself alone?

CHRISTY: I did, God help me, and there I'd be as happy as
the sunshine of St Martin's Day, watching the light passing the north or the patches of fog, till I'd hear a rabbit

starting to screech and I'd go running in the furze. Then, when I'd my full share, I'd come walking down where you'd see the ducks and geese stretched sleeping on the highway of the road, and before I'd pass the dunghill, I'd hear himself snoring out – a loud, lonesome snore he'd be making all times, the while he was sleeping; and he a man'd be raging all times, the while he was waking, like a gaudy officer you'd hear cursing and damning and swearing oaths.

PEGEEN: Providence and Mercy, spare us all!

CHRISTY: It's that you'd say surely if you seen him and he after drinking for weeks, rising up in the red dawn, or before it maybe, and going out into the yard as naked as an ash-tree in the moon of May, and shying clods against the visage of the stars he'd till put the fear of death into the banbhs and the screeching sows.

PEGEEN: I'd be well-nigh afeard of that lad myself, I'm thinking. And there was no one in it but the two of you alone?

CHRISTY: The divil a one, though he'd sons and daughters walking all great states and territories of the world, and not a one of them, to this day, but would say their seven curses on him, and they rousing up to let a cough or sneeze, maybe, in the deadness of the night.

PEGEEN [nodding her head]: Well, you should have been a queer lot. I never cursed my father the like of that, though I'm twenty and more years of age.

CHRISTY: Then you'd have cursed mine, I'm telling you, and he a man never gave peace to any, saving when he'd get two months or three, or be locked in the asylums for battering peelers or assaulting men [with depression], the way it was a bitter life he led me till I did up a Tuesday and halve his skull.

PEGEEN [putting her hand on his shoulder]: Well, you'll have peace in this place, Christy Mahon, and none to trouble you, and it's near time a fine lad like you should have your good share of the earth.

CHRISTY: It's time surely, and I a seemly fellow with great strength in me and bravery of . . . [Someone knocks.]

CHRISTY [*clinging to Pegeen*]: Oh, glory! it's late for knocking, and this last while I'm in terror of the peelers, and
the walking dead. [*Knocking again.*]

PEGEEN: Who's there?

VOICE [*outside*]: Me.

PEGEEN: Who's me?

VOICE: The Widow Quin.

PEGEEN [*jumping up and giving him the bread and milk*]:
Go on now with your supper, and let on to be sleepy, for
if she found you were such a warrant to talk, she'd be
stringing gabble till the dawn of day.

  [*He takes bread and sits shyly with his back to the
  door.*]

PEGEEN [*opening the door, with temper*]: What ails you, or
what is it you're wanting at this hour of the night?

WIDOW QUIN [*coming in a step and peering at Christy*]: I'm
after meeting Shawn Keogh and Father Reilly below,
who told me of your curiosity man, and they fearing by
this time he was maybe roaring, romping on your hands
with drink.

PEGEEN [*pointing to Christy*]: Look now is he roaring, and
he stretched out drowsy with his supper and his mug of
milk. Walk down and tell that to Father Reilly and to
Shaneen Keogh.

WIDOW QUIN [*coming forward*]: I'll not see them again, for
I've their word to lead that lad forward for to lodge with
me.

PEGEEN [*in blank amazement*]: This night is it?

WIDOW QUIN [*going over*]: This night. 'It isn't fitting,' says
the priesteen, 'to have his likeness lodging with an
orphaned girl.' [*To Christy*] God save you, mister!

CHRISTY [*shyly*]: God save you kindly!

WIDOW QUIN [*looking at him with half-amused curiosity*]:
Well, aren't you a little smiling fellow? It should have
been great and bitter torments did rouse your spirits to
a deed of blood.

CHRISTY [*doubtfully*]: It should, maybe.

WIDOW QUIN: It's more than 'maybe' I'm saying, and
it'd soften my heart to see you sitting so simple with

your cup and cake, and you fitter to be saying your
catechism than slaying your da.

PEGEEN [*at counter, washing glasses*]: There's talking when
any'd see he's fit to be holding his head high with the
wonders of the world. Walk on from this, for I'll not have
him tormented, and he destroyed travelling since Tuesday was a week.

WIDOW QUIN [*peaceably*]: We'll be walking surely when
his supper's done, and you'll find we're great company,
young fellow, when it's of the like of you and me you'd
hear the penny poets singing in an August Fair.

CHRISTY [*innocently*]: Did you kill your father?

PEGEEN [*contemptuously*]: She did not. She hit himself with
a worn pick, and the rusted poison did corrode his blood
the way he never overed it, and died after. That was a
sneaky kind of murder did win small glory with the boys
itself. [*She crosses to Christy's left.*]

WIDOW QUIN [*with good humour*]: If it didn't, maybe all
knows a widow woman has buried her children and destroyed her man is a wiser comrade for a young lad than
a girl, the like of you, who'd go helter-skeltering after
any man would let you a wink upon the road.

PEGEEN [*breaking out into a wild rage*]: And you'll say that,
Widow Quin, and you gasping with the rage you had
racing the hill beyond to look on his face.

WIDOW QUIN [*laughing derisively*]: Me, is it? Well, Father
Reilly has cuteness to divide you now. [*She pulls Christy
up.*] There's great temptation in a man did slay his da,
and we'd best be going, young fellow; so rise up and come
with me.

PEGEEN [*seizing his arm*]: He'll not stir. He's pot-boy in
this place, and I'll not have him stolen off and kidnapped
while himself's abroad.

WIDOW QUIN: It'd be a crazy pot-boy'd lodge him in the
shebeen where he works by day, so you'd have a right
to come on, young fellow, till you see my little houseen,
a perch off on the rising hill.

PEGEEN: Wait till morning, Christy Mahon. Wait till you
lay eyes on her leaky thatch is growing more pasture for

her buck goat than her square of fields, and she without a tramp itself to keep in order her place at all.

WIDOW QUIN: When you see me contriving in my little gardens, Christy Mahon, you'll swear the Lord God formed me to be living alone, and that there isn't my match in Mayo for thatching, or mowing, or shearing a sheep.

PEGEEN [*with noisy scorn*]: It's true the Lord God formed you to contrive indeed. Doesn't the world know you reared a black ram at your own breast, so that the Lord Bishop of Connaught felt the elements of a Christian, and he eating it after in a kidney stew? Doesn't the world know you've been seen shaving the foxy skipper from France for a threepenny-bit and a sop of grass tobacco would wring the liver from a mountain goat you'd meet leaping the hills?

WIDOW QUIN [*with amusement*]: Do you hear her now, young fellow? Do you hear the way she'll be rating at your own self when a week is by?

PEGEEN [*to Christy*]: Don't heed her. Tell her to go on into her pigsty and not plague us here.

WIDOW QUIN: I'm going; but he'll come with me.

PEGEEN [*shaking him*]: Are you dumb, young fellow?

CHRISTY [*timidly to Widow Quin*]: God increase you; but I'm pot-boy in this place, and it's here I liefer stay.

PEGEEN [*triumphantly*]: Now you have heard him, and go on from this.

WIDOW QUIN [*looking round the room*]: It's lonesome this hour crossing the hill, and if he won't come along with me, I'd have a right maybe to stop this night with yourselves. Let me stretch out on the settle, Pegeen Mike; and himself can lie by the hearth.

PEGEEN [*short and fiercely*]: Faith, I won't. Quit off or I will send you now.

WIDOW QUIN [*gathering her shawl up*]: Well, it's a terror to be aged a score. [*To Christy*] God bless you now, young fellow, and let you be wary, or there's right torment will await you here if you go romancing with her like, and she waiting only, as they bade me say, on a sheepskin parchment to be wed with Shawn Keogh of Killakeen.

CHRISTY [*going to Pegeen as she bolts door*]: What's that she's after saying?

PEGEEN: Lies and blather, you've no call to mind. Well, isn't Shawn Keogh an impudent fellow to send up spying on me? Wait till I lay hands on him. Let him wait, I'm saying.

CHRISTY: And you're not wedding him at all?

PEGEEN: I wouldn't wed him if a bishop came walking for to join us here.

CHRISTY: That God in glory may be thanked for that.

PEGEEN: There's your bed now. I've put a quilt upon you I'm after quilting a while since with my own two hands, and you'd best stretch out now for your sleep, and may God give you a good rest till I call you in the morning when the cocks will crow.

CHRISTY [*as she goes to inner room*]: May God and Mary and St Patrick bless you and reward you for your kindly talk. [*She shuts the door behind her. He settles his bed slowly, feeling the quilt with immense satisfaction.*] Well, it's a clean bed and soft with it, and it's great luck and company I've won me in the end of time – two fine women fighting for the likes of me – till I'm thinking this night wasn't I a foolish fellow not to kill my father in the years gone by.

CURTAIN

Act Two

Scene as before. Brilliant morning light.

[CHRISTY, *looking bright and cheerful, is cleaning a girl's boots.*]

CHRISTY [*to himself, counting jugs on dresser*]: Half a hundred beyond. Ten there. A score that's above. Eighty jugs. Six cups and a broken one. Two plates. A power of glasses. Bottles, a schoolmaster'd be hard set to count, and enough in them, I'm thinking, to drunken all the wealth and wisdom of the county Clare. [*He puts down the boot carefully.*] There's her boots now, nice and decent for her evening use, and isn't it grand brushes she has? [*He puts them down and goes by degrees to the looking-glass.*] Well, this'd be a fine place to be my whole life talking out with swearing Christians, in place of my old dogs and cat; and I stalking around, smoking my pipe and drinking my fill, and never a day's work but drawing a cork an odd time, or wiping a glass, or rinsing out a shiny tumbler for a decent man. [*He takes the looking-glass from the wall and puts it on the back of a chair; then sits down in front of it and begins washing his face.*] Didn't I know rightly, I was handsome, though it was the divil's own mirror we had beyond, would twist a squint across an angel's brow; and I'll be growing fine from this day, the way I'll have a soft lovely skin on me and won't be the like of the clumsy young fellows do be ploughing all times in the earth and dung. [*He starts.*] Is she coming again? [*He looks out.*] Stranger girls. God help me, where'll I hide myself away and my long neck naked to the world? [*He looks out.*] I'd best go to the room maybe till I'm dressed again.

[*He gathers up his coat and the looking-glass, and runs into the inner room. The door is pushed open, and* SUSAN BRADY *looks in, and knocks on door.*]

SUSAN: There's nobody in it. [*Knocks again.*]

NELLY [*pushing her in and following her, with* HONOR BLAKE *and* SARA TANSEY]: It'd be early for them both to be out walking the hill.

SUSAN: I'm thinking Shawn Keogh was making game of us, and there's no such man in it at all.

HONOR [*pointing to straw and quilt*]: Look at that. He's been sleeping there in the night. Well, it'll be a hard case if he's gone off now, the way we'll never set our eyes on a man killed his father, and we after rising early and destroying ourselves running fast on the hill.

NELLY: Are you thinking them's his boots?

SARA [*taking them up*]: If they are, there should be his

father's track on them. Did you never read in the papers
the way murdered men do bleed and drip?

SUSAN: Is that blood thère, Sara Tansey?

SARA [*smelling it*]: That's bog water, I'm thinking; but it's
his own they are, surely, for I never seen the like of them
for whitey mud, and red mud, and turf on them, and the
fine sands of the sea. That man's been walking, I'm
telling you.

[*She goes down right, putting on one of his boots.*]

SUSAN [*going to window*]: Maybe he's stolen off to Bel-
mullett with the boots of Michael James, and you'd have
a right so to follow after him, Sara Tansey, and you the
one yoked the ass cart and drove ten miles to set your
eyes on the man bit the yellow lady's nostril on the
northern shore. [*She looks out.*]

SARA [*running to window, with one boot on*]: Don't be talking, and we fooled today. [*Putting on the other boot.*]
There's a pair do fit me well and I'll be keeping them for
walking to the priest, when you'd be ashamed this place,
going up winter and summer with nothing worth while
to confess at all.

HONOR [*who has been listening at door*]. Whisht! there's
someone inside the room. [*She pushes door a chink open.*]
It's a man.

[SARA *kicks off boots and puts them where they were.
They all stand in a line looking through chink.*]

SARA: I'll call him. Mister! Mister! [*He puts in his head.*]
Is Pegeen within?

CHRISTY [*coming in as meek as a mouse, with the looking-
glass held behind his back*]: She's above on the cnuceen,
seeking the nanny goats, the way she'd have a sup of
goat's milk for to colour my tea.

SARA: And asking your pardon, is it you's the man killed
his father?

CHRISTY [*sidling towards the nail where the glass was hanging*]: I am, God help me!

SARA [*taking eggs she has brought*]: Then my thousand
welcomes to you, and I've run up with a brace of duck's
eggs for your food today. Pegeen's ducks is no use, but

these are the real rich sort. Hold out your hand and you'll
see it's no lie I'm telling you.

CHRISTY [*coming forward shyly, and holding out his left
hand*]: They're a great and weighty size.

SUSAN: And I run up with a pat of butter, for it'd be a poor
thing to have you eating your spuds dry, and you after
running a great way since you did destroy your da.

CHRISTY: Thank you kindly.

HONOR: And I brought you a little cut of a cake, for you
should have a thin stomach on you, and you that length
walking the world.

NELLY: And I brought you a little laying pullet – boiled
and all she is – was crushed at the fall of night by the
curate's car. Feel the fat of that breast, mister.

CHRISTY: It's bursting, surely. [*He feels it with the back of
his hand, in which he holds the presents.*]

SARA: Will you pinch it? Is your right hand too sacred for
to use at all? [*She slips round behind him.*] It's a glass he
has. Well, I never seen to this day a man with a looking-
glass held to his back. Them that kills their fathers is a
vain lot surely.

[GIRLS *giggle.*]

CHRISTY [*smiling innocently and piling presents on glass*]:
I'm very thankful to you all today. . . .

WIDOW QUIN [*coming in quickly, at door*]: Sara Tansey,
Susan Brady, Honor Blake! What in glory has you here
at this hour of day?

GIRLS [*giggling*]: That's the man killed his father.

WIDOW QUIN [*coming to them*]: I know well it's the man;
and I'm after putting him down in the sports below for
racing, leaping, pitching, and the Lord knows what.

SARA [*exuberantly*]: That's right, Widow Quin. I'll bet my
dowry that he'll lick the world.

WIDOW QUIN: If you will, you'd have a right to have him
fresh and nourished in place of nursing a feast. [*Taking
presents.*] Are you fasting or fed, young fellow?

CHRISTY: Fasting, if you please.

WIDOW QUIN [*loudly*]: Well, you're the lot. Stir up now
and give him his breakfast. [*To Christy*] Come here to

me [*she puts him on bench beside her while the* GIRLS *make
tea and get his breakfast*], and let you tell us your story
before Pegeen will come, in place of grinning your ears
off like the moon of May.

CHRISTY [*beginning to be pleased*]: It's a long story; you'd
be destroyed listening.

WIDOW QUIN: Don't be letting on to be shy, a fine, gamey,
treacherous lad the like of you. Was it in your house
beyond you cracked his skull?

CHRISTY [*shy but flattered*]: It was not. We were digging
spuds in his cold, sloping, stony, divil's patch of a field.

WIDOW QUIN: And you went asking money of him, or
making talk of getting a wife would drive him from his
farm?

CHRISTY: I did not, then; but there I was digging and
digging, and 'You squinting idiot,' says he, 'let you
walk down now and tell the priest you'll wed the Widow
Casey in a score of days.'

WIDOW QUIN: And what kind was she?

CHRISTY [*with horror*]: A walking terror from beyond the
hills, and she two score and five years, and two hundred-
weights and five pounds in the weighing scales, with a
limping leg on her, and a blinded eye, and she a woman
of noted misbehaviour with the old and young.

GIRLS [*clustering round him, serving him*]: Glory be.

WIDOW QUIN: And what did he want driving you to wed
with her? [*She takes a bit of the chicken.*]

CHRISTY [*eating with growing satisfaction*]: He was letting
on I was wanting a protector from the harshness of
the world, and he without a thought the whole while
but how he'd have her hut to live in and her gold to
drink.

WIDOW QUIN: There's maybe worse than a dry hearth and
a widow woman and your glass at night. So you hit him
then?

CHRISTY [*getting almost excited*]: I did not. 'I won't wed
her,' says I, 'when all know she did suckle me for six
weeks when I came into the world, and she a hag this
day with a tongue on her has the crows and seabirds

scattered, the way they wouldn't cast a shadow on her garden with the dread of her curse.'

WIDOW QUIN [*teasingly*]: That one should be right company.

SARA [*eagerly*]: Don't mind her. Did you kill him then?

CHRISTY: 'She's too good for the like of you,' says he, 'and go on now or I'll flatten you out like a crawling beast has passed under a dray.' 'You will not if I can help it,' says I. 'Go on,' says he, 'or I'll have the divil making garters of your limbs tonight.' 'You will not if I can help it,' says I. [*He sits up brandishing his mug.*]

SARA: You were right surely.

CHRISTY [*impressively*]: With that the sun came out between the cloud and the hill, and it shining green in my face. 'God have mercy on your soul,' says he, lifting a scythe. 'Or on your own,' said I, raising the loy.

SUSAN: That's a grand story.

HONOR: He tells it lovely.

CHRISTY [*flattered and confident, waving bone*]: He gave a drive with the scythe, and I gave a lep to the east. Then I turned around with my back to the north, and I hit a blow on the ridge of his skull, laid him stretched out, and he split to the knob of his gullet. [*He raises the chicken bone to his Adam's apple.*]

GIRLS [*together*]: Well, you're a marvel! Oh, God bless you! You're the lad, surely!

SUSAN: I'm thinking the Lord God sent him this road to make a second husband to the Widow Quin, and she with a great yearning to be wedded, though all dread her here. Lift him on her knee, Sara Tansey.

WIDOW QUIN: Don't tease him.

SARA [*going over to the dresser and counter very quickly, and getting two glasses and porter*]: You're heroes, surely, and let you drink a supeen with your arms linked like the outlandish lovers in the sailor's song. [*She links their arms and gives them the glasses.*] There now. Drink a health to the wonders of the western world, the pirates, preachers, poteen-makers, with the jobbing jockies; parching peelers, and the juries fill their stomachs selling judgments of the English law. [*Brandishing the bottle.*]

WIDOW QUIN: That's a right toast, Sara Tansey. Now, Christy.

[*They drink with their arms linked, he drinking with his left hand, she with her right. As they are drinking,* PEGEEN MIKE *comes in with a milk-can and stands aghast. They all spring away from Christy. He goes down left.* WIDOW QUIN *remains seated.*]

PEGEEN [*angrily, to Sara*]: What is it you're wanting?

SARA [*twisting her apron*]: An ounce of tobacco.

PEGEEN: Have you tuppence?

SARA: I've forgotten my purse.

PEGEEN: Then you'd best be getting it and not be fooling us here. [*To the Widow Quin, with more elaborate scorn.*] And what is it you're wanting, Widow Quin?

WIDOW QUIN [*insolently*]: A penn'orth of starch.

PEGEEN [*breaking out*]: And you without a white shift or a shirt in your whole family since the drying of the flood. I've no starch for the like of you, and let you walk on now to Killamuck.

WIDOW QUIN [*turning to Christy, as she goes out with the girls*]: Well, you're mighty huffy this day, Pegeen Mike, and you, young fellow, let you not forget the sports and racing when the noon is by. [*They go out.*]

PEGEEN [*imperiously*]: Fling out that rubbish and put them cups away. [CHRISTY *tidies away in great haste.*] Shove in the bench by the wall. [*He does so.*] And hang that glass on the nail. What disturbed it at all?

CHRISTY [*very meekly*]: I was making myself decent only, and this a fine country for young lovely girls.

PEGEEN [*sharply*]: Whisht your talking of girls. [*Goes to counter on right.*]

CHRISTY: Wouldn't any wish to be decent in a place . . .

PEGEEN: Whisht, I'm saying.

CHRISTY [*looks at her face for a moment with great misgivings, then as a last effort takes up a loy, and goes towards her, with feigned assurance*]: It was with a loy the like of that I killed my father.

PEGEEN [*still sharply*]: You've told me that story six times since the dawn of day.

CHRISTY [*reproachfully*]: It's a queer thing you wouldn't care to be hearing it and them girls after walking four miles to be listening to me now.

PEGEEN [*turning round astonished*]: Four miles?

CHRISTY [*apologetically*]: Didn't himself say there were only bona fides living in the place?

PEGEEN: It's bona fides by the road they are, but that lot came over the river lepping the stones. It's not three perches when you go like that, and I was down this morning looking on the papers the post-boy does have in his bag. [*With meaning and emphasis*] For there was great news this day, Christopher Mahon. [*She goes into room on left.*]

CHRISTY [*suspiciously*]: Is it news of my murder?

PEGEEN [*inside*]: Murder, indeed.

CHRISTY [*loudly*]: A murdered da?

PEGEEN [*coming in again and crossing right*]: There was not, but a story filled half a page of the hanging of a man. Ah, that should be a fearful end, young fellow, and it worst of all for a man destroyed his da; for the like of him would get small mercies, and when it's dead he is they'd put him in a narrow grave, with cheap sacking wrapping him round, and pour down quicklime on his head, the way you'd see a woman pouring any frish-frash from a cup.

CHRISTY [*very miserably*]: Oh, God help me. Are you thinking I'm safe? You were saying at the fall of night I was shut of jeopardy and I here with yourselves.

PEGEEN [*severely*]: You'll be shut of jeopardy no place if you go talking with a pack of wild girls the like of them do be walking abroad with the peelers, talking whispers at the fall of night.

CHRISTY [*with terror*]: And you're thinking they'd tell?

PEGEEN [*with mock sympathy*]: Who knows, God help you?

CHRISTY [*loudly*]: What joy would they have to bring hanging to the likes of me?

PEGEEN: It's queer joys they have, and who knows the thing they'd do, if it'd make the green stones cry itself to think of you swaying and swiggling at the butt of a rope, and you with a fine, stout neck, God bless you! the way you'd be a half an hour, in great anguish, getting your death.

CHRISTY [*getting his boots and putting them on*]: If there's that terror of them, it'd be best, maybe, I went on wandering like Esau or Cain and Abel on the sides of Neifin or the Erris plain.

PEGEEN [*beginning to play with him*]: It would, maybe, for I've heard the Circuit Judges this place is a heartless crew.

CHRISTY [*bitterly*]: It's more than Judges this place is a heartless crew. [*Looking up at her.*] And isn't it a poor thing to be starting again, and I a lonesome fellow will be looking out on women and girls the way the needy fallen spirits do be looking on the Lord?

PEGEEN: What call have you to be that lonesome when there's poor girls walking Mayo in their thousands now?

CHRISTY [*grimly*]: It's well you know what call I have. It's well you know it's a lonesome thing to be passing small towns with the lights shining sideways when the night is down, or going in strange places with a dog noising before you and a dog noising behind, or drawn to the cities where you'd hear a voice kissing and talking deep love in every shadow of the ditch, and you passing on with an empty, hungry stomach failing from your heart.

PEGEEN: I'm thinking you're an odd man, Christy Mahon. The oddest walking fellow I ever set my eyes on to this hour today.

CHRISTY: What would any be but odd men and they living lonesome in the world?

PEGEEN: I'm not odd, and I'm my whole life with my father only.

CHRISTY [*with infinite admiration*]: How would a lovely, handsome woman the like of you be lonesome when all men should be thronging around to hear the sweetness of your voice, and the little infant children should be pestering your steps, I'm thinking, and you walking the roads.

PEGEEN: I'm hard set to know what way a coaxing fellow the like of yourself should be lonesome either.

CHRISTY: Coaxing.

PEGEEN: Would you have me think a man never talked with the girls would have the words you've spoken today? It's only letting on you are to be lonesome, the way you'd get around me now.

CHRISTY: I wish to God I was letting on; but I was lonesome all times, and born lonesome, I'm thinking, as the moon of dawn. [*Going to door.*]

PEGEEN [*puzzled by his talk*]: Well, it's a story I'm not understanding at all why you'd be worse than another, Christy Mahon, and you a fine lad with the great savagery to destroy your da.

CHRISTY: It's little I'm understanding myself, saving only that my heart's scalded this day, and I going off stretching out the earth between us, the way I'll not be waking near you another dawn of the year till the two of us do arise to hope or judgement with the saints of God, and now I'd best be going with my wattle in my hand, for hanging is a poor thing [*turning to go*], and it's little welcome only is left me in this house today.

PEGEEN [*sharply*]: Christy. [*He turns round.*] Come here to me. [*He goes towards her.*] Lay down that switch and throw some sods on the fire. You're pot-boy in this place, and I'll not have you mitch off from us now.

CHRISTY: You were saying I'd be hanged if I stay.

PEGEEN [*quite kindly at last*]: I'm after going down and reading the fearful crimes of Ireland for two weeks or three, and there wasn't a word of your murder. [*Getting up and going over to the counter.*] They've likely not found the body. You're safe so with ourselves.

CHRISTY [*astonished, slowly*]: It's making game of me you were [*following her with fearful joy*], and I can stay so, working at your side, and I not lonesome from this mortal day.

PEGEEN: What's to hinder you staying, except the widow woman or the young girls would inveigle you off?

CHRISTY [*with rapture*]: And I'll have your words from this

day filling my ears, and that look is come upon you meeting
my two eyes, and I watching you loafing around in the
warm sun, or rinsing your ankles when the night is come.

PEGEEN [*kindly, but a little embarrassed*]: I'm thinking
you'll be a loyal young lad to have working around, and
if you vexed me a while since with your leaguing with
the girls, I wouldn't give a thraneen for a lad hadn't a
mighty spirit in him and a gamey heart.

[SHAWN KEOGH *runs in carrying a cleeve on his back
followed by the* WIDOW QUIN.]

SHAWN [*to Pegeen*]: I was passing below, and I seen your
mountainy sheep eating cabbages in Jimmy's field. Run
up or they'll be bursting, surely.

PEGEEN: Oh, God mend them! [*She puts a shawl over her
her head and runs out.*]

CHRISTY [*looking from one to the other. Still in high spirits*]:
I'd best go to her aid maybe. I'm handy with ewes.

WIDOW QUIN [*closing the door*]: She can do that much, and
there is Shaneen has long speeches for to tell you now.
[*She sits down with an amused smile.*]

SHAWN [*taking something from his pocket and offering it to*
CHRISTY]: Do you see that, mister?

CHRISTY [*looking at it*]: The half of a ticket to the Western
States!

SHAWN [*trembling with anxiety*]: I'll give it to you and my
new hat [*pulling it out of hamper*]; and my breeches with
the double seat [*pulling it out*]; and my new coat is
woven from the blackest shearings for three miles
around [*giving him the coat*]; I'll give you the whole of
them, and my blessing, and the blessing of Father Reilly
itself, maybe, if you'll quit from this and leave us in the
peace we had till last night at the fall of dark.

CHRISTY [*with a new arrogance*]: And for what is it you're
wanting to get shut of me?

SHAWN [*looking to the Widow for help*]: I'm a poor scholar
with middling faculties to coin a lie, so I'll tell you the
truth, Christy Mahon. I'm wedding with Pegeen beyond, and I don't think well of having a clever, fearless
man the like of you dwelling in her house.

CHRISTY [*almost pugnaciously*]: And you'd be using bribery for to banish me?

SHAWN [*in an imploring voice*]: Let you not take it badly, mister honey: isn't beyond the best place for you, where you'll have golden chains and shiny coats and you riding upon hunters with the ladies of the land. [*He makes an eager sign to the widow Quin to come to help him.*]

WIDOW QUIN [*coming over*]: It's true for him, and you'd best quit off and not have that poor girl setting her mind on you, for there's Shaneen thinks she wouldn't suit you, though all is saying that she'll wed you now.

[CHRISTY *beams with delight.*]

SHAWN [*in terrified earnest*]: She wouldn't suit you, and she with the divil's own temper the way you'd be strangling one another in a score of days. [*He makes the movement of strangling with his hands.*] It's the like of me only that she's fit for; a quiet simple fellow wouldn't raise a hand upon her if she scratched itself.

WIDOW QUIN [*putting Shawn's hat on Christy*]: Fit them clothes on you anyhow, young fellow, and he'd maybe loan them to you for the sports. [*Pushing him towards inner door.*] Fit them on and you can give your answer when you have them tried.

CHRISTY [*beaming, delighted with the clothes*]: I will then. I'd like herself to see me in them tweeds and hat. [*He goes into room and shuts the door.*]

SHAWN [*in great anxiety*]: He'd like herself to see them. He'll not leave us, Widow Quin. He's a score of divils in him the way it's well-nigh certain he will wed Pegeen.

WIDOW QUIN [*jeeringly*]: It's true all girls are fond of courage and do hate the like of you.

SHAWN [*walking about in desperation*]: Oh, Widow Quin, what'll I be doing now? I'd inform again him, but he'd burst from Kilmainham and he'd be sure and certain to destroy me. If I wasn't so God-fearing, I'd near have courage to come behind him and run a pike into his side, Oh, it's a hard case to be an orphan and not to have your father that you're used to, and you'd easy kill and make yourself a hero in the sight of all. [*Coming up to*

her.] Oh, Widow Quin, will you find me some contrivance
when I've promised you a ewe?

WIDOW QUIN: A ewe's a small thing, but what would you
give me if I did wed him and did save you so?

SHAWN [*with astonishment*]: You?

WIDOW QUIN: Aye. Would you give me the red cow you
have and the mountainy ram, and the right of way across
your rye path, and a load of dung at Michaelmas, and
turbary upon the western hill?

SHAWN [*radiant with hope*]: I would, surely, and I'd give
you the wedding-ring I have, and the loan of a new suit,
the way you'd have him decent on the wedding-day. I'd
give you two kids for your dinner, and a gallon of poteen,
and I'd call the piper on the long car to your wedding
from Crossmolina or from Ballina. I'd give you . . .

WIDOW QUIN: That'll do, so, and let you wisht, for he's
coming now again.

[CHRISTY *comes in very natty in the new clothes.*
WIDOW QUIN *goes to him admiringly.*]

WIDOW QUIN: If you seen yourself now, I'm thinking you'd
be too proud to speak to at all, and it'd be a pity
surely to have your like sailing from Mayo to the western
world.

CHRISTY [*as proud as a peacock*]: I'm not going. If this is a
poor place itself, I'll make myself contented to be lodging here.

[WIDOW QUIN *makes a sign to Shawn to leave them.*]

SHAWN: Well, I'm going measuring the racecourse while
the tide is low, so I'll leave you the garments and my
blessing for the sports today. God bless you! [*He
wriggles out.*]

WIDOW QUIN [*admiring Christy*]: Well, you're mighty
spruce, young fellow. Sit down now while you're quiet
till you talk with me.

CHRISTY [*swaggering*]: I'm going abroad on the hillside for
to seek Pegeen.

WIDOW QUIN: You'll have time and plenty for to seek
Pegeen, and you heard me saying at the fall of night the
two of us should be great company.

CHRISTY: From this out I'll have no want of company when all sorts is bringing me their food and clothing [*he swaggers to the door, tightening his belt*], the way they'd set their eyes upon a gallant orphan cleft his father with one blow to the breeches belt. [*He opens door, then staggers back.*] Saints of glory! Holy angels from the throne of light!

WIDOW QUIN [*going over*]: What ails you?

CHRISTY: It's the walking spirit of my murdered da!

WIDOW QUIN [*looking out*]: Is it that tramper?

CHRISTY [*wildly*]: Where'll I hide my poor body from that ghost of hell?

[*The door is pushed open, and* OLD MAHON *appears on threshold.* CHRISTY *darts in behind door.*]

WIDOW QUIN [*in great amusement*]: God save you, my poor man.

MAHON [*gruffly*]: Did you see a young lad passing this way in the early morning or the fall of night?

WIDOW QUIN: You're a queer kind to walk in not saluting at all.

MAHON: Did you see the young lad?

WIDOW QUIN [*stiffly*]: What kind was he?

MAHON: An ugly young streeler with a murderous gob on him, and a little switch in his hand. I met a tramper seen him coming this way at the fall of night.

WIDOW QUIN: There's harvest hundreds do be passing these days for the Sligo boat. For what is it you're wanting him, my poor man?

MAHON: I want to destroy him for breaking the head on me with the clout of a loy. [*He takes off a big hat, and shows his head in a mass of bandages and plaster, with some pride.*] It was he did that, and amn't I a great wonder to think I've traced him ten days with that rent in my crown?

WIDOW QUIN [*taking his head in both hands and examining it with extreme delight*]: That was a great blow. And who hit you? A robber maybe?

MAHON: It was my own son hit me, and he the divil a robber, or anything else, but a dirty, stuttering lout.

WIDOW QUIN [*letting go his skull and wiping her hands in her apron*]: You'd best be wary of a mortified scalp, I think they call it, lepping around with that wound in the splendour of the sun. It was a bad blow, surely, and you should have vexed him fearful to make him strike that gash in his da.

MAHON: Is it me?

WIDOW QUIN [*amusing herself*]: Aye. And isn't it a great shame when the old and hardened do torment the young?

MAHON [*raging*]: Torment him is it? And I after holding out with the patience of a martyred saint till there's nothing but destruction on, and I'm driven out in my old age with none to aid me.

WIDOW QUIN [*greatly amused*]: It's a sacred wonder the way that wickedness will spoil a man.

MAHON: My wickedness, is it? Amn't I after saying it is himself has me destroyed, and he a lier on walls, a talker of folly, a man you'd see stretched the half of the day in the brown ferns with his belly to the sun.

WIDOW QUIN: Not working at all?

MAHON: The divil a work, or if he did itself, you'd see him raising up a haystack like the stalk of a rush, or driving our last cow till he broke her leg at the hip, and when he wasn't at that he'd be fooling over little birds he had – finches and felts – or making mugs at his own self in the bit of a glass we had hung on the wall.

WIDOW QUIN [*looking at Christy*]: What way was he so foolish? It was running wild after the girls maybe?

MAHON [*with a shout of derision*]: Running wild, is it? If he seen a red petticoat coming swinging over the hill, he'd be off to hide in the sticks, and you'd see him shooting out his sheep's eyes between the little twigs and the leaves, and his two ears rising like a hare looking out through a gap. Girls, indeed!

WIDOW QUIN: It was drink maybe?

MAHON: And he a poor fellow would get drunk on the smell of a pint. He'd a queer rotten stomach, I'm telling you, and when I gave him three pulls from my pipe a while since, he was taken with contortions till I had to send him in the ass-cart to the females' nurse.

WIDOW QUIN [*clasping her hands*]: Well, I never, till this day, heard tell of a man the like of that!

MAHON: I'd take a mighty oath you didn't, surely, and wasn't he the laughing joke of every female woman where four baronies meet, the way the girls would stop their weeding if they seen him coming the road to let a roar at him, and call him the looney of Mahon's.

WIDOW QUIN: I'd give the world and all to see the like of him. What kind was he?

MAHON: A small, low fellow.

WIDOW QUIN: And dark?

MAHON: Dark and dirty.

WIDOW QUIN [*considering*]: I'm thinking I seen him.

MAHON [*eagerly*]: An ugly young blackguard.

WIDOW QUIN: A hideous, fearful villain, and the spit of you.

MAHON: What way is he fled?

WIDOW QUIN: Gone over the hills to catch a coasting steamer to the north or south.

MAHON: Could I pull up on him now?

WIDOW QUIN: If you'll cross the sands below where the tide is out, you'll be in it as soon as himself, for he had to go round ten miles by the top of the bay. [*She points to the door.*] Strike down by the head beyond and then follow on the roadway to the north and east.

[MAHON *goes abruptly.*]

WIDOW QUIN [*shouting after him*]: Let you give him a good vengeance when you come up with him, but don't put yourself in the power of the law, for it'd be a poor thing to see a judge in his black cap reading out his sentence on a civil warrior the like of you. [*She swings the door to and looks at Christy, who is cowering in terror, for a moment, then she bursts into a laugh.*] Well, you're the walking Playboy of the Western World, and that's the poor man you had divided to his breeches belt.

CHRISTY [*looking out; then, to her*]: What'll Pegeen say when she hears that story? What'll she be saying to me now?

WIDOW QUIN: She'll knock the head of you, I'm thinking, and drive you from the door. God help her to be taking you for a wonder, and you a little schemer making up a story you destroyed your da.

CHRISTY [*turning to the door, nearly speechless with rage, half to himself*]: To be letting on he was dead, and coming back to his life, and following after me like an old weasel tracing a rat, and coming in here laying desolation between my own self and the fine women of Ireland, and he a kind of carcase that you'd fling upon the sea . . .

WIDOW QUIN [*more soberly*]: There's talking for a man's one only son.

CHRISTY [*breaking out*]: His one son, is it? May I meet him with one tooth and it aching, and one eye to be seeing seven and seventy divils in the twists of the road, and one old timber leg on him to limp into the scalding grave. [*Looking out.*] There he is now crossing the strands, and that the Lord God would send a high wave to wash him from the world.

WIDOW QUIN [*scandalized*]: Have you no shame? [*putting her hand on his shoulder and turning him round*] What ails you? Near crying, is it?

CHRISTY [*in despair and grief*]: Amn't I after seeing the love-light of the star of knowledge shining from her brow, and hearing words would put you thinking on the holy Brigid speaking to the infant saints, and now she'll be turning again, and speaking hard words to me, like an old woman with a spavindy ass she'd have, urging on a hill.

WIDOW QUIN: There's poetry talk for a girl you'd see itching and scratching, and she with a stale stink of poteen on her from selling in the shop.

CHRISTY [*impatiently*]: It's her like is fitted to be handling merchandise in the heavens above, and what'll I be doing now, I ask you, and I a kind of wonder was jilted by the heavens when a day was by.

[*There is a distant noise of* GIRLS' *voices.* WIDOW QUIN *looks from window and comes to him, hurriedly.*]

WIDOW QUIN: You'll be doing like myself, I'm thinking,

when I did destroy my man, for I'm above many's the
day, odd times in great spirits, abroad in the sunshine,
darning a stocking or stitching a shift; and odd times
again looking out on the schooners, hookers, trawlers is
sailing the sea, and I thinking on the gallant hairy fellows
are drifting beyond, and myself long years living alone.

CHRISTY [*interested*]: You're like me, so.

WIDOW QUIN: I am your like, and it's for that I'm taking
a fancy to you, and I with my little houseen above where
there'd be myself to tend you, and none to ask were you
a murderer or what at all.

CHRISTY: And what would I be doing if I left Pegeen?

WIDOW QUIN: I've nice jobs you could be doing – gathering
shells to make a white-wash for our hut within, building
up a little goosehouse, or stretching a new skin on an old
curagh I have, and if my hut is far from all sides, it's
there you'll meet the wisest old men, I tell you, at the
corner of my wheel, and it's there yourself and me will
have great times whispering and hugging. . . .

VOICES [*outside, calling far away*]: Christy! Christy Mahon!
Christy!

CHRISTY: Is it Pegeen Mike?

WIDOW QUIN: It's the young girls, I'm thinking, coming to
bring you to the sports below, and what is it you'll have
me to tell them now?

CHRISTY: Aid me for to win Pegeen. It's herself only that
I'm seeking now. [WIDOW QUIN *gets up and goes to window.*] Aid me for to win her, and I'll be asking God to
stretch a hand to you in the hour of death, and lead you
short cuts through the Meadows of Ease, and up the
floor of Heaven to the Footstool of the Virgin's Son.

WIDOW QUIN: There's praying!

VOICES [*nearer*]: Christy! Christy Mahon!

CHRISTY [*with agitation*]: They're coming. Will you swear
to aid and save me, for the love of Christ?

WIDOW QUIN [*looks at him for a moment*]: If I aid you, will
you swear to give me a right of way I want, and a
mountainy ram, and a load of dung at Michaelmas, the
time that you'll be master here?

CHRISTY: I will, by the elements and stars of night.

WIDOW QUIN: Then we'll not say a word of the old fellow, the way Pegeen won't know your story till the end of time.

CHRISTY: And if he chances to return again?

WIDOW QUIN: We'll swear he's a maniac and not your da. I could take an oath I seen him raving on the sands today.

[GIRLS *run in.*]

SUSAN: Come on to the sports below. Pegeen says you're to come.

SARA TANSEY: The lepping's beginning, and we've a jockey's suit to fit upon you for the mule race on the sands below.

HONOR: Come on, will you?

CHRISTY: I will then if Pegeen's beyond.

SARA: She's in the boreen making game of Shaneen Keogh.

CHRISTY: Then I'll be going to her now. [*He runs out, followed by the* GIRLS.]

WIDOW QUIN: Well, if the worst comes in the end of all, it'll be great game to see there's none to pity him but a widow woman, the like of me, has buried her children and destroyed her man. [*She goes out.*]

CURTAIN

Act Three

Scene as before. Later in the day.

[JIMMY *comes in, slightly drunk.*]

JIMMY [*calls*]: Pegeen! [*Crosses to inner door.*] Pegeen Mike! [*Comes back again into the room.*] Pegeen! [PHILLY *comes in in the same state. To Philly*] Did you see herself?

PHILLY: I did not; but I sent Shawn Keogh with the ass-

cart for to bear him home. [*Trying cupboards, which are
locked.*] Well, isn't he a nasty man to get into such
staggers at a morning wake; and isn't herself the divil's
daughter for locking, and she so fussy after that young
gaffer, you might take your death with drouth and none
to heed you?

JIMMY: It's little wonder she'd be fussy, and he after
bringing bankrupt ruin on the roulette man, and the
trick-o'-the-loop man, and breaking the nose of the
cockshot-man, and winning all in the sports below,
racing, lepping, dancing, and the Lord knows what! He's
right luck, I'm telling you.

PHILLY: If he has, he'll be rightly hobbled yet, and he not
able to say ten words without making a brag of the way
he killed his father, and the great blow he hit with the
loy.

JIMMY: A man can't hang by his own informing, and his
father should be rotten by now.

[OLD MAHON *passes the window slowly.*]

PHILLY: Supposing a man's digging spuds in that field with
a long spade, and supposing he flings up the two halves of
that skull, what'll be said then in the papers and the
courts of law?

JIMMY: They'd say it was an old Dane, maybe, was
drowned in the flood. [OLD MAHON *comes in and sits
down near door listening.*] Did you never hear tell of the
skulls they have in the city of Dublin, ranged out like
blue jugs in a cabin of Connaught?

PHILLY: And you believe that?

JIMMY [*pugnaciously*]: Didn't a lad see them and he after
coming from harvesting in the Liverpool boat? 'They
have them there,' says he, 'making a show of the great
people there was one time walking the world. White
skulls and black skulls and yellow skulls, and some with
full teeth, and some haven't only but one.'

PHILLY: It was no lie, maybe, for when I was a young lad
there was a graveyard beyond the house with the
remnants of a man who had thighs as long as your arm.
He was a horrid man, I'm telling you, and there was

many a fine Sunday I'd put him together for fun, and he
with shiny bones, you wouldn't meet the like of these
days in the cities of the world.

MAHON [*getting up*]: You wouldn't, is it? Lay your eyes on
that skull, and tell me where and when there was another
the like of it, is splintered only from the blow of a loy.

PHILLY: Glory be to God! And who hit you at all?

MAHON [*triumphantly*]: It was my own son hit me. Would
you believe that?

JIMMY: Well, there's wonders hidden in the heart of man!

PHILLY [*suspiciously*]: And what way was it done?

MAHON [*wandering about the room*]: I'm after walking
hundreds and long scores of miles, winning clean beds
and the fill of my belly four times in the day, and I doing
nothing but telling stories of that naked truth. [*He comes
to them a little aggressively.*] Give me a supeen and I'll tell
you now.

[WIDOW QUIN *comes in and stands aghast behind him.
He is facing Jimmy and Philly, who are on the left.*]

JIMMY: Ask herself beyond. She's the stuff hidden in her
shawl.

WIDOW QUIN [*coming to Mahon quickly*]: You here, is it?
You didn't go far at all?

MAHON: I seen the coasting steamer passing, and I got a
drouth upon me and a cramping leg, so I said, 'The divil
go along with him,' and turned again. [*Looking under her
shawl.*] And let you give me a supeen, for I'm destroyed
travelling since Tuesday was a week.

WIDOW QUIN [*getting a glass, in a cajoling tone*]: Sit down
then by the fire and take your ease for a space. You've
a right to be destroyed indeed, with your walking, and
fighting, and facing the sun [*giving him poteen from a
stone jar she has brought in*]. There now is a drink for you,
and may it be to your happiness and length of life.

MAHON [*taking glass greedily, and sitting down by fire*]:
God increase you!

WIDOW QUIN [*taking men to the right stealthily*]: Do you
know what? That man's raving from his wound today, for
I met him a while since telling a rambling tale of a tinker

had him destroyed. Then he heard of Christy's deed, and he up and and says it was his son had cracked his skull. Oh, isn't madness a fright, for he'll go killing someone yet, and he thinking it's the man has struck him so?

JIMMY [*entirely convinced*]: It's a fright surely. I knew a party was kicked in the head by a red mare, and he went killing horses a great while, till he eat the insides of a clock and died after.

PHILLY [*with suspicion*]: Did he see Christy?

WIDOW QUIN: He didn't. [*With a warning gesture.*] Let you not be putting him in mind of him, or you'll be likely summoned if there's murder done. [*Looking round at Mahon.*] Whisht! He's listening. Wait now till you hear me taking him easy and unravelling all. [*She goes to Mahon.*] And what way are you feeling, mister? Are you in contentment now?

MAHON [*slightly emotional from his drink*]: I'm poorly only, for it's a hard story the way I'm left today, when it was I did tend him from his hour of birth, and he a dunce never reached his second book, the way he'd come from school, many's the day, with his legs lamed under him, and he blackened with his beatings like a tinker's ass. It's a hard story, I'm saying, the way some do have their next and nighest raising up a hand of murder on them, and some is lonesome getting their death with lamentation in the dead of night.

WIDOW QUIN [*not knowing what to say*]: To hear you talking so quiet, who'd know you were the same fellow we seen pass today?

MAHON: I'm the same surely. The wrack and ruin of three-score years; and it's a terror to live that length, I tell you, and to have your sons going to the dogs against you, and you wore out scolding them, and skelping them, and God knows what.

PHILLY [*to Jimmy*]: He's not raving. [*To Widow Quin*] Will you ask him what kind was his son?

WIDOW QUIN [*to Mahon with a peculiar look*]: Was your son that hit you a lad of one year and a score maybe, a great hand at racing and lepping and licking the world?

MAHON [*turning on her with a roar of rage*]: Didn't you hear
me say he was the fool of men, the way from this out he'll
know the orphan's lot, with old and young making game
of him, and they swearing, raging, kicking at him like a
mangy cur.

[*A great burst of cheering outside, some way off.*]

MAHON [*putting his hands to his ears*]: What in the name of
God do they want roaring below?

WIDOW QUIN [*with the shade of a smile*]: They're cheering
a young lad, the champion Playboy of the Western
World.

[*More cheering.*]

MAHON [*going to the window*]: It'd split my heart to hear
them, and I with pulses in my brain-pan for a week gone
by. Is it racing they are?

JIMMY [*looking from door*]: It is, then. They are mounting
him for the mule race will be run upon the sands. That's
the playboy on the winkered mule.

MAHON [*puzzled*]: That lad, is it? If you said it was a fool
he was, I'd have laid a mighty oath he was the likeness of
my wandering son. [*Uneasily, putting his hand to his
head.*] Faith, I'm thinking I'll go walking for to view the
race.

WIDOW QUIN [*stopping him, sharply*]: You will not. You'd
best take the road to Belmullet, and not be dilly-dallying
in this place where there isn't a spot you could sleep.

PHILLY [*coming forward*]: Don't mind her. Mount there on
the bench and you'll have a view of the whole. They're
hurrying before the tide will rise, and it'd be near over if
you went down the pathway through the crags below.

MAHON [*mounts on bench, WIDOW QUIN beside him*]: That's
a right view again the edge of the sea. They're coming
now from the point. He's leading. Who is he at all?

WIDOW QUIN: He's the champion of the world, I tell you,
and there isn't a hap'orth isn't falling lucky to his hands
today.

PHILLY [*looking out, interested in the race*]: Look at that.
They're pressing him now.

JIMMY: He'll win it yet.

PHILLY: Take your time, Jimmy Farrel. It's too soon to say.

WIDOW QUIN [*shouting*]: Watch him taking the gate. There's riding.

JIMMY [*cheering*]: More power to the young lad!

MAHON: He's passing the third.

JIMMY: He'll lick them yet.

WIDOW QUIN: He'd lick them if he was running races with a score itself.

MAHON: Look at the mule he has, kicking the stars.

WIDOW QUIN: There was a lep! [*Catching hold of Mahon in her excitement.*] He's fallen? He's mounted again! Faith, he's passing them all!

JIMMY: Look at him skelping her!

PHILLY: And the mountain girls hooshing him on!

JIMMY: It's the last turn! The post's cleared for them now!

MAHON: Look at the narrow place. He'll be into the bogs! [*With a yell.*] Good rider! He's through it again!

JIMMY: He neck and neck!

PHILLY: Good boy to him! Flames, but he's in! [*Great cheering, in which all join.*]

MAHON [*with hesitation*]: What's that? They're raising him up. They're coming this way. [*With a roar of rage and astonishment.*] It's Christy, by the stars of God! I'd know his way of spitting and he astride the moon. [*He jumps down and makes a run for the door, but* WIDOW QUIN *catches him and pulls him back.*]

WIDOW QUIN: Stay quiet, will you? That's not your son. [*To Jimmy.*] Stop him, or you'll get a month for the abetting of manslaughter and be fined as well.

JIMMY: I'll hold him.

MAHON [*struggling*]: Let me out! Let me out, the lot of you, till I have my vengeance on his head today.

WIDOW QUIN [*shaking him, vehemently*]: That's not your son. That's a man is going to make a marriage with the daughter of this house, a place with fine trade, with a licence, and with poteen too.

MAHON [*amazed*]: That man marrying a decent and a moneyed girl! Is it mad yous are? Is it in a crazy-house for females that I'm landed now?

WIDOW QUIN: It's mad yourself is with the blow upon your head. That lad is the wonder of the western world.

MAHON: I seen it's my son.

WIDOW QUIN: You seen that you're mad. [*Cheering outside.*] Do you hear them cheering him in the zig-zags of the road? Aren't you after saying that your son's a fool, and how would they be cheering a true idiot born?

MAHON [*getting distressed*]: It's maybe out of reason that that man's himself. [*Cheering again.*] There's none surely will go cheering him. Oh, I'm raving with a madness that would fright the world! [*He sits down with his hand to his head.*] There was one time I seen ten scarlet divils letting on they'd cork my spirit in a gallon can: and one time I seen rats as big as badgers sucking the lifeblood from the butt of my lug; but I never till this day confused that dribbling idiot with a likely man. I'm destroyed surely.

WIDOW QUIN: And who'd wonder when it's your brain-pan that is gaping now?

MAHON: Then the blight of the sacred drouth upon myself and him, for I never went mad to this day, and I not three weeks with the Limerick girls drinking myself silly and parlatic from the dusk to dawn. [*To Widow Quin, suddenly*] Is my visage astray?

WIDOW QUIN: It is, then. You're a sniggering maniac, a child could see.

MAHON [*getting up more cheerfully*]: Then I'd best be going to the union beyond, and there'll be a welcome before me, I tell you [*with great pride*], and I a terrible and fearful case, the way that there I was one time, screeching in a straightened waistcoat, with seven doctors writing out my sayings in a printed book. Would you believe that?

WIDOW QUIN: If you're a wonder itself, you'd best be hasty, for them lads caught a maniac one time and pelted the poor creature till he ran out, raving and foaming, and was drowned in the sea.

MAHON [*with philosophy*]: It's true mankind is the divil when your head's astray. Let me out now and I'll slip down the boreen, and not see them so.

WIDOW QUIN [*showing him out*]: That's it. Run to the right, and not a one will see.

[*He runs off.*]

PHILLY [*wisely*]: You're at some gaming, Widow Quin; but I'll walk after him and give him his dinner and a time to rest, and I'll see then if he's raving or as sane as you.

WIDOW QUIN [*annoyed*]: If you go near that lad, let you be wary of your head, I'm saying. Didn't you hear him telling he was crazed at times?

PHILLY: I heard him telling a power; and I'm thinking we'll have right sport before night will fall. [*He goes out.*]

JIMMY: Well, Philly's a conceited and foolish man. How could that madman have his senses and his brain-pan slit? I'll go after them and see him turn on Philly now. [*He goes;* WIDOW QUIN *hides poteen behind counter. Then hubbub outside.*]

VOICES: There you are! Good jumper! Grand lepper! Darlint boy! He's the racer! Bear him on, will you!

[CHRISTY *comes in, in jockey's dress, with* PEGEEN MIKE, SARA, *and other* GIRLS *and* MEN.]

PEGEEN [*to crowd*]: Go on now and don't destroy him and he drenching with sweat. Go along, I'm saying, and have your tug-of-warring till he's dried his skin.

CROWD: Here's his prizes! A bagpipes! A fiddle was played by a poet in the years gone by! A flat and three-thorned blackthorn would lick the scholars out of Dublin town!

CHRISTY [*taking prizes from the Men*]: Thank you kindly, the lot of you. But you'd say it was little only I did this day if you'd seen me a while since striking my one single blow.

TOWN CRIER [*outside ringing a bell*]: Take notice, last event of this day! Tug-of-warring on the green below! Come on, the lot of you! Great achievements for all Mayo men!

PEGEEN: Go on and leave him for to rest and dry. Go on, I tell you, for he'll do no more. [*She hustles crowd out;* WIDOW QUIN *following them.*]

MEN [*going*]: Come on, then. Good luck for the while!

PEGEEN [*radiantly, wiping his face with her shawl*]: Well,

you're the lad, and you'll have great times from this out
when you could win that wealth of prizes, and you
sweating in the heat of noon!

CHRISTY [*looking at her with delight*]: I'll have great times
if I win the crowning prize I'm seeking now, and that's
your promise that you'll wed me in a fortnight, when our
banns is called.

PEGEEN [*backing away from him*]: You've right daring to
go ask me that, when all knows you'll be starting to
some girl in your own townland, when your father's
rotten in four months, or five.

CHRISTY [*indignantly*]: Starting from you, is it? [*He follows
her.*] I will not, then, and when the airs is warming, in
four months or five, it's then yourself and me should be
pacing Neifin in the dews of night, the times sweet smells
do be rising, and you'd see a little, shiny new moon,
maybe, sinking on the hills.

PEGEEN [*looking at him playfully*]: And it's that kind of a
poacher's love you'd make, Christy Mahon, on the sides
of Neifin, when the night is down?

CHRISTY: It's little you'll think if my love's a poacher's, or
an earl's itself, when you'll feel my two hands stretched
around you, and I squeezing kisses on your puckered
lips, till I'd feel a kind of pity for the Lord God is all ages
sitting lonesome in His golden chair.

PEGEEN: That'll be right fun, Christy Mahon, and any girl
would walk her heart out before she'd meet a young man
was your like for eloquence, or talk at all.

CHRISTY [*encouraged*]: Let you wait, to hear me talking,
till we're astray in Erris, when Good Friday's by, drinking a sup from a well, and making mighty kisses with our
wetted mouths, or gaming in a gap of sunshine, with
yourself stretched back unto your necklace, in the
flowers of the earth.

PEGEEN [*in a low voice, moved by his tone*]: I'd be nice so,
is it?

CHRISTY [*with rapture*]: If the mitred bishops seen you
that time, they'd be the like of the holy prophets, I'm
thinking, do be straining the bars of Paradise to lay eyes

on the Lady Helen of Troy, and she abroad, pacing back and forward, with a nosegay in her golden shawl.

PEGEEN [*with real tenderness*]: And what is it I have, Christy Mahon, to make me fitting entertainment for the like of you, that has such poet's talking, and such bravery of heart.

CHRISTY [*in a low voice*]: Isn't there the light of seven heavens in your heart alone, the way you'll be an angel's lamp to me from this out, and I abroad in the darkness, spearing salmons in the Owen or the Carrowmore?

PEGEEN: If I was your wife I'd be along with you those nights, Christy Mahon, the way you'd see I was a great hand at coaxing bailiffs, or coining funny nicknames for the stars of night.

CHRISTY: You, is it? Taking your death in the hailstones, or in the fogs of dawn.

PEGEEN: Yourself and me would shelter easy in a narrow bush [*with a qualm of dread*]; but we're only talking, maybe, for this would be a poor, thatched place to hold a fine lad is the like of you.

CHRISTY [*putting his arm round her*]: If I wasn't a good Christian, it's on my naked knees I'd be saying my prayers and paters to every jackstraw you have roofing your head, and every stony pebble is paving the laneway to your door.

PEGEEN [*radiantly*]: If that's the truth I'll be burning candles from this out to the miracles of God that have brought you from the south today, and I with my gowns bought ready, the way that I can wed you, and not wait at all.

CHRISTY: It's miracles, and that's the truth. Me there toiling a long while, and walking a long while, not knowing at all I was drawing all times nearer to this holy day.

PEGEEN: And myself, a girl, was tempted often to go sailing the seas till I'd marry a Jew-man, with ten kegs of gold, and I not knowing at all there was the like of you drawing nearer, like the stars of God.

CHRISTY: And to think I'm long years hearing women talking that talk, to all bloody fools, and this the first

time I've heard the like of your voice talking sweetly for
my own delight.

PEGEEN: And to think it's me is talking sweetly, Christy
Mahon, and I the fright of seven townlands for my biting
tongue. Well, the heart's a wonder; and, I'm thinking,
there won't be our like in Mayo, for gallant lovers, from
this hour today. [*Drunken singing is heard outside.*]
There's my father coming from the wake, and when he's
had his sleep we'll tell him, for he's peaceful then.
[*They separate.*]

MICHAEL [*singing outside*]:
> The jailer and the turnkey
> They quickly ran us down,
> And brought us back as prisoners
> Once more to Cavan town.

[*He comes in supported by* SHAWN.]
> There we lay bewailing
> All in a prison bound. . . .

[*He sees Christy. Goes and shakes him drunkenly by the
hand, while* PEGEEN *and* SHAWN *talk on the left.*]

MICHAEL [*to Christy*]: The blessing of God and the holy
angels on your head, young fellow. I hear tell you're
after winning all in the sports below; and wasn't it a
shame I didn't bear you along with me to Kate Cassidy's
wake, a fine, stout lad, the like of you, for you'd never
see the match of it for flows of drink, the way when we
sunk her bones at noonday in her narrow grave, there
were five men, aye, and six men, stretched out retching
speechless on the holy stones.

CHRISTY [*uneasily, watching Pegeen*]: Is that the truth?

MICHAEL: It is, then; and aren't you a louty schemer to go
burying your poor father unbeknownst when you'd a
right to throw him on the crupper of a Kerry mule and
drive him westwards, like holy Joseph in the days gone
by, the way we could have given him a decent burial,
and not have him rotting beyond, and not a Christian
drinking a smart drop to the glory of his soul?

CHRISTY [*gruffly*]: It's well enough he's lying, for the likes
of him.

MICHAEL [*slapping him on the back*]: Well, aren't you a
hardened slayer? It'll be a poor thing for the household
man where you go sniffing for a female wife; and [*pointing
to Shawn*] look beyond at that shy and decent Christian
I have chosen for my daughter's hand, and I after getting
the gilded dispensation this day for to wed them now.

CHRISTY: And you'll be wedding them this day, is it?

MICHAEL [*drawing himself up*]: Aye. Are you thinking, if
I'm drunk itself, I'd leave my daughter living single with
a little frisky rascal is the like of you?

PEGEEN [*breaking away from Shawn*]: Is it the truth the
dispensation's come?

MICHAEL [*triumphantly*]: Father Reilly's after reading it in
gallous Latin, and 'It's come in the nick of time,' says
he; 'so I'll wed them in a hurry, dreading that young
gaffer who'd capsize the stars.'

PEGEEN [*fiercely*]: He's missed his nick of time, for it's that
lad, Christy Mahon, that I'm wedding now.

MICHAEL [*loudly, with horror*]: You'd be making him a son
to me, and he wet and crusted with his father's blood?

PEGEEN: Aye. Wouldn't it be a bitter thing for a girl to go
marrying the like of Shaneen, and he a middling kind of
a scarecrow, with no savagery or fine words in him at
all?

MICHAEL [*gasping and sinking on a chair*]: Oh, aren't you a
heathen daughter to go shaking the fat of my heart, and
I swamped and drownded with the weight of drink?
Would you have them turning on me the way that I'd
be roaring to the dawn of day with the wind upon my
heart? Have you not a word to aid me, Shaneen? Are
you not jealous at all?

SHAWN [*in great misery*]: I'd be afeard to be jealous of a
man did slay his da?

PEGEEN: Well, it'd be a poor thing to go marrying your
like. I'm seeing there's a world of peril for an orphan girl,
and isn't it a great blessing I didn't wed you before himself came walking from the west or south?

SHAWN: It's a queer story you'd go picking a dirty tramp
up from the highways of the world.

PEGEEN [*playfully*]: And you think you're a likely beau to
   go straying along with the shiny Sundays of the opening
   year, when it's sooner on a bullock's liver you'd put a
   poor girl thinking than on the lily or the rose?

SHAWN: And have you no mind of my weight of passion,
   and the holy dispensation, and the drift of heifers I'm
   giving, and the golden ring?

PEGEEN: I'm thinking you're too fine for the like of me,
   Shawn Keogh of Killakeen, and let you go off till you'd
   find a radiant lady with droves of bullocks on the plains
   of Meath, and herself bedizened in the diamond jewel-
   leries of Pharaoh's ma. That'd be your match, Shaneen.
   So God save you now!
   [*She retreats behind Christy.*]

SHAWN: Won't you hear me telling you . . . ?

CHRISTY [*with ferocity*]: Take yourself from this, young
   fellow, or I'll maybe add a murder to my deeds today.

MICHAEL [*springing up with a shriek*]: Murder is it? Is it
   mad yous are? Would you go making murder in this
   place, and it piled with poteen for our drink to-night? Go
   on to the foreshore if it's fighting you want, where the
   rising tide will wash all traces from the memory of man.
   [*Pushing Shawn towards Christy.*]

SHAWN [*shaking himself free, and getting behind Michael*]:
   I'll not fight him, Michael James. I'd liefer live a bache-
   lor, simmering in passions to the end of time, than face
   a lepping savage the like of him has descended from the
   Lord knows where. Strike him yourself, Michael James,
   or you'll lose my drift of heifers and my blue bull from
   Sneem.

MICHAEL: Is it me fight him, when it's father-slaying he's
   bred to now? [*Pushing Shawn.*] Go on, you fool, and fight
   him now.

SHAWN [*coming forward a little*]: Will I strike him with my
   hand?

MICHAEL: Take the loy is on your western side.

SHAWN: I'd be afeard of the gallows if I struck with that.

CHRISTY [*taking up the loy*]: Then I'll make you face the
   gallows or quit off from this. [SHAWN *flies out of the door.*]

CHRISTY: Well, fine weather be after him [*going to Michael, coaxingly*], and I'm thinking you wouldn't wish to have that quaking blackguard in your house at all. Let you give us your blessing and hear her swear her faith to me, for I'm mounted on the spring-tide of the stars of luck, the way it'll be good for any to have me in the house.

PEGEEN [*at the other side of Michael*]: Bless us now, for I swear to God I'll wed him, and I'll not renege.

MICHAEL [*standing up in the centre, holding on to both of them*]: It's the will of God, I'm thinking, that all should win an easy or a cruel end, and it's the will of God that all should rear up lengthy families for the nurture of the earth. What's a single man, I ask you, eating a bit in one house and drinking a sup in another, and he with no place of his own, like an old braying jackass strayed upon the rocks? [*To Christy*] It's many would be in dread to bring your like into their house for to end them, maybe, with a sudden end; but I'm a decent man of Ireland, and I liefer face the grave untimely and I seeing a score of grandsons growing up little gallant swearers by the name of God, than go peopling my bedside with puny weeds the like of what you'd breed, I'm thinking, out of Shaneen Keogh. [*He joins their hands.*] A daring fellow is the jewel of the world, and a man did split his father's middle with a single clout should have the bravery of ten, so may God and Mary and St Patrick bless you, and increase you from this mortal day.

CHRISTY *and* PEGEEN: Amen, O Lord!

[*Hubbub outside.* OLD MAHON *rushes in, followed by all the crowd, and* WIDOW QUIN. *He makes a rush at* CHRISTY, *knocks him down, and begins to beat him.*]

PEGEEN [*dragging back his arm*]: Stop that, will you? Who are you at all?

MAHON: His father, God forgive me!

PEGEEN [*drawing back*]: Is it rose from the dead?

MAHON: Do you think I look so easy quenched with the tap of a loy? [*Beats Christy again.*]

PEGEEN [*glaring at Christy*]: And it's lies you told, letting on you had him slitted, and you nothing at all.

CHRISTY [*catching Mahon's stick*]: He's not my father. He's
a raving maniac would scare the world. [*Pointing to
Widow Quin.*] Herself knows it is true.

CROWD: You're fooling Pegeen! The Widow Quin seen him
this day, and you likely knew! You're a liar!

CHRISTY [*dumbfounded*]: It's himself was a liar, lying
stretched out with an open head on him, letting on he
was dead.

MAHON: Weren't you off racing the hills before I got my
breath with the start I had seeing you turn on me at all?

PEGEEN: And to think of the coaxing glory we had given
him, and he after doing nothing but hitting a soft blow
and chasing northward in a sweat of fear. Quit off from
this.

CHRISTY [*piteously*]: You've seen my doings this day, and
let you save me from the old man; for why would you
be in such a scorch of haste to spur me to destruction
now?

PEGEEN: It's there your treachery is spurring me, till I'm
hard set to think you're the one I'm after lacing in my
heart-strings half an hour gone by. [*To Mahon*] Take
him on from this, for I think bad the world should see
me raging for a Munster liar, and the fool of men.

MAHON: Rise up now to retribution, and come on with me.

CROWD [*jeeringly*]: There's the playboy! There's the lad
thought he'd rule the roost in Mayo! Slate him now,
mister.

CHRISTY [*getting up in shy terror*]: What is it drives you to
torment me here, when I'd asked the thunders of the
might of God to blast me if I ever did hurt to any saving
only that one single blow.

MAHON [*loudly*]: If you didn't, you're a poor good-for-
nothing, and isn't it by the like of you the sins of the
whole world are committed?

CHRISTY [*raising his hands*]: In the name of the Almighty
God . . .

MAHON: Leave troubling the Lord God. Would you have
Him sending down droughts, and fevers, and the old hen
and the cholera morbus?

CHRISTY [*to Widow Quin*]: Will you come between us and protect me now?

WIDOW QUIN: I've tried a lot, God help me, and my share is done.

CHRISTY [*looking round in desperation*]: And I must go back into my torment is it, or run off like a vagabond straying through the unions with the dust of August making mudstains in the gullet of my throat; or the winds of March blowing on me till I'd take an oath I felt them making whistles of my ribs within?

SARA: Ask Pegeen to aid you. Her like does often change.

CHRISTY: I will not, then, for there's torment in the splendour of her like, and she a girl any moon of midnight would take pride to meet, facing southwards on the heaths of Keel. But what did I want crawling forward to scorch my understanding at her flaming brow?

PEGEEN [*to Mahon, vehemently, fearing she will break into tears*]: Take him on from this or I'll set the young lads to destroy him here.

MAHON [*going to him, shaking his stick*]: Come on now if you wouldn't have the company to see you skelped.

PEGEEN [*half-laughing, through her tears*]: That's it, now the world will see him pandied, and he an ugly liar was playing off the hero, and the fright of men.

CHRISTY [*to Mahon, very sharply*]: Leave me go!

CROWD: That's it now, Christy. If them two set fighting, it will lick the world.

MAHON [*making a grab at Christy*]: Come here to me.

CHRISTY [*more threateningly*]: Leave me go, I'm saying.

MAHON: I will, maybe, when your legs is limping, and your back is blue.

CROWD: Keep it up, the two of you. I'll back the old one. Now the playboy.

CHRISTY [*in low and intense voice*]: Shut your yelling, for if you're after making a mighty man of me this day by the power of a lie, you're setting me now to think if it's a poor thing to be lonesome it's worse, maybe, go mixing with the fools of earth.

[MAHON *makes a movement towards him.*]

CHRISTY [*almost shouting*]: Keep off . . . lest I do show a
blow unto the lot of you would set the guardian angels
winking in the clouds above.
  [*He swings round with a sudden rapid movement and
  picks up a loy.*]
CROWD [*half-frightened, half-amused*]: He's going mad!
Mind yourselves! Run from the idiot!
CHRISTY: If I am an idiot, I'm after hearing my voice this
day saying words would raise the top-knot on a poet in a
merchant's town. I've won your racing, and your lep-
ping, and . . .
MAHON: Shut your gullet and come on with me.
CHRISTY: I'm going, but I'll stretch you first. [*He runs at
  OLD MAHON with the loy, chases him out of the door
  followed by crowd and WIDOW QUIN. There is a great noise
  outside, then a yell, and dead silence for a moment.
  CHRISTY comes in, half-dazed, and goes to fire.*]
WIDOW QUIN [*coming in hurriedly, and going to him*]:
They're turning again you. Come on, or you'll be hanged,
indeed.
CHRISTY: I'm thinking, from this out, Pegeen'll be giving
me praises, the same as in the hours gone by.
WIDOW QUIN [*impatiently*]: Come by the back door. I'd
think bad to have you stifled on the gallows tree.
CHRISTY [*indignantly*]: I will not, then. What good'd be
my lifetime if I left Pegeen?
WIDOW QUIN: Come on, and you'll be no worse than you
were last night; and you with a double murder this time
to be telling to the girls.
CHRISTY: I'll not leave Pegeen Mike.
WIDOW QUIN [*impatiently*]: Isn't there the match of her in
every parish public, from Binghamstown unto the plain
of Meath? Come on, I tell you, and I'll find you finer
sweethearts at each waning moon.
CHRISTY: It's Pegeen I'm seeking only, and what'd I care
if you brought me a drift of chosen females, standing in
their shifts itself, maybe, from this place to the eastern
world?
SARA [*runs in, pulling off one of her petticoats*]: They're

going to hang him. [*Holding out petticoat and shawl.*] Fit these upon him, and let him run off to the east.

WIDOW QUIN: He's raving now; but we'll fit them on him, and I'll take him to the ferry to the Achill boat.

CHRISTY [*struggling feebly*]: Leave me go, will you? when I'm thinking of my luck today, for she will wed me surely, and I a proven hero in the end of all.

[*They try to fasten petticoat round him.*]

WIDOW QUIN: Take his left hand, and we'll pull him now. Come on, young fellow.

CHRISTY [*suddenly starting up*]: You'll be taking me from her? You're jealous, is it, of her wedding me? Go on from this. [*He snatches up a stool, and threatens them with it.*]

WIDOW QUIN [*going*]: It's in the madhouse they should put him, not in jail, at all. We'll go by the back door to call the doctor, and we'll save him so.

[*She goes out, with* SARA, *through inner room.* MEN *crowd in the doorway.* CHRISTY *sits down again by the fire.*]

MICHAEL [*in a terrified whisper*]: Is the old lad killed surely?

PHILLY: I'm after feeling the last gasps quitting his heart. [*They peer in at Christy.*]

MICHAEL [*with a rope*]: Look at the way he is. Twist a hangman's knot on it, and slip it over his head, while he's not minding at all.

PHILLY: Let you take it, Shaneen. You're the soberest of all that's here.

SHAWN: Is it me to go near him, and he the wickedest and the worst with me? Let you take it, Pegeen Mike.

PEGEEN: Come on, so. [*She goes forward with the others, and they drop the double hitch over his head.*]

CHRISTY: What ails you?

SHAWN [*triumphantly, as they pull the rope tight on his arms*]: Come on to the peelers, till they stretch you now.

CHRISTY: Me!

MICHAEL: If we took pity on you the Lord God would, maybe, bring us ruin from the law today, so you'd best come easy, for hanging is an easy and a speedy end.

CHRISTY: I'll not stir. [*To Pegeen*] And what is it you'll say to me, and I after doing it this time in the face of all?

PEGEEN: I'll say, a strange man is a marvel, with his mighty talk; but what's a squabble in your backyard, and the blow of a loy, have taught me that there's a great gap between a gallous story and a dirty deed. [*To Men.*] Take him on from this, or the lot of us will be likely put on trial for his deed today.

CHRISTY [*with horror in his voice*]: And it's yourself will send me off, to have a horny-fingered hangman hitching his bloody slipknots at the butt of my ear.

MEN [*pulling rope*]: Come on, will you?

[*He is pulled down on the floor.*]

CHRISTY [*twistings his legs round the table*]: Cut the rope, Pegeen, and I'll quit the lot of you, and live from this out, like the madmen of Keel, eating muck and green weeds on the faces of the cliffs.

PEGEEN: And leave us to hang, is it, for a saucy liar, the like of you? [*To Men*] Take him on, out from this.

SHAWN: Pull a twist on his neck, and squeeze him so.

PHILLY: Twist yourself. Sure he cannot hurt you, if you keep your distance from his teeth alone.

SHAWN: I'm afeard of him. [*To Pegeen*] Lift a lighted sod, will you, and scorch his leg.

PEGEEN [*blowing the fire with a bellows*]: Leave go now, young fellow, or I'll scorch your shins.

CHRISTY: You're blowing for to torture me. [*His voice rising and growing stronger.*] That's your kind, is it? Then let the lot of you be wary, for, if I've to face the gallows, I'll have a gay march down, I tell you, and shed the blood of some of you before I die.

SHAWN [*in terror*]: Keep a good hold, Philly. Be wary, for the love of God. For I'm thinking he would liefest wreak his pains on me.

CHRISTY [*almost gaily*]: If I do lay my hands on you, it's the way you'll be at the fall of night, hanging as a scarecrow for the fowls of hell. Ah, you'll have a gallous jaunt, I'm saying, coaching out through Limbo with my father's ghost.

SHAWN [*to Pegeen*]: Make haste, will you? Oh, isn't he a holy terror, and isn't it true for Father Reilly, that all drink's a curse that has the lot of you so shaky and uncertain now?

CHRISTY: If I can wring a neck among you, I'll have a royal judgement looking on the trembling jury in the courts of law. And won't there be crying out in Mayo the day I'm stretched upon the rope, with ladies in their silks and satins snivelling in their lacy kerchiefs, and they rhyming songs and ballads on the terror of my fate? [*He squirms round on the floor and bites Shawn's leg.*]

SHAWN [*shrieking*]: My leg's bit on me. He's the like of a mad dog, I'm thinking, the way that I will surely die.

CHRISTY [*delighted with himself*]: You will, then, the way you can shake out hell's flags of welcome for my coming in two weeks or three, for I'm thinking Satan hasn't many have killed their da in Kerry, and in Mayo too.
    [OLD MAHON *comes in behind on all fours and looks on unnoticed.*]

MEN [*to Pegeen*]: Bring the sod, will you?

PEGEEN [*coming over*]: God help him so. [*Burns his leg.*]

CHRISTY [*kicking and screaming*]: Oh, glory be to God!
    [*He kicks loose from the table, and they all drag him towards the door.*]

JIMMY [*seeing old Mahon*]: Will you look what's come in?
    [*They all drop Christy and run left.*]

CHRISTY [*scrambling on his knees face to face with Old Mahon*]: Are you coming to be killed a third time, or what ails you now?

MAHON: For what is it they have you tied?

CHRISTY: They're taking me to the peelers to have me hanged for slaying you.

MICHAEL [*apologetically*]: It is the will of God that all should guard their little cabins from the treachery of law, and what would my daughter be doing if I was ruined or was hanged itself?

MAHON [*grimly, loosening Christy*]: It's little I care if you put a bag on her back, and went picking cockles till the

hour of death; but my son and myself will be going our
own way, and we'll have great times from this out telling
stories of the villainy of Mayo, and the fools is here. [*To
Christy, who is freed*] Come on now.

CHRISTY: Go with you, is it? I will then, like a gallant
captain with his heathen slave. Go on now and I'll see
you from this day stewing my oatmeal and washing my
spuds, for I'm master of all fights from now. [*Pushing
Mahon.*] Go on, I'm saying.

MAHON: Is it me?

CHRISTY: Not a word out of you. Go on from this.

MAHON [*walking out and looking back at Christy over his
shoulder*]: Glory be to God! [*With a broad smile.*] I am
crazy again. [*Goes.*]

CHRISTY: Ten thousand blessings upon all that's here, for
you've turned me a likely gaffer in the end of all, the way
I'll go romancing through a romping lifetime from this
hour to the dawning of the judgement day. [*He goes out.*]

MICHAEL: By the will of God, we'll have peace now for our
drinks. Will you draw the porter, Pegeen?

SHAWN [*going up to her*]: It's a miracle Father Reilly can
wed us in the end of all, and we'll have none to trouble
us when his vicious bite is healed.

PEGEEN [*hitting him a box on the ear*]: Quit my sight.
[*Putting her shawl over her head and breaking out into wild
lamentations*] Oh, my grief, I've lost him surely. I've lost
the only Playboy of the Western World.

                                                CURTAIN

Notes

Source Material: In *The Aran Islands* (1906), Synge records the following story told him by the oldest man on the isle of Inishmaan:

He often tells me about a Connaught man who killed his father with the blow of a spade when he was in a passion, and then fled to this island and threw himself on the mercy of some of the natives with whom he was said to be related. They hid him in a hole – which the old man has shown me – and kept him safe for weeks, though the police came and searched for him, and he could hear their boots grinding on the stones over his head. In spite of a reward which was offered, the island was incorruptible, and after much trouble the man was safely shipped to America.

This impulse to protect the criminal is universal in the west. It seems partly due to the association between justice and the hated English jurisdiction, but more directly to the primitive feeling of these people, who are never criminals yet always capable of crime, that a man will not do wrong unless he is under the influence of a passion which is as irresponsible as a storm on the sea. If a man has killed his father, and is already sick and broken with remorse, they can see no reason why he should be dragged away and killed by the law.

Act One

75 *creel cart*: cart with high movable sides.

76 *wake*: a farewell party for the dead, with the corpse laid out on a table.

76 *Father Reilly's dispensation*: a dispensation was necessary for a marriage in Lent.

78 *Stooks of the Dead Women*: Stook-like rocks on the strand where a boat bearing twelve dead women was reputed to have landed.

81 *bona fide*: a genuine traveller to whom a drink could be sold outside the licensed hours.

81 *strong farmer*: farmer with productive land.
81 *butt of his tail-pocket*: the very bottom of the pocket of a swallow-tailed coat.
84 *loy*: spade with a long thin blade.
84 *poteen*: whiskey from an illegal still.
87 *scribes of bog*: strips of peat-land.
87 *streleen*: chatter.
89 *banbhs*: piglets. (Pronounced *bonives*.)
91 *penny poets*: ballad-sellers.
91 *shebeen*: low-grade wayside tavern.
92 *sheepskin parchment*: the dispensation to marry mentioned earlier.

Act Two

95 *cnuceen*: little hill.
98 *the western world*: the province of Connaught.
100 *frish-frash*: froth.
101 *Neifin*: a mountain in Mayo.
101 *Erris*: a district in north-west Mayo.
102 *mitch off*: skulk away.
103 *thraneen*: bit of thread.
103 *the Western States*: the United States of America.
104 *Kilmainham*: a jail in Dublin.
105 *turbary*: the right to cut peat.
105 *the western world*: here the phrase means the United States of America.
106 *streeler*: loafer.
107 *a lier on walls*: probably one who leans on a wall and boasts.
107 *felts*: thrushes.
109 *spavindy*: lame in the hocks.
110 *curagh*: boat made of wickerwork covered with hides.
110 *wheel*: spinning-wheel.
111 *boreen*: lane.

Act Three

112 *the trick-o'-the-loop man*: the man in charge of the hoop-la sideshow at a fair.

112 *cockshot-man*; one who allows missiles to be thrown at him for money as a fairground pastime.

113 *supeen*: little drink.

115 *Belmullet*: peninsula on the coast of Mayo.

117 *parlatic*: paralytic.

117 *union*: workhouse.

119 *townland*: district.

119 *when Good Friday's by*: 'when Lent is over,' i.e. when love-making is permissible.

120 *paters*: paternosters.

125 *old hen*: influenza.

126 *pandied*: beaten.

127 *eastern world*: the province of Leinster.

129 *gallous*: wild, worthy of the gallows.

Cock-a-doodle Dandy

The best introduction to *Cock-a-doodle Dandy* is an article entitled 'O'Casey's Lively Credo' which the playwright himself published in the *New York Times* on 9 November 1958. 'It is only through an Irish scene,' he confesses, 'that my imagination can weave a way, within the Irish shadows or out in the Irish sunshine . . . if it is to have full, or at least a fair chance.' In *Cock-a-doodle Dandy* the shadows gradually eclipse the sunshine, for O'Casey is mainly preoccupied with flaws and anomalies in contemporary Irish life and culture. The achievement of independence, for instance, has not halted the flow of emigrants from Eire; in 1947, its population was 150,000 less than it was in 1911. The majority of the emigrants are young men and women, and a large proportion of them leave Ireland to escape from the repressive influence of the type of parish priest who restricts the hours of dances and the number of occasions and places where members of the opposite sexes may meet. The Censorship of Publications Board instituted by the government of Eire is stricter than the Papal Index and has banned many of the works of the ablest American and European writers, including the first two volumes of O'Casey's autobiography. Though there is no official censorship of plays, clerical opinion is always a force to be reckoned with; in 1958, for instance, it caused the withdrawal of *Bloomsday*, a dramatization of James Joyce's *Ulysses*, from the Dublin International Theatre Festival.

Though O'Casey has been resident in England since 1926, he has kept in touch with developments in his native land, and 'O'Casey's Lively Credo' reveals that many episodes in *Cock-a-doodle Dandy* have a factual basis, notably those in which Father Domineer fells a man who defies him, in which Loreleen is manhandled merely for having been seen in a car with a married man, in which Shanaar spreads fear and superstition, and in which Marthraun and Mahan haggle for higher profits. The recent social history of Eire could also provide parallels to the arranged marriage of Marthraun and Lorna, to Domineer's attempt to confiscate Loreleen's copy of *Ulysses*, to Julia's fruitless pilgrimage to Lourdes, and to the decision of Loreleen, Lorna, Marion, and Robin to emigrate to England.

To O'Casey, however, as he declares in the 'Lively Credo', 'what is called naturalism, or even realism, isn't enough,' and *Cock-a-doodle Dandy* is a satiric fantasy in the spirit of Aristophanes and Swift, making extended use of the symbolic and expressionist techniques which he first essayed in the second act of *The Silver Tassie*. The play begins symbolically with the dancing entry and exit of the Cock, with his crimson crest, black plumage, and yellow feet and ankles. His face has *the look of a cynical jester*, for he represents those instinctive and creative urges which men suppress at their peril, and is associated throughout the play with sexual love, poetry, music, dancing, laughter, and the sheer joy of living. O'Casey's choice of this bird-symbol was evidently influenced by W. B. Yeats, whose lines,

> Lift up the head
> And clap the wings
> Red Cock, and crow!

are approvingly quoted at the end of 'O'Casey's Lively Credo'. In Yeats's plays and poems, birds are persistently used to symbolize the culture of those periods in the cycle of history when the individual frees himself for a time from the dogmas and restrictions of ascetic religions.

In *Cock-a-doodle Dandy*, however, the devotees of the Cock are a harassed minority and eventually decide to emigrate to England, 'where life resembles life more than it does here'. The setting of the play is the village of Nyadnanave, whose Gaelic name means 'Nest of Saints' but suggests the pun 'Nest of Knaves'. It may also be a wry comment on the traditional description of Ireland as 'the land of saints and scholars'. The village is ruled by Father Domineer, a man who cannot smile. His harangue in Scene Two, condemning dancing, films, plays, books, singing, and bright attire, shows that he is the antithesis of the values represented by the Cock. His puritanism is supported by the Civic Guard and abetted by the superstition of the old and the hypocrisy of the young as represented by Shanaar ('Old Man') and One-Eyed Larry.

O'Casey judges his characters in terms of their reaction to the Cock. As the symbolic accessories of their costumes suggest, Loreleen, Marion, and the Messenger, Robin Adair, are in sympathy with him from the outset. Loreleen suffers for her adherence to the life-principle represented by the Cock. At one point, she is aptly compared to Deirdre; she, too, returns to her native land only to find grief and disillusion. Significantly, she reconciles the Dionysian humanism of the Cock with Christianity; echoing the Bible, she warns Marthraun and Mahan against laying up 'treasures on earth', and she tells Domineer that suppressing books is 'thryin' to keep God from talkin'. The Messenger resembles the legendary love-god, Angus; his music and songs symbolize a poetic principle. The turning-point of the play comes in Scene Two when Loreleen and Marion lure Mahan and Marthraun away from their bickering about money, and, dancing with them to the music of the Messenger's accordion, are on the point of humanizing them when Domineer enters and breaks the spell. Lorna, however, acquires courage and hope through contact with Loreleen and leaves for England with her at the end of the play.

These serious themes lie below the surface of a play coruscating with action, sudden changes of light and colour, and stage tricks which include collapsible chairs, a quaking house, a whiskey bottle whose contents will not spill, and a blast of wind which deprives a Civic Guard of his trousers. There is method in these fantasticalities, however. They illustrate either the mischievousness of the Cock or the hallucinations which torment repressed and superstitious minds.

                                                                W.A.A.

Cock-a-doodle Dandy

Sean O'Casey

To James Stephens
the jesting poet with a radiant star
in's coxcomb

Characters

THE COCK

MICHAEL MARTHRAUN, *a small farmer, now the owner of a lucrative bog*

SAILOR MAHAN, *once a sailor, now the owner of a fleet of lorries carrying turf from bog to town*

LORNA, *second young wife of Marthraun*

LORELEEN, *Marthraun's daughter by his first young wife*

MARION, *helper in Lorna's house*

SHANAAR, *a 'very wise old crawthumper', really a dangerous old cod*

1ST ROUGH FELLOW ⎫
2ND ROUGH FELLOW ⎭ *peasants working on the bog*

FATHER DOMINEER, *the parish priest of Nyadnanave*

THE SERGEANT, *of the Civic Guard*

JACK, *Mahan's foreman lorry driver*

JULIA, *Lorna's sister, a paralytic on a visit to Lourdes*

HER FATHER

ONE-EYED LARRY, *a peasant lad and potential sacristan*

A MAYOR

A MACE-BEARER

THE MESSENGER, *in love with Marion*

THE BELLMAN, *a kind of town crier*

A PORTER, *of a general store in the near-by town*

Scenes

Scene One. The front garden outside Michael Marthraun's house, in Nyadnanave. Morning.

Scene Two. The same. Midday.

Scene Three. The same. Dusk.

Cock-a-doodle Dandy was first performed at the People's
Theatre, Newcastle-on-Tyne, on 10 December 1949. The main
roles were taken as follows:

THE COCK   Peter Andrews Collier
MICHAEL MARTHRAUN   Jack Percy
SAILOR MAHAN   Tom Rutherford
LORELEEN   Margaret Wilson
SHANAAR   James Garbutt
MARION   Nancy O'Kane
THE MESSENGER   W. R. Nicholson
LORNA   Helen Paterson
FATHER DOMINEER   John Lilburne

Scene One

Part of the garden outside the house of Michael Marthraun. It is rough and uncared-for, with tough grass everywhere, sprinkled with buttercups and daisies. It is surrounded by a stone wall, three to four feet high, which is pierced by a wooden gate to the right of any visitor entering the garden. To the left, a little way from the gate, a clump of sunflowers, in full bloom, stand stiff and stately, their blossoms big as shields, the petals raying out widely and sharply, like rays from an angry sun. Glancing farther to the left, a visitor would see the gable-end of the house, with a porch jutting from it, and a window above the porch. The porch is supported by twisted pillars of wood, looking like snakes, which are connected with lattice-work shaped like noughts and crosses. These are painted a dazzling white. The framework of the window above is a little on the skew, and the sashwork holding the glass is twisted into irregular lines. A little way from the porch, towards the wall, is a dignified-looking bronze urn holding a stand-offish, cynical-looking evergreen. Farther up, near the wall, the Irish Tricolour flutters from a flag-pole. The house itself is black in colour, the sash and frame of the window in it is a brilliant red.

It is a brilliantly fine day in summer, and as there is nothing in the garden to provide a shade, the place is a deep pool of heat, which, seemingly, has lasted for some time, for the grass has turned to a deep yellow hue, save where the house and porch throw a rich black shadow. Stretching away in the distance, beyond the wall, is a bog of a rich purple colour, dabbed here and there with black patches. The sky above it is a silvery grey, glittering like an oriental canopy.

Some little distance away, an accordion is heard playing a dance tune, and, a few moments after, the COCK *comes dancing in around the gable of the house, circles the dignified urn, and disappears round the farther end of the gable-end as the music ceases.*

He is of a deep black plumage, fitted to his agile and slender body like a glove on a lady's hand; yellow feet and ankles, bright-green flaps like wings, and a stiff cloak falling like a tail behind him. A big crimson crest flowers over his head, and crimson flaps hang from his jaws. His face has the look of a cynical jester.

MICHAEL MARTHRAUN, *followed by* SAILOR MAHAN, *comes into the garden by the porch. Each carries a kitchen chair, which they set down some way from the house. Michael is a man who is well over sixty years of age, clean-shaven, lean, and grim-looking. His lips twitch nervously whenever he forgets to keep his mouth tightly closed. He is dressed in a blackish tweed suit, and his legs are encased in black leggings. A heavy gold chain stretches across his waistcoat, and he wears a wide-leafed collar, under which a prim black bow is tied.*

Sailor Mahan is a little over fifty, stouter than his companion, and of a more serene countenance. He has a short, pointed beard, just beginning to show signs of greyness. His face is of a ruddier hue, and shows that the wind and the stress of many storms have made it rugged, but in no way unpleasant. There is, maybe, a touch of the sea-breeze in his way of talking and his way of walking. He is wearing light-grey flannel trousers, a double-breasted royal blue coat, and has a white scarf round his neck, over a light-blue shirt. They come to the two chairs, and stand there facing each other.

MICHAEL: Come out here, come on out here, where a body can talk free. There's whispers an' whispers in that house, upsettin' a man's mind.

MAHAN [*puzzled*]: Whispers? What kinda whispers?

MICHAEL: Sthrange kinds; whispers good for neither soul nor body.

MAHAN: But there's no one in the house but your wife, Lorna, Marion the maid, and your own girl Loreleen?

MICHAEL: Ay, so you think; but I know different.

MAHAN [*breezily*]: Nonsense, Mick; you're haulin' on a rope that isn't there!

MICHAEL [*raising his voice*]: You don't live in th' house, do you? [*Mahan is silent.*] You don't live in th' house, do you?

MAHAN [*raising his voice too*]: I know I don't live in it, an' if it's like what you say, I don't want to live in it!

MICHAEL: Well, then, keep quiet when a man speaks of what he knows.

MAHAN: I know as much about a whisper as you do.

MICHAEL: You know about th' whispers of wind an' wave, harmless an' innocent things; but I'm talkin' about whispers ebbin' an' flowin' about th' house, with an edge of evil on them, since that painted one, that godless an' laughin' little bitch left London to come here for a long an' leering holiday.

MAHAN: Loreleen? Why, man, she's your own daughter by your first young wife!

MICHAEL: So it was said at th' time, an' so it's believed still; but I had me doubts then, and I've more doubts now. I dhread meetin' her, dhread it, dhread it. [*With a frightened laugh*] Michael Marthraun's daughter! [*Gripping Mahan's arm*] Is she anyone's daughter, man?

MAHAN [*impatiently*]: She must be somebody's daughter, man!

MICHAEL [*impatiently*]: Why must she be, man? Remember what th' Missioner said last night: Sthrange things are foisted by the powers of evil into th' life o' man. Since that one come back from England, where evil things abound, there's sinisther signs appearin' everywhere, evil evocations floatin' through every room.

MAHAN [*puzzled*]: What kinda evocation an' significality is there?

MICHAEL [*looking suspiciously at the porch, then at the window above it, and drawing Mahan farther away from the house*]: Looka, Sailor Mahan [*he speaks furtively*], there's always a stern commotion among th' holy objects of th' house, when that one, Loreleen, goes sailin' by; an invisible wind blows th' pictures out, an' turns their frenzied faces to th' wall; once I seen the statue of St Crankarius standin' on his head to circumvent th' lurin' quality of her presence; an' another time, I seen th' image

of our own St Pathrick makin' a skelp at her with his
crozier; fallin' flat on his face, stunned, when he missed!

MAHAN [*doubtful, but a little impressed*]: Good God, them's
serious things, Michael Marthraun! [*A pause.*] Are you
sure, now, Mick, you're not deludin' yourself?

MICHAEL: Have sense, man! An' me own wife, Lorna
Marthraun, is mixin' herself with th' disordher, fondlin'
herself with all sorts o' dismayin' decorations. Th' other
day, I caught her gapin' into a lookin'-glass, an' when I
looked meself, I seen gay-coloured horns branchin' from
her head!

MAHAN: No! Oh, Mick, you're fancyin' things. Lorna's a
fine, upstandin' woman, an' should be respected.

MICHAEL: Are you gone on her, too? I tell you, I seen the
way th' eyes of young men stare at her face, an' follow
th' movements of her lurin' legs – there's evil in that
woman!

MAHAN: But there's nothin' evil in a pretty face, or in a
pair of lurin' legs.

MICHAEL: Oh, man, your religion should tell you th'
biggest fight th' holy saints ever had was with tempta-
tions from good-lookin' women.

MAHAN [*getting nervous, and eager to change the subject*]:
Looka, let's sit down, an' thry to settle about what
you're willin' to pay for th' cartage of th' turf.

MICHAEL [*ignoring Mahan's attempt to change the tide of
talk*]: Up there in that room [*he points to the window above
the porch*] she often dances be herself, but dancin' in her
mind with hefty lads, plum'd with youth, an' spurred
with looser thoughts of love. [*As he speaks, the sounds of
a gentle waltz are heard, played by harp, lute, or violin, or
by all three, the sounds coming, apparently, from the room
whose window is above the porch. Bitterly*] There, d'ye
hear that, man! Mockin' me. She'll hurt her soul, if she
isn't careful.

MAHAN: She's young enough yet to nourish th' need o'
dancin'. An' anyway, why did you insist on marryin'
her, an' she so young; an' she so gay? She was all again'
it herself.

MICHAEL: She consented to it, at last, didn't she?

MAHAN: Ay, when you, her father, an' th' priest had
badgered th' girl's mind into disordered attention over
th' catch she was gettin'.

MICHAEL: Oh, well you know, Sailor Mahan, that she had
her blue eye on th' fat little farm undher me feet; th'
taut roof over me head; an' th' kind cushion I had in
th' bank, against a hard day.

MAHAN: I seen you meself throtting afther her from star-
board to port, from poop to quarther-deck, hoistin'
before her th' fancy of ribbon an' lace, silver-buckled
shoes, an' a silk dhress for Sunday.

MICHAEL: An' what had she but a patched petticoat, a
worn look, an' broken brogues to wear to Mass on
Sundays? An' didn't I give her oul' fella fifty solid
pounds so that her ailin' sisther could thravel to Lourdes
to get undher th' aegis of th' Blessed Virgin? An' what
did I get for them but a scraggy oul' bog of two hundhred
acres?

MAHAN: An' you're makin' a good thing out of it since turf
came into its own. It's made you a Councillor, a Justice
of th' Peace, an' th' fair-haired boy of th' clergy.

MICHAEL: As you mentioned turf, we'd betther settle this
question of you demandin', for carting it, an exthra
amount I couldn't possibly pay.

MAHAN [*stiffness coming into his voice*]: You'll have to,
Michael Marthraun, for it can't be done now for a cent less.

MICHAEL: We'll have a drink while we're discussin'. I have
a bottle of th' best, ten years maturin', inside. Sit down
there till I get it. [*He goes into the porch and, after a few
moments, comes quickly out again, his mouth twitching, his
voice toned to fear and hate.*] That one, Loreleen's comin'
down th' stairs, an' I don't want to come too near her.
We'll wait till she goes. Let's talk of our affairs, quietly,
while she passes by. Th' thing to do, as Shanaar would
tell you, when you hear a sound or see a shape of anything evil, is to take no notice of it. [*Whispering impatiently*] Sit down, man!

MAHAN [*sitting down – dubiously*]: Are you sure, Mick, you

have a close-hauled comprehension of th' way you're
thinkin?'

MICHAEL: Ay, am I sure; as sure as I am that a cock crows!
[*A cock suddenly crows lustily as* LORELEEN *appears in
the doorway of the porch. She is a very attractive young
woman with an air of her own. A jaunty air it is,
indicating that it is the sign of a handsome, gay, and
intelligent woman. She is dressed in a darkish green
dress, with dark-red flashes on bodice and side of skirt. A
saucy hat of a brighter green than the dress sports a
scarlet ornament, its shape suggestive of a cock's crimson
crest. Her legs – very charming ones – are clad in brown
silk stockings; brown that flashes a golden sheen.*
MICHAEL, *who has sat down, jumps startled to his feet
at the sudden sound of the cock's crow and, stretching over
the table, grips Mahan by the shoulder.*]

MICHAEL: What's that, what's that?

MAHAN [*startled by Michael's frightened movement*]: What's
what, man?

MICHAEL [*trying to recover himself*]: Nothin', I heard
nothin'. What was it you were sayin'? [*In a whisper*] Get
goin' on th' turf, man.

MAHAN [*mystified, but doing his best*]: You'll have to grant
th' two shillin's additional on each load, Mick. I'd work
me lorries at a loss if I took less. [*Placing an affectionate
hand on Michael's shoulder*] An' you know well, you're
such an oul' an' valued friend, I'd do it for affection's
sake, if I only could.

MICHAEL [*forgetting about Loreleen*]: Don't I know that
well, Sailor Mahan; an' I'd do th' same, an' more, be
you; but if I surrendhered two shillin's, I might as well
give you th' bog as well. I have to live, Sailor Mahan.

MAHAN: Damn it, man, haven't I to live too? How th' hell
am I goin' to give th' men a shillin' more without th'
exthra two shillin's from you? Pray to th' saints to let
them fall like rain from heaven, eh?

MICHAEL [*putting his face closer to Mahan's, hotly*]: Looka
here, Sailor Mahan, you're not goin' to magicfy me into
th' dhream of believin' you're not addin', every hurryin'

week, a fine bundle o' notes to th' jubilant store you've there already, forcin' overtime on th' poor men o' th' bank, flickin' th' notes into imperial ordher.

MAHAN [*as fiercely – standing up to say it, his face close to the face of Michael*]: An' you yourself, Michael Marthraun, aren't worn away with th' punishment of poverty! Puttin' on a poor mouth, an' if you set out to count graciously all you have in hidlins, you'd be workin' many a long, glad day, without supper or sleep, be daylight an' candle-light, till your mind centhred on th' sum dominated be th' last note fluttherin' from your fingers!

LORELEEN [*who has strolled slowly over to the gate, listening to the talk the while, turning at the gate to watch as well as listen*]: Lay not up for yourselves treasures upon earth, where moth and rust doth corrupt, and where thieves break through and steal!

MICHAEL [*in a frightened whisper*]: Don't turn your head; take no notice. Don't pretend to hear her lyin' hallucinations!

[*A young,* ROUGH-LOOKING FELLOW, *well-set and strong, comes running along the pathway to the gate. He is wearing dark-brown corduroy trousers, belted at waist, grey shirt, and scarf of bright green, with yellow dots. He pushes Loreleen aside.*]

1ST ROUGH FELLOW [*pushing Loreleen out of his way*]: Outa me way, woman! [*He sees how charming she is as he swings her aside.*] Be God, but you're th' good-lookin' lass! What are you doin' in this hole?

LORELEEN: Seeking happiness, an' failing to find it.

1ST ROUGH FELLOW: It isn't here you should be, lost among th' rough stones, th' twisty grass, an' th' moody misery of th' brown bog; but it's lyin' laughin' you should be where th' palms are tall, an' wherever a foot is planted, a scarlet flower is crushed; where there's levity living its life, an' not loneliness dyin' as it is here.

LORELEEN [*dropping him a deep curtsy*]: Thank you, sir knight, for th' silken compliments to your handmaiden. [*She turns to go out, and the* ROUGH FELLOW *hurries in through the gate, down to the two men.*

1ST ROUGH FELLOW [*going through the gate down to where the two men are, and turning to speak up to Loreleen, still standing at the gate*]: If you wait till I'm done with these fellas [*he indicates Michael and Mahan*] I could go to th' bend o' th' road with you, for it's meself would sur- rendher a long spell of heaven's ease to go a long day's journey with a lass like you!

> [ANOTHER ROUGH FELLOW *hurries in along the path- way outside to the gate, pulling Loreleen aside when he finds her in his way. He wears light-brown corduroy trousers, check shirt, and has a scarf of light yellow, with green stripes, round his neck.*]

2ND ROUGH FELLOW [*pulling Loreleen out of his way*]: Eh, there, woman – outa me way! [*He sees, as she swings around, how charming she is.*] Arra, what winsome wind blew such a flower into this dread, dhried-up desert? Deirdre come to life again, not to sorrow, but to dance! If Eve was as you are, no wondher Adam fell, for a lass like you could shutther th' world away with a kiss! [*He goes through the gate, and down to the other man, pausing to look up at Loreleen again.*]

2ND ROUGH FELLOW [*to Loreleen*]: Wait, lass, till I'm done with these fellas, an' I'll go with you till youth's a shadow a long way left behind!

LORELEEN [*down to the two Rough Fellows*]: I'm not for you, friends, for I'm not good for decent men. The two old cronies will tell you a kiss from me must be taken undher a canopy of dangerous darkness. [*She kisses a hand to them.*] Goodbye! [*She goes out.*]

MICHAEL } [*together*]: What d'ye th' two of yous want here?
MAHAN   }   Why aren't yous at work?

1ST ROUGH FELLOW [*laying a hand sternly on the shoulder of Mahan*]: Looka, you; you give us th' exthra shillin', or we leave your lorries standin', helpless an' naked on th' roads!

2ND ROUGH FELLOW [*laying a hand sternly on Michael's shoulder*]: Looka, you; looka that! [*He throws a cheque contemptuously on to the table.*] Dy'e think a good week's wages is in a cheque for tuppence?

MICHAEL: You didn't work a week, because of th' rain, an' canteen contribution an' insurance brought your wage for the week to tuppence.

2ND ROUGH FELLOW: Tell me how I'm goin' to live a week on tuppence?

1ST ROUGH FELLOW: Seein' th' both of them's Knights o' Columbanus, they should be able to say.

MICHAEL: That's a social question to be solved by th' Rerum Novarum.

2ND ROUGH FELLOW: Fifty years old; not worth much when it was born, an' not worth a damn now. You give a guaranteed week, or th' men come off your bog! [*He goes off towards the gate.*]

1ST ROUGH FELLOW [*going to the gate – to Mahan*]: Take our demand serious, or your lorries stand still on th' highways!

2ND ROUGH FELLOW [*impatiently*]: Looka, there she is! [*He points a finger in front.*] Let's hurry, an' we'll ketch up on th' fine, fair lady.

[*They hurry along the path, but suddenly stop to stare ahead.*]

1ST ROUGH FELLOW [*with awe in his voice*]: What's happenin' to her? A cloud closin' in on her, flashes like lightning whirlin' round her head, an' her whole figure ripplin'!

2ND ROUGH FELLOW [*frightened*]: Jasus, she's changin' into th' look of a fancy-bred fowl! It's turnin' to face us; it's openin' its bake as big as a bayonet!

[*The crow of a cock is heard in the distance*].

1ST ROUGH FELLOW [*frightened*]: Here, man, th' other way for us! It's an omen, a warnin', a reminder of what th' Missioner said last night that young men should think of good-lookin' things in skirts only in th' presence of, an' undher th' guidance of, old and pious people.

[*The two of them hurry away in the opposite direction.*]

MICHAEL [*to Mahan*]: Did you hear that? I'm askin' you, Sailor Mahan, did you hear what them two graspin' rascals said?

MAHAN: I heard, but I can see no significality in it, unless th' two of them had dhrink taken.

MICHAEL [*warningly*]: Looka, Sailor Mahan, if you aren't
careful, your wilful disbelief in things'll lead you
asthray! Loreleen isn't me daughter; she isn't even a
woman: she's either undher a spell, or she's a possessed
person.

MAHAN [*with contempt*]: Aw, for God's sake, Mick, have
sense, an' get that bottle o' whiskey out to put a spell
on us.

MICHAEL [*almost shouting*]: Have you forgotten already th'
case of th' Widow Malone who could turn, twinklin',
into a dog or a hare, when she wanted to hide herself?
An' how, one day, th' dogs followed what they thought
was a hare that made for th' widow's cottage, an' dived
through an open window, one o' th' dogs snappin' a
leg off before it could get through. An' when th' door
was burst open, there was th' oul' witch-widow screamin'
on her oul' bed, one leg gone, with blood spoutin' from
th' stump, so that all th' people heard her last screechin'
as she went sliddherin' down to hell!

MAHAN: I heard tell of it months after, when I come back
from Valparaiso.

MICHAEL: Well, if you heard of it, you know it must have
happened. An' here you are, thinkin' only of whiskey,
and showin' how ready you are to ruin me be askin'
more than I'm able to give. You, a good Christian, a
Knight of St Columbanus, a student in th' Circle
studyin' th' Rerum Novarum, you should show a sign
of charity an' justice, recognizin' th' needs of th' people
rather than your own. [*Suddenly*] Here, I'll add thrup-
pence, an' make th' offer ninepence. Hold out th' hand,
an' clinch th' bargain.

MAHAN: I'll be scuppered if I will! You'll not use me like
th' oul father of th' good woman within, who sold you
th' bog when he thought it was derelict, though you're
makin' thousands out of it now.

MICHAEL: You forget I gave th' oul' cod enough to bring
his other daughter to Lourdes for a cure!

MAHAN: You know th' way th' men are actin' now – goin'
slow, an' doin' two journeys where they used to do three.

MICHAEL: An' aren't my men threatenin' to come off th'
bog altogether? It's this materialism's doin' it – edgin'
into revolt against Christian conduct. If they'd only
judge o' things in th' proper Christian way, as we do,
there'd be no disputes. Now let's be good sons of
Columbanus – you thinkin' of my difficulties, an' me
thinkin' of yours.

MAHAN: Make your offer one an' sixpence, an' I'll hoist
th' pennant of agreement?

MICHAEL: I couldn't. Looka, Sailor Mahan, it would ruin
me.

MAHAN [*viciously*]: You'd rather throw th' money after a
tall-hat so that you could controvert yourself into a
dapper disturbance th' time the president comes to view
th' workin' of th' turf. Talk about Loreleen castin' a
spell! Th' whole disthrict'll be paralysed in a spell when
your top-hat comes out to meet the president's top-hat,
th' two poor things tryin' to keep people from noticin'
what's undher them! Two shillin's, now, or nothin'. [*He
sits down in disgust.*]

> [*Behind the wall,* SHANAAR *is seen coming along the
> road; he opens the gate, and comes slowly down to where
> the two men are. He is a very, very old man, wrinkled like
> a walnut, bent at the shoulders, with longish white hair
> and a white beard – a bit dirty – reaching to his belly.
> He is dressed peasant-wise, thin, threadbare frieze coat,
> patched blackish corduroy trousers, thick boots, good and
> strong, a vivid blue muffler round his neck, and a sack-
> cloth waistcoat, on which hangs a brass cross, suspended
> round his neck by twine. A round, wide-brimmed, black
> hat is on his head.*]

SHANAAR [*lifting his hat as he comes in by the gate*]: God save
all here! God save all that may be in th' house, barrin'
th' cat an' th' dog!

MICHAEL [*with great respect*]: An' you, too, Shanaar, old,
old man, full of wisdom an' th' knowledge of deeper
things.

SHANAAR: Old is it? Ever so old, thousands of years,
thousands of years if all were told.

MICHAEL: Me an' Sailor Mahan here were talkin' some time ago, about th' sthrange dodges of unseen powers, an' of what the Missioner said about them last night, but th' easiness of his mind hasn't been hindhered.

SHANAAR [*bending lower, and shoving his bearded face between the two men*]: If it doesn't hindher th' easiness of his mind now, it will one day! Maybe this very day in this very place.

MICHAEL [*to Mahan*]: What d'ye say to that, now?

MAHAN [*trying to be firm, but a little uneasy*]: Nothin', nothin'.

SHANAAR [*shoving his face closer to Mahan's*]: Ah, me friend, for years an' years I've thravelled over hollow lands an' hilly lands, an' I know. Big powers of evil, with their little powers, an' them with their littler ones, an' them with their littlest ones, are everywhere. You might meet a bee that wasn't a bee; a bird that wasn't a bird; or a beautiful woman who wasn't a woman at all.

MICHAEL [*excitedly*]: I'm tellin' him that, I'm tellin' him that all along!

MAHAN [*a little doubtfully – to Shanaar*]: An' how's a poor body to know them?

SHANAAR [*looking round cautiously, then speaking in a tense whisper*]: A sure sign, if only you can get an all-round glimpse of them. [*He looks round him again.*] *Daemones posteriora non habent* – they have no behinds!

MICHAEL [*frightened a lot*]: My God, what an awe-inspiring, expiring experience!

MAHAN [*frightened too, but trying to appear brave*]: That may be, but I wouldn't put innocent birds or bees in that category.

SHANAAR [*full of pitying scorn for ignorance*]: You wouldn't! Innocent birds! Listen all: There was a cuckoo once that led a holy brother to damnation. Th' cuckoo's call enticed th' brother to a silent glade where th' poor man saw a lovely woman, near naked, bathin' her legs in a pool, an' in an instant th' holy man was taken with desire. Lost! She told him he was handsome, but he must have money if he wanted to get her. Th'

brother entered a noble's house, an' demanded a hundhred crowns for his convent; but the noble was a wise
old bird, an' said he'd have to see the prior first. There-
upon, th' brother up with an axe, hidden undher his
gown, an' cleft th' noble from skull to chin; robbed th'
noble, dhressed himself in rare velvets, an' searched out
all th' rosy rottenness of sin with th' damsel till th' money
was gone. Then they caught him. Then they hanged
him, an', mind you [*the three heads come closer together*],
while this poor brother sobbed on the scaffold, everyone
heard th' mocking laughter of a girl and th' calling of a
cuckoo!

[*As Shanaar is speaking the three last things, the mocking
laughter of a girl is heard, the call of a cuckoo, and a
young man's sobbing, one after the other, at first, then
they blend together for a few moments, and cease. Shanaar
stands as stiff as his bent back will allow, and the other two
rise slowly from their chairs, stiff, too, and frightened.*]

SHANAAR [*in a tense whisper*]: Say nothing; take no notice.
Sit down. Thry to continue as if yous hadn't heard!

MAHAN [*after a pause*]: Ay, a cuckoo, maybe; but that's a
foreign bird: no set harbour or home. No genuine decent
Irish bird would do a thing like that on a man.

MICHAEL: Looka here, Sailor Mahan, when th' powers of
evil get goin', I wouldn't put anything past an ordinary
hen!

SHANAAR: An' you'd be right, Mr Marthraun, though, as
a rule, hens is always undher th' eye an' comprehension
of a Christian. Innocent-looking things are often th'
most dangerous. Looka th' lad whose mother had set her
heart on him bein' a priest, an' one day, at home, he
suddenly saw a corncrake flyin' into a house be an open
window. Climbin' in afther it, he spied a glittherin'
brooch on a table, an' couldn't resist th' temptation o'
thievin' it. That lad spent th' next ten years in a reforma-
tory; his mother died of a broken heart, and his father
took to dhrink.

[*During the recital of Shanaar's story, the 'crek crek, crek
crek' of a corncrake is heard.*]

MICHAEL [*in a tense whisper – to Mahan*]: D'ye hear that, Sailor Mahan?

SHANAAR [*warningly*]: Hush! Take no vocal notice. When yous hear anything or see anything suspicious, give it no notice, unless you know how to deal with it.

MICHAEL [*solemnly*]: A warnin' we'll remember. But supposin' a hen goes wrong, what are we to do?

SHANAAR [*thoughtfully*]: It isn't aysey to say, an' you have to go cautious. The one thing to do, if yous have the knowledge, is to parley with th' hens in a Latin dissertation. If among th' fowl there's an illusion of a hen from Gehenna, it won't endure th' Latin. She can't face th' Latin. Th' Latin downs her. She tangles herself in a helluva disordher. She busts asundher, an' disappears in a quick column of black an' blue smoke, a thrue ear ketchin' a screech of agony from its centre!

MICHAEL [*tremendously impressed*]: Looka that now. See what it is to know! [*A commotion is heard within the house: a loud cackling, mingled with a short, sharpened crow of a cock; the breaking of delf; the half-angry, half-frightened cries of women. A cup, followed by a saucer, flies out through the open window, over the porch, past the heads of the three men, who duck violently, and then crouch, amazed, and a little frightened.*] What th' hell's happenin' now?

[MARION *rushes to the door of the porch, frightened and alarmed. She is a young girl of twenty or so, and very good-looking. Her skirts come just to her knees, for they are nice legs, and she likes to show them – and why shouldn't she? And when she does so, she can add the spice of a saucy look to her bright blue eyes. Instead of the usual maid's cap, she wears a scarf-bandeau round her head, ornamented with silver strips, joined in the centre above her forehead, with an enamelled stone, each strip extending along the bandeau as far as either ear. She wears a dark-green uniform, flashed with a brighter green on the sleeves and neck, and the buttons of the bodice are of the same colour. Her stockings and shoes are black. A*] *small, neat, white apron, piped with green, protects her uniform.*]

MARION [*excitedly – to the men*]: It's flyin' about th' house, an' behavin' outrageous! I guessed that that Loreleen's cluck, cluck, cluckin' would upset th' bird's respectable way of livin'!

MICHAEL [*frightened*]: What's wrong with you, girl; what's up?

MARION: Will one of yous come in, an' ketch it, for God's sake, before it ruins th' house?

MAHAN [*shouting*]: Ketch what, ketch what, woman?

MARION: A wild goose! It's sent th' althar light flyin'; it's clawed the holy pictures; an' now it's peckin at th' tall-hat!

MICHAEL: A wild goose? Are you sure it was a wild one?

MARION [*in great distress*]: I dunno, I dunno – maybe it's a wild duck. It's some flyin' thing tearin' th' house asundher.

MICHAEL [*trembling – to Shanaar*]: D'ye think it might be what you know?

SHANAAR [*his knees shaking a little*]: It might be, Mr Marthraun! It might be, God help us!

MAHAN [*nervous himself*]: Keep your heads, keep your heads! It's nothin'.

MICHAEL [*beside himself with anxiety and dread – shaking Marion roughly by the shoulders*]: Conthrol yourself, girl, an' speak sensibly. Is it a goose or a duck or a hen, or what is it?

MARION [*wildly*]: It's a goose – no, it's a hen, it must be a hen! We thried to dhrive it out with flyin' cups and flyin' saucers, but it didn't notice them. Oh, someone should go in, or it'll peck th' place to pieces!

SHANAAR [*prayerfully*]: So long as it's not transmuted, so long as it's not been transmuted!

MICHAEL [*shaking Marion again*]: Where's Lorna, where's Lorna?

MARION [*responding to the shaking listlessly*]: Last I seen of her, she was barricadin' herself undher th' banisters!

MICHAEL [*pleadingly – to Mahan*]: You've been free with

whales an' dolphins an' octopususas, Sailor Mahan – you run in, like a good man, an' enthrone yourself on top of th' thing!

MAHAN [*indignant*]: Is it me? I'm not goin' to squandher meself conthrollin' live land-fowl!

MICHAEL [*to Shanaar – half-commandingly*]: In case it's what we're afraid of, you pop in, Shanaar, an' liquidate whatever it is with your Latin.

SHANAAR [*backing towards the wall*]: No good in th' house: it's effective only in th' open air.

MICHAEL [*in a fury – to Marion – pushing her violently towards the gate*]: You go, you gapin', frightened fool, an' bring Father Domineer quick!

[*All this time, intermittent cackling has been heard, cackling with a note of satisfaction, or even victory in it, interspersed with the whirring sound of wings.*

As MARION *rushes out through the gate, she runs into the arms of the* MESSENGER, *who carries a telegram in his hand. He clasps Marion tight in his arms, and kisses her. He wears a silvery-grey coat, buttoned over his breast, and trousers. On the right side of the coat is a flash of a pair of scarlet wings. A bright-green beret is set jauntily on his head and he is wearing green-coloured sandals.*

MICHAEL *and* MAHAN *have moved farther from the house, and* SHANAAR *has edged to the gateway, where he stares at the house, ready to run if anything happens. His hands are piously folded in front of him, and his lips move as if he prayed.*]

MESSENGER [*to Marion*]: Ah, lovely one of grace an' gladness, whose kiss is like a honied flame, where are you rushin' to in such a hurry?

MICHAEL [*angrily – up to the Messenger*]: Let her go, you – she's runnin' for th' priest!

MESSENGER: Th' priest – why?

[*The cackling breaks into intensity, the whirring of wings becomes louder, and a plate flies out through the window, followed by a squeal from Lorna.*]

MESSENGER [*astonished, but not startled*]: What's goin' on in th' house?

MICHAEL: There's a wild goose, or somethin', asthray in th' house, an' it's sent th' althar bowl flyin'!

MARION: An' it's peckin' th' holy pictures hangin' on th' walls.

MAHAN: Some think it's a wild duck.

SHANAAR: It may be a hen, only a hen.

MESSENGER [*releasing Marion, and handing the telegram to Michael*]: Here's a telegram for you. [MICHAEL *takes it mechanically, and stuffs it in a pocket.*] Is it losin' your senses yous are to be afraid of a hen? [*He goes towards the porch.*] I'll soon settle it!

SHANAAR [*who is now outside, behind the wall*]: If you value your mortal life, lad, don't go in, for th' hen in there isn't a hen at all!

MESSENGER: If th' hen, that isn't a hen, in there, isn't a hen, then it must be a cock. I'll settle it! [*He rushes into the house.*]

MICHAEL [*in agony*]: If it's a cock, we're done!

SHANAAR [*fervently*]: *Oh, rowelum randee, horrida aidus, sed spero spiro specialii spam!*

[*The head of the* COCK, *with its huge, handsome crimson comb, is suddenly thrust through the window above the porch, and lets out a violent and triumphant crow.* SHANAAR *disappears behind the wall, and* MAHAN *and* MICHAEL *fall flat in the garden, as if in a dead faint.*]

MICHAEL [*as he is falling*]: Holy saints preserve us – it's th' Cock!

SHANAAR [*from behind the wall*]: *Oh, dana eirebus, heniba et galli scatterum in multus parvum avic asthorum!*

[*The* COCK'*s head is as suddenly withdrawn, and a louder commotion is heard to be going on in the house; the* MESSENGER *shouting, a* WOMAN'*s squeal. Then silence for a few moments as puffs of blue-black smoke jet out through the window. When the smoke has gone, the* MESSENGER *comes from the house into the garden. His cap is awry on his head, his face is a little flushed, and his mouth is smiling. He carries in his right hand what might have been a broomstick, but is now a silver staff, topped with a rosette of green and red ribbons. He is followed out by the* COCK *whom he is leading by a green ribbon, the other end circling the Cock's neck. The* COCK *follows the Messenger meekly, stopping when he stops, and moving when the Messenger moves.*]

SHANAAR [*peeping over the wall*]: Boys an' girls, take no notice of it, or you're done! Talk only of th' first thing entherin' your minds.

MESSENGER [*looking with astonishment at the two men sitting up now on the ground, as far as possible from the house, and moving away when the Cock comes nearer*]: What's th' matther with yous? Why are yous dodgin' about on your bums? Get up, get up, an' be sensible.

[MICHAEL *and* MAHAN *scramble to their feet, hurry out through the gate, and stand, warily, beside Shanaar.* LORNA'S *head appears at the window above the porch, and it is at once evident that she is much younger than her husband, very good-looking still, but the bright and graceful contours of her face are somewhat troubled by a vague aspect of worry and inward timidity. Her face shows signs of excitement, and she speaks rather loudly down to the Messenger.*]

LORNA [*to the Messenger*]: Robin Adair, take that bird away at once. Hand him over to th' Civic Guard, or someone fit to take charge of him.

MESSENGER [*up to Lorna*]: Looka, lovely lady, there's no danger, an' there never was. He was lonely, an' was only goin' about in quest o' company. Instead of shyin' cups an' saucers at him, if only you'd given him your lily-white hand, he'd have led you through a wistful an' wondherful dance. But you frightened th' poor thing!

LORNA: Frightened him, is it? It was me was frightened when I seen him tossin' down delf, clawin' holy pictures, and peckin' to pieces th' brand new tall-hat that Mr Marthraun bought to wear, goin' with the Mayor to greet His Brightness, th' President of Eire, comin' to inaugerate th' new canteen for th' turf workers.

MICHAEL [*enraged*]: Is it me new hat he's desthroyed?

SHANAAR [*pulling Michael's arm in warning*]: Damnit, man, take no notice!

MICHAEL [*turning indignantly on Shanaar*]: How'd you
like your sumptuous, silken hat to be mangled into a
monstrosity!

SHANAAR [*with concentrated venom*]: Hush, man, hush!

MARION [*who has been looking at the Cock with admiration*]:
Sure, he's harmless when you know him.

MESSENGER [*stroking its back*]: 'Course he is! Just a gay
bird, that's all. A bit unruly at times, but conthrollable
be th' right persons. [*To the Cock*] Go on, comrade, lift
up th' head an' clap th' wings, black cock, an' crow!
[*The* COCK *lifts up his head, claps his wings, and lets out
a mighty crow, which is immediately followed by a
rumbling roll of thunder.*]

MICHAEL [*almost in a state of collapse*]: Aw, we're done for!

SHANAAR [*violently*]: No notice, no notice!

LORNA [*from the window*]: God bless us, what's that?
[*Down to the Messenger*] Robin, will you take that
damned animal away, before things happen that God
won't know about!

MESSENGER [*reassuringly – up to Lorna*]: Lovely lady, you
can let your little hands lie with idle quietness in your
lap, for there's no harm in him beyond gaiety an' fine
feelin'. [*To the Cock*] You know th' goose-step done be
the Irish Militia in th' city of Cork more'n a hundhred
years ago? Well, we'll go home doin' it, to show there's
nothing undher th' sun Ireland didn't know, before th'
world sensed it. Ready? One, two – quick march!
[*The* MESSENGER *and the* COCK *march off doing the
goose-step.* MARION *follows them, imitating the step, as
far as the end of the garden; then she stands looking after
them, waving them farewell.* MICHAEL *and* MAHAN
*come slowly and stealthily into the garden as the Cock
goes out. They go to the chairs, on which they sit,
exhausted, wiping their foreheads with their handker-
chiefs.* SHANAAR *comes towards them more slowly, keeping an eye in the direction taken by the Cock and the
Messenger. When the place is clear, he anchors himself
behind the table.*]

LORNA [*down to Marion*]: Marion, dear, come on in, an'

help me to straighten things up a little. [*She goes away from the window.*]

MARION [*going slowly towards the house, after having given a last farewell – gleefully*]: Wasn't it a saucy bird! An' th' stately way he done th' goose-step! [*She playfully shakes Michael's shoulder.*] Did you see it, sir? [MICHAEL *takes no notice.*] God forgive me, but it gave us all an hilarious time – didn't it, sir?

MICHAEL [*coldly*]: Your misthress called you.

MARION: I heard her, sir. What a clatther it all made! An yous' all quakin', an' even Sailor Mahan there, shakin' in his shoes, sure it was somethin' sinisther!

MAHAN [*angrily*]: You go in to your misthress, girl!

MARION [*giggling*]: Th' bould sailor lad! An' he gettin' rocked in th' cradle of th' deep! Me faltherin' tongue can't impart th' fun I felt at seein' yous all thinkin' th' anchor was bein' weighed for th' next world!

MICHAEL [*loudly*]: Go to your misthress when you're told.

MARION [*giggling more than ever*]: An' oul' dodderin' Shanaar, there, concoctin' his Latin, an' puttin' th' wall between himself an' th' blast! Well, while yous sit all alone there in th' gloamin', yous won't be in heart for singin'. [*She chants*] 'Only to see his face again, only to hear him crow!' [*She runs merrily in.*]

SHANAAR [*warily – in a warning whisper*]: Watch that one!

MICHAEL: Th' ignorant, mockin', saucy face of her afther us bein' in danger of thransportation to where we couldn't know ourselves with agony an' consternation!

SHANAAR [*fervently*]: Sweet airs of heaven be round us all! Watch that one, Mr Marthraun. Women is more flexible towards th' ungodly than us men, an' well th' old saints knew it. I'd recommend you to compel her, for a start, to lift her bodice higher up, an' pull her skirt lower down; for th' circumnambulatory nature of a woman's form often has a detonatin' effect on a man's idle thoughts.

MICHAEL [*pensively*]: How thrue, how thrue that is!

SHANAAR: What we have to do now, is to keep thought from dwellin' on th' things seen an' heard this day; for dwellin' on it may bring th' evil back again. So don't let any thought of it, *ab initio extensio*, remain in your minds, though, as a precaution, when I'm passin' th' barracks, I'll acquaint the Civic Guard. Now I must be off, for I've a long way to thravel. [*He goes as far as the gate, and returns.*] Mr Marthraun, don't forget to have th' room, where th' commotion was manifested, *turbulenta concursio cockalorum*, purified an' surified be an understandin' clergyman. Goodbye. [*Again he goes as far as the gate, and returns.*] Be on your guard against any unfamiliar motion or peculiar conspicuosity or quasi-modical addendum, perceivable in any familiar thing or creature common to your general recognisances. A cat barkin' at a dog, or a dog miaouin' be a fire would atthract your attention, give you a shock, but don't, for th' love of God, notice it! It's this scourge of materialism sweepin' th' world, that's incantatin' these evils to our senses and our doorsteps.

MAHAN [*pensively*]: That's th' way th' compass is pointin', Shanaar – everyone only thinkin', thinkin' of himself.

SHANAAR: An' women's wily exhilarations are abettin' it, so that a man's measure of virtue is now made with money, used to buy ornaments, bestowed on girls to give a gaudy outside to the ugliness of hell.

MICHAEL [*fervently*]: Oh, how thrue, how thrue that is!

SHANAAR: An' th' coruscatin' conduct in th' dance-halls is completin' th' ruin.

MAHAN [*solemnly*]: Wise words from a wiser man! Afther a night in one of them, there isn't an ounce of energy left in a worker!

SHANAAR [*whispering*]: A last warnin' – Don't forget that six thousand six hundhred an' sixty-six evil spirits can find ready lodgin's undher th' skin of a single man!

MICHAEL [*horrified*]: What an appallin' thought!

SHANAAR: So be on your guard. Well, goodbye.

MICHAEL [*offering him a note*]: Here's a pound to help you on your way.

SHANAAR [*setting the note aside*]: No, thanks. If I took it, I couldn't fuse th' inner with th' outher vision; I'd lose th' power of spiritual scansion. If you've a shillin' for a meal in th' town till I get to the counthry, where I'm always welcome, I'll take it, an' thank you. [MICHAEL *gives him a shilling.*]

SHANAAR: Thank you kindly. [*He goes out through the gate, and along the pathway outside. Just as he is about to disappear, he faces towards the two men, and stretches out a hand in a gesture of blessing. Fervently*] *Ab tormentum sed absolvo, non revolvo, cockalorum credulum hibernica!*

MICHAEL [*with emotion*]: You too, Shanaar, oul' son; you too! [SHANAAR *goes off.*]

MAHAN [*after a pause – viciously*]: That Latin-lustrous oul' cod of a prayer-blower is a positive danger goin' about th' country!

MICHAEL [*startled and offended*]: Eh? I wouldn't go callin' him a cod, Sailor Mahan. A little asthray in a way, now an' again, but no cod. You should be th' last to call th' man a cod, for if it wasn't for his holy Latin aspirations, you mightn't be here now.

MAHAN [*with exasperation*]: Aw, th' oul' fool, pipin' a gale into every breeze that blows! I don't believe there was ever anything engenderogically evil in that cock as a cock, or denounceable either! Lardin' a man's mind with his killakee Latin! An' looka th' way he slights th' women. I seen him lookin' at Lorna an' Marion as if they'd horns on their heads!

MICHAEL [*doubtfully*]: Maybe he's too down on th' women, though you have to allow women is temptin'.

MAHAN: They wouldn't tempt man if they didn't damn well know he wanted to be tempted!

MICHAEL: Yes, yes; but we must suffer th' temptation accordin' to the cognisances of th' canon law. But let's have a dhrink, for I'm near dead with th' drouth, an' we can sensify our discussion about th' increased price you're demandin' for carryin' th' turf; though, honest to God, Sailor Mahan, I can't add a ha'penny more to what I'm givin'.

MAHAN: A dhrink would be welcome, an' we can talk over th' matter, though, honest to God, Michael Marthraun, blast th' penny less I'll take than what I'm askin'.

MICHAEL [*going to the porch, and shouting into the house*]:
Marion, bring th' bottle of ten years' maturin', an' two
glasses! [*He returns.*] It's th' principle I'm thinkin' of.

MAHAN: That's what's troublin' me, too. [MARION *comes
in with the bottle of whiskey and the two glasses. She places
them on the table, getting between the two men to do so.
Reading the label*] Flanagan's First! Nyav na Nyale – th'
heaven of th' clouds! An' brought be a lass who's a
Flanagan's first too!

MARION [*in jovial mood*]: G'long with you – you an' your
blarney!

MICHAEL [*enthusiastically*]: Had you lived long ago, Emer
would have been jealous of you! [*He playfully pinches
her bottom.*]

MARION [*squealing*]: Ouch! [*She breaks away, and makes for
the porch.*] A pair o' naughty men! [*She goes into the
house.*]

MICHAEL [*calling after her*]: I forgot th' soda, Marion;
bring th' siphon, lass.

MAHAN [*complacently*]: I could hold that one in me arms
for a long time, Mick.

MICHAEL: Th' man would want to be dead who couldn't.

MAHAN [*enthusiastically*]: I'd welcome her, even if I seen
her through th' vision of oul' Shanaar – with horns
growin' out of her head!

[MARION *returns with the siphon which she places on the
table. The two men, looking in front of them, have silly,
sly grins on their faces.*

*The ornament which Marion wears round her head
has separated into two parts, each of which has risen over
her head, forming two branching horns, apparently
sprouting from her forehead. The two men, slyly gazing
in front, or at the table, do not see the change. Marion's
face has changed too, and now seems to wear a mocking,
cynical look, fitting the aspect of her face to the horns.*]

MARION [*joking*]: Two wild men – it's afraid I am to come
near yous.

[MICHAEL *puts his right arm round her waist, and*
MAHAN *his left one.*]

MAHAN [*slyly*]: What about a kiss on your rosy mouth, darlin', to give a honied tang to th' whiskey?

MICHAEL: An' one for me, too?

MARION [*with pretended demureness*]: A thrue gentleman'll rise up an' never expect a thrue lady to bend down for a kiss. [*With vigour*] Up an' take it, before yous grow cold!

> [*They rise from their chairs, foolish grins on their faces, settle themselves for a kiss, and then perceive the change that has taken place. They flop back on to the chairs, fright and dismay sweeping over their faces.*]

MAHAN ⎫
MICHAEL ⎬ [*together*]: Good God!

> [*They slump in the chairs, overcome, their hands folded in front of their chests, palm to palm, as if in prayer. MARION looks at them in some astonishment.*]

MARION: What ails yous? Was th' excitement too much for yous, or what?

MICHAEL [*plaintively*]: Saints in heaven help us now!

MARION: What's come over yous? Th' way yous slumped so sudden down, you'd think I'd horns on me, or somethin'!

MICHAEL [*hoarsely*]: G'way, g'way! Shanaar, Shanaar, where are you now!

MARION [*going over to Mahan, and putting an arm round his neck*]: What about you, gay one?

MAHAN [*gurgling with fright*]: You're sthranglin' me! G'way, g'way, girl!

MARION: Looka, a kiss would do yous good. Yous think too much of th' world!

MAHAN [*chokingly*]: St Christopher, mainstay of mariners, be with me now!

> [LORNA *thrusts her head out from the window over the porch.*]

LORNA [*down to Marion*]: Let them two oul' life-frighteners fend for themselves, an' come in. From th' back window, I can see th' crowd gathered to give Julia a send-off to Lourdes, so come in to tidy if you want to join them with me.

MARION [*half to herself – as she runs into the house*]: God
forgive me – I near forgot! Here we are followin'
laughter, instead of seekin' succour from prayer! [*She
runs in, and* LORNA *takes her head back into the room
again.*]

MICHAEL [*frightened and very angry*]: Now, maybe, you'll
quit your jeerin' at oul' Shanaar! Now, maybe, you'll
let your mind concentrate on higher things! Now, maybe,
you won't be runnin' loose afther girls!

MAHAN [*indignantly*]: Damnit, man, you were as eager for
a cuddle as I was!

MICHAEL [*lifting his eyes skywards*]: Oh, d'ye hear that! I
was only toleratin' your queer declivity, like a fool. An'
afther all th' warnin's given be wise oul' Shanaar!
Looka, Sailor Mahan, you'll have to be more on your
guard!

MAHAN [*trying to defend himself*]: How could any man
suspect such a thing? We'll have to think this thing
out.

MICHAEL [*with exasperation*]: Think it out! Oh, man,
Sailor Mahan, have you nothin' more sensible to say
than that we'll have to think it out?

MAHAN: Let's have a dhrink, for God's sake, to steady us
down!

MICHAEL [*hurriedly putting bottle and glasses under the
table*]: What're you thinkin' of, Sailor Mahan? We
can't dispense ourselves through a scene of jollification
an' poor Julia passin' on her way to Lourdes!
[*Along the path, on a stretcher, carried by the two
ROUGH FELLOWS, comes JULIA, followed by her father.
The stretcher is borne to the gate, and there laid down, so
that the head of it is flush with the gate-posts, and the rest
of it within the garden. The framework of the gate makes
a frame for Julia, who is half sitting up, her head
supported by a high pillow. Her face is a sad yellowish
mask, pierced by wide eyes, surrounded by dark circles.
Her father is a sturdy fellow of fifty, a scraggly greyish
beard struggling from his chin. He is roughly dressed
as a poorer peasant might be, and his clothes are patched*

in places. He wears a brown muffler, and a faded black
trilby-hat is on his head. All the time, he looks straight
in front with a passive and stony stare.

Before the stretcher walks the MAYOR, *rather stout,*
clean-shaven, wearing a red robe over rough clothing; he
has a very wide three-cornered hat, laced with gold, on his
head. Behind him walks the MACE-BEARER, *a big silver*
and black mace on his shoulder. He is tall, and wears
a bright blue robe, trimmed with silver, on his head is a
huge cocked hat, laced, too, with silver. These two do not
enter the garden, but walk on, and stand waiting near the
house, beside the flag-pole, but without the wall.

LORNA, *followed by* MARION, *comes out of the house.*
Instead of the bright headgear worn before, they have
black kerchiefs, worn peasant-wise on their heads – that
is, they have been folded triangularly, draped over their
heads, with the ends tied beneath their chins.

LORNA *runs over to the stretcher, kneels down beside*
it, and kisses Julia.]

LORNA [*affectionately*]: My sister, my little Julia, oh, how
sorry I am that you have to go on this long, sad journey!

JULIA [*her voice is low, but there is a hectic note of hope in it*]:
A long journey, Lorna darlin', but not a sad one; oh,
no, not a sad one. Hope, Lorna, will have me be the
hand all the long way. I go to kneel at the feet of the
ever Blessed Virgin.

LORNA: Oh, she will comfort you, me darlin'.

JULIA: Yes, she will comfort me, Lorna [*after a pause*]; an'
cure me too. Lorna, say she will cure me too.

LORNA [*stifling a sob*]: An' cure you, too.

JULIA [*to Michael*]: Give me your good wishes, Mr Marthraun.

MICHAEL [*with genuine emotion*]: Julia, me best wishes go
with you, an' me best prayers'll follow all th' long way!

JULIA [*to Mahan*]: An' you, Sailor Mahan – have you no
good wish for the poor voyager?

MAHAN [*fervently*]: Young lass, may you go through
healin' wathers, an' come back a clipper, with ne'er a
spar, a sail, or a rope asthray!

[FATHER DOMINEER *comes quickly in on the path out-side. He is a tall, rather heavily built man of forty. He has a breezy manner now, heading the forlorn hope. He is trying to smile now, but crack his mouth as he will, the tight, surly lines of his face refuse to furnish one. He is dressed in the usual clerical, outdoor garb, and his hard head is covered with a soft, rather widely brimmed black hat.*]

FATHER DOMINEER [*as happily as he can*]: Now, now, no halts on th' road, little daughter! The train won't wait, an' we must have a few minutes to spare to make you comfortable. Bring her along, Brancardiers! Forward, in th' name o' God and of Mary, ever Virgin, ever blessed, always bending to help poor, banished children of Eve!

[*The two* ROUGH MEN *take up the stretcher and carry it along the pathway outside, the* MAYOR, *followed by his* MACE-BEARER, *leading it on.* FATHER DOMINEER *follows immediately behind; then come* LORNA *and* MARION, *followed by* MICHAEL *and* MAHAN.

As the stretcher moves along the pathway outside, a band in the distance is heard playing 'Star of the Sea', to which is added the voice of a crowd singing the words:

Hail, Queen of Heaven, the ocean Star!
Guide of the wand'rer here below!
Thrown on life's surge, we claim thy care –
Save us from peril and from woe.

Mother of Christ, Star of the Sea,
Pray for the wanderer, pray for me.]

FATHER DOMINEER [*enthusiastically*]: Julia will bring us back a miracle, a glorious miracle! To Lourdes!

                                          END OF SCENE ONE

Scene Two

*The Scene is the same as before, though the sunshine isn't
quite so bright and determined. The Irish Tricolour flies
breezily from its flag-pole; the table and chairs stand where
they were, and the bottle and glasses are still under it.*

*No one is in the garden, all, apparently, having gone to see
Julia away on her long, long journey. Away in the distance
the band is playing 'Star of the Sea', and the tune can be
softly heard from the garden.*

After a few moments, LORNA *and* MARION *come along the
path outside, enter by the gate, and cross over into the house.*

MARION [*anxiously*]: What d'ye think of th' chance of a
cure?

LORNA: I'm afraid th' chance is a poor one; but we won't
talk about it.

MARION [*piously*]: Well, it was a grand send-off, an' God
is good.

LORNA [*coldly*]: An' th' devil's not a bad fella either.
[*They both go into the house, and, a few moments later,*
MICHAEL *and* MAHAN *stroll along the path, come into
the garden, and go to where the table and chairs are.*]

MAHAN: Well, th' anchor's weighed.

MICHAEL: It was an edifyin' spectacle, Sailor Mahan,
thrustin' us outa this world for th' time bein'. Julia's
asked for a sign, Sailor Mahan, an', believe me, she'll
get it.

MAHAN: She will, she will, though I wouldn't like to bet
on it.

MICHAEL: She'll get what she's afther – a complete cure.
Me own generous gift of fifty pounds for th' oul' bog'll
be rewarded; an' th' spate o' prayin' goin' on, from th'
Mayor to the Bellman, is bound to get th' higher saints
goin', persuadin' them to furnish a suitable answer to
all we're askin'.

MAHAN [*impatiently*]: Arra, man alive, d'ye think th'
skipper aloft an' his glitterin' crew is goin' to bother
their heads about a call from a tiny town an' disthrict
thryin' hard to thrive on turf?

MICHAEL [*indignantly*]: Looka, if you were only versed in
th' endurin' promulgacity of th' gospels, you'd know
th' man above's concerned as much about Nyadnanave
as he is about a place where a swarm of cardinals
saunther secure, decoratin' th' air with all their purple
an' gold!

MAHAN [*as indignantly*]: Are you goin' to tell me that th'
skipper aloft an' his hierarchilogical crew are concerned
about th' Mayor, the Messenger, Marion, me, an' you as
much as they are about them who've been promoted to
th' quarter-deck o' th' world's fame? Are you goin' to
pit our palthry penances an' haltin' hummin' o' hymns
against th' piercin' pipin' of the' rosary be Bing Bang
Crosby an' other great film stars, who side-stepped from
published greatness for a holy minute or two to send a
blessed blast over th' wireless, callin' all Catholics to
perpetuatin' prayer!

MICHAEL [*sitting down on a chair*]: Sailor Mahan, I ask you
to thry to get your thoughts ship-shaped in your mind.
[*While they have been talking, the* MESSENGER *has come
running along the path outside, and is now leaning on
the gate, listening to the two men, unnoticed by them.*]

MAHAN [*plumping down on the other chair – indignantly*]:
D'ye remember who you're talkin' to, man! Ship-shape
in me mind! Isn't a man bound to have his mind fitted
together in a ship-shape way, who, forced out of his
thrue course be a nautical cathastrope, to wit, videliket,
an act o' God, ploughed a way through th' Sargasso Sea,
reachin' open wathers, long afther hope had troubled
him no longer?

MICHAEL [*wearily*]: Aw, Sailor Mahan, what's them things
got to do with th' things tantamount to heaven?

MESSENGER [*over to them*]: Mick's right – them things
can't be tantamount to anything bar themselves.

MAHAN [*turning fiercely on the Messenger*]: What do you

want? What're you doin' here? Your coalition of ignorant
knowledge can't comprehend th' things we talk about!

MESSENGER [*with some excitement*]: Listen, boys – I've a
question to ask yous.

MICHAEL [*with a gesture signifying this isn't the time to ask
it*]: Ask it some time more convenient. An' don't refer to
us as 'boys' – we're gentlemen to you!

MAHAN [*to Michael*]: Looka, Mick, if you only listened to
Bing Crosby, th' mighty film star, croonin' his Irish
lullaby, [*he chants*] 'Tooral ooral ooral, tooral ooral ay',
you'd have th' visuality to see th' amazin' response he'd
have from millions of admirers, if he crooned a hymn!

MESSENGER: I was never sthruck be Bing Crosby's
croonin'.

MICHAEL [*wrathfully – to Messenger*]: You were never
sthruck! An' who th' hell are you to be consulted?
Please don't stand there interferin' with the earnest
colloquy of betther men. [*To Mahan*] Looka, Sailor
Mahan, any priest'll tell you that in th' eyes of heaven
all men are equal an' must be held in respect an'
reverence.

MAHAN [*mockingly*]: Ay, they'll say that to me an' you, but
will they say it to Bing Crosby, or any other famous
film star?

MESSENGER: Will they hell! Honour be th' clergy's regu-
lated by how much a man can give!

MICHAEL [*furiously – to the Messenger*]: Get to hell outa
here! With that kinda talk, we won't be able soon to sit
steady on our chairs. Oh!

[*The chair he is sitting on collapses, and he comes down
to the ground on his arse.*]

MAHAN [*astonished*]: Holy saints, what's happened?

MICHAEL [*in a fierce whisper – to Mahan*]: Take no notice of
it, fool. Go on talkin'!

MAHAN [*a little confused*]: I'll say you're right, Mick; th'
way things are goin' we won't be able much longer to
sit serene on our chairs. Oh!

[*The chair collapses under Mahan, and he, too, comes
down to the ground.*]

MICHAEL [*in a fierce whisper*]: Don't notice it; go on's if nothin' happened!

MESSENGER [*amused*]: Well, yous have settled down now, anyhow! Will I get yous chairs sturdy enough to uphold th' wisdom of your talkin'?

MICHAEL [*angrily – to Messenger*]: There's nothin' wrong with th' chairs we have! You get outa here! Nothin's wrong with th' chairs at all. Get outa here! I don't trust you either!

MESSENGER: I've somethin' important to ask yous.

MICHAEL: Well, ask it at some more convenient time. [*To Mahan*] It's a blessin' that so many lively-livin' oul' holy spots are still in th' land to help us an' keep us wary.

MESSENGER [*scornfully*]: An' where are th' lively holy spots still to be found? Sure, man, they're all gone west long ago, an' the whole face o' th' land is pock-marked with their ruins!

MICHAEL [*shouting at the Messenger*]: Where are th' lost an' ruined holy places? We've always cared for, an' honoured, our holy spots! Mention one of them, either lost or ruined!

MESSENGER [*shouting back*]: There are thousands of them, man; places founded be Finian, Finbarr, an' th' rest; places that are now only an oul' ruined wall, blighted be nettle an' dock, their only glory th' crimson berries of th' bright arbutus! Where's th' Seven Churches of Glendalough? Where's Durrow of Offally, founded be Columkille himself? Known now only be the name of the Book of Durrow.

MICHAEL [*ferociously*]: Book o' Durrow! It's books that have us half th' woeful way we are, fillin' broody minds with loose scholasticality, infringin' th' holy beliefs an' thried impositions that our fathers' fathers' fathers gave our fathers' fathers, who gave our fathers what our fathers gave to us!

MESSENGER: Faith, your fathers' faith is fear, an' now fear is your only fun.

MAHAN [*impatiently*]: Let him go, Mick, an' let's have that dhrink you mentioned a year ago.

[MARION's *head appears at the window, looking down at the Messenger. The decorations on her head have now declined to their first place.*]

MARION [*down to the Messenger*]: Hallo, Robin Adair! [*He looks up.*] Where are th' two oul' woeful wondhers? [*He points to where they are.*] Oh, they've brought the unsteady chairs out, and now they've broken them up! [*To Michael – angrily*] You knew well th' chairs in the hall were there only to present an appearance.

MESSENGER [*up to her*]: Oh, Marion, Marion, sweet Marion, come down till I give you a kiss havin' in it all the life an' longin' of th' greater lovers of th' past!

MARION [*leaving the window*]: Now, now, naughty boy!

MICHAEL [*sourly*]: You'd do well to remember, lad, the month in jail you got for kissin' Marion, an' the forty-shillin' fine on Marion, for kissing you in a public place at th' cross-roads.

[MARION *comes from the house, goes towards the* MESSENGER, *who seizes her in his arms and kisses her.*]

MESSENGER: I'd do a year an' a day in a cold cell of pressed-in loneliness, an' come out singin' a song, for a kiss from a lass like Marion!

MARION: Don't think too much of me, Robin Adair, for I've some of th' devil in me, an' th' two fostherers of fear, there, think I wear horns on holy days.

MICHAEL [*impressively*]: See – she's warnin' you, herself, young man!

MARION [*to the Messenger*]: An' what has you here arguin' with them two oul' fools?

MESSENGER: I came to ask a question of them, but they were buried in their prayers. Did you see him? Did he come this way?

MICHAEL [*suddenly alarmed*]: Come where?

MAHAN [*alarmed*]: See who?

MESSENGER: Th' Cock.

MAHAN ⎫
MICHAEL ⎭ [*together*]: Th' Cock!

[*They carefully creep away from the broken chairs, and stand up when they are some distance from them.*]

MESSENGER: Ay. I thought he'd make for here first.

MICHAEL [*echoing the Messenger*]: Make for here first!
[*In the distance, the loud, exultant crow of the Cock is heard.*]

MESSENGER [*excitedly*]: There he is! Away in the direction east of th' bog! I'll go get him, an' fetch him home.

MARION [*kissing the Messenger*]: Bring him here first, Robin, an' I'll have a wreath of roses ready to hang round his neck.

MESSENGER [*rushing away*]: I will, I will, fair one! [*He goes off. She takes the broken chairs into the house.*]

MARION [*carrying in the chairs*]: Next time, you boyos, take out two steady ones.

MICHAEL [*horrified*]: Did you hear what she said, Sailor Mahan? Hang a wreath of roses round his neck! Well, I'll have th' gun ready! Ay, now! [*He goes over to the porch, but* MAHAN *lays a restraining hand on his arm.*]

MAHAN: What good would th' gun be? Have you forgot what Shanaar told us? Your bullet would go clean through him, an' leave him untouched. Now that we're in peace here, let's have th' dhrink we were to have, an' which we both need.

MICHAEL [*halting*]: You're right, Sailor Mahan. If he comes here, what we have to do is to take no notice. Look through him, past him, over him, but never at him. [*He prepares the bottle of whiskey and the glasses.*] There's sinisther enchantments all around us. God between us an' all harm! We'll have to be for ever on our guard.

MAHAN [*impatiently*]: Yis, yis; fill out th' dhrink for God's sake!

MICHAEL: May it give us courage. [*He tilts the bottle over the glass, but none of it spills out.*] Good God, th' bottle's bewitched too!

MAHAN: Bottle bewitched? How could a bottle be bewitched? Steady your nerves, man. Thry givin' it a shake.

MICHAEL [*who has left the bottle back on the table – retreating away from it*]: Thry givin' it a shake yourself, since you're so darin'.

[MAHAN *goes over to the table with a forced swagger, and reaches out a cautious hand for the bottle. As he touches it, its colour changes to a glowing red.*]

MAHAN [*fervent and frightened*]: St Christopher, pathron of all mariners, defend us – th' bottle's changed its colour!

MICHAEL: There's evil things cantherin' an' crawlin' about this place! You saw th' seal on th' bottle showin' it was untouched since it left th' store. Flanagan's finest, Jameson's best, ten years maturin' – an' look at it now.

MAHAN: How are we goin' to prevent ourselves from bein' the victims of sorcery an' ruin? You'd think good whiskey would be exempt from injury even be th' lowest of th' low.

MICHAEL: It's th' women who're always intherceptin' our good intentions. Evil things is threatenin' us every-where. Th' one safe method of turnin' our back to a power like this is to go forward an' meet it half-way. [*He comes close to Mahan, and whispers hoarsely*] Selah!

MAHAN [*mystified and frightened at what he thinks may be something sinister*]: Selah?

MICHAEL [*emphatically*]: Selah!

MAHAN [*agonizingly*]: Good God!

MICHAEL: Now, maybe, you'll believe what th' Missioner said last night.

MAHAN [*a little dubiously*]: He might have been exagger-atin' a bit, Mick.

MICHAEL: Look at th' bottle, man! Demons can hide in th' froth of th' beer a man's dhrinkin'. An' all th' time, my turf-workers an' your lorry drivers are screwin' all they can out of us so that they'll have more to spend on pictures an' in th' dance halls, leavin' us to face th' foe alone.

MAHAN [*abjectly*]: What's a poor, good-livin', virtuous man to do then?

MICHAEL: He must always be thinkin' of th' four last things – hell, heaven, death, an' th' judgement.

MAHAN [*pitifully*]: But that would sthrain a man's nerves, an' make life hardly worth livin'.

MICHAEL: It's plain, Sailor Mahan, you're still hankerin'

afther th' things o' th' world, an' the soft, stimulatin'
touch of th' flesh. You're puttin' th' two of us in peril,
Sailor Mahan.

MAHAN [*protesting*]: You're exaggeratin' now.

MICHAEL: I am not. I seen your eyes followin' that Loreleen when she's about, hurtin' th' tendher muscles of
your eye squintin' down at her legs. You'll have to curb
your conthradictions, for you're puttin' us both in dire
peril, Sailor Mahan. Looka what I've lost already! Me
fine silk hat torn to shreds, so that Lorna's had to tele-
pone th' Firm for another, that I may suitably show
meself when I meet his Brightness, the President; an'
looka th' whiskey there – forced into a misundher-
standin' of itself be some minor demon devisin' a spell
on it! Guess how much good money I surrendhered to
get that bottle, Sailor Mahan?

MAHAN: I've no idea of what whiskey is a gallon now.

MICHAEL [*impatiently*]: What whiskey is a gallon now? Is
there some kinda spell on you, too, Sailor Mahan? You
can't think of whiskey in gallons now; you have to think
of it in terms of sips; an' sips spaced out from each other
like th' holy days of obligation.

MAHAN: An' how are we goin' to get rid of it? We're in
some danger while it's standin' there.

MICHAEL: How th' hell do I know how we'll get rid of it?
We'll have to get Shanaar to deal with it, an', mind you,
don't go too near it.

[*The* PORTER *appears on the sidewalk outside the wall.
He is a middle-aged man with an obstinate face, the chin
hidden by a grizzled beard. He is wearing a pair of old
brown trousers, an older grey coat, and an old blue shirt.
On his head is a big cap, with a long, wide peak jutting
out in front of it. The crown of the cap is a high one, and
around the crown is a wide band of dazzling scarlet. He
is carrying a parcel wrapped in brown paper, either side
of which is a little torn. He looks north, south, west,
and then, turning east, he sees the two men in the garden.*]

PORTER [*to the two men*]: Isn't it handy now that I've
clapped eyes on two human bein's in this god-forsaken

hole! I've been trudghin' about for hours thryin' to find
th' one that'll claim what's in this parcel I'm bearin', an',
maybe, th' two of yous, or maybe, one of yous, can tell
me where I'll find him. I'm on th' thrack of an oul' fella
callin' himself a Councillor an' a Jay Pee.

MICHAEL: What's his name?

PORTER: That's more than I can say, for th' chit of th' girl
in th' shop, who took th' ordher, forgot to write down
th' name, an' then forgot th' name itself when she
started to write it down. All I know is that in this
disthrict I'm seekin' a Mr Councillor So-an'-so; one
havin' Councillor at his head an' Jay Pee at his tail.

MICHAEL [*with importance*]: I'm a Councillor and a Jay
Pee.

PORTER [*with some scorn*]: D'ye tell me that now? [*He
bends over the wall to come closer to Michael.*] Listen, me
good man, me journey's been too long an' too dangerous
for me to glorify any cod-actin'! It would be a quare
place if you were a councillor. You'll have to grow a few
more grey hairs before you can take a rise outa me!

MICHAEL [*indignantly*]: Tell us what you've got there,
fella, an', if it's not for us, be off about your business!

PORTER [*angrily*]: Fella yourself! An' mend your manners,
please! It's hardly th' like of you would be standin' in
need of a silky, shinin' tall-hat.

MICHAEL: If it's a tall-hat, it's for me! I'm Mr Councillor
Marthraun, Jay Pee – ordhered to be sent express by th'
firm of Buckley's.

PORTER [*with a quick conciliatory change*]: That's th' firm.
I guessed you was th' man at once, at once. That man's
a leadher in th' locality, I said, as soon as I clapped me
eye on you. A fine, clever, upstandin' individual, I says
to meself.

MICHAEL [*shortly*]: Hand over th' hat, and you can go.

PORTER: Hould on a minute, sir; wait till I tell you: I'm
sorry, but th' hat's been slightly damaged in thransit.
[*He begins to take the hat from the paper.*]

MICHAEL: Damaged? How th' hell did you damage it?

PORTER: Me, is it? No, not me, sir. [*He stretches over the wall towards them.*] When I was bringin' it here, someone shot a bullet through it, east be west!

MICHAEL: Nonsense, man, who'd be shootin' bullets round here?

PORTER: Who indeed? That's th' mystery. Bullet it was. People told me the Civic Guards were out thryin' to shoot down an evil spirit flyin' th' air in th' shape of a bird.

MICHAEL [*alarmed*]: Th' Cock.

PORTER [*placing the tall-hat on the wall carefully*]: An' seein' how things are, an' th' fright I got, it's welcome a dhrink would be from th' handsome bottle I see paradin' on th' table.

MICHAEL [*in a loud whisper*]: To touch it is to go in danger of your life – th' bottle's bewitched!

PORTER: Th' bottle bewitched? What sort of a place have me poor, wandherin 'feet sthrayed into at all? Before I ventured to come here at all, I should have stayed at home. I'm already as uneasy as th' place itself! [*A shot is heard, and the tall-hat is knocked from the wall on to the road.*] Saints in glory, there's another one!

MAHAN [*excitedly*]: It's your hat, man, th' red band on your hat!

PORTER [*to Michael – speaking rapidly, picking the tall-hat from the road and offering it to Michael*]: Here, take your hat, sir, an' keep it safe, an' I'll be goin'.

MICHAEL [*frightened and angry*]: Take it back; its damaged; take it back, fella!

PORTER [*loudly and with anger*]: Fella yourself! Is it takin' th' risk I'd be of a bullet rushin' through me instead of th' oul' hat? [*He flings it towards the two men.*] Here, take your oul' hat an' th' risk along with it! Do what you want with it; do what you like with it; do what you can with it – I'm off! [*He runs off in the direction he came from, while the two men gaze doubtfully at the hat lying in the garden.*]

MICHAEL [*tremulously*]: The cowards that are in this counthry – leavin' a poor man alone in his dilemma! I'd be afraid to wear it now.

MAHAN: Aw, give yourself a shake, Mick. You're not afraid of a poor tall-hat. An' throw away ten good pounds. [*He goes forward where the hat is, but* MICHAEL *holds him by the arm.*]

MICHAEL [*with warning and appeal*]: No, don't touch it till we see further.

> [*The* SERGEANT *appears on the pathway outside. He has a rifle in his hands; he leans against the wall looking towards the two. He is obviously anxious, and in a state of fear.*]

SERGEANT: Yous didn't see it? It didn't come here, did it?

MICHAEL [*breathless with the tension of fear*]: No, no; not yet. [*With doleful appeal*] Oh, don't be prowlin' round here – you'll only be attractin' it to th' place!

SERGEANT [*ignoring appeal*]: Three times I shot at it; three times th' bullets went right through it; and twice th' thing flew away crowing.

MICHAEL [*excitedly*]: Did you get it th' third time, did you get it then?

SERGEANT: Wait till I tell yous: sthrange things an' unruly are happenin' in this holy land of ours this day! Will I ever forget what happened th' third time I hot it! Never, never. Isn't it a wondher an' a mercy of God that I'm left alive afther th' reverberatin' fright I got!

MICHAEL [*eagerly*]: Well, what happened when you hot it then?

MAHAN [*eagerly*]: When you hot it for th' third time?

SERGEANT: Yous could never guess?

MICHAEL [*impatiently*]: Oh, we know we'd never guess; no one can go guessin' about demonological disturbances.

MAHAN: Tell us, will you, without any more of your sthructural suggestions!

SERGEANT: As sure as I'm standin' here; as sure as sure as this gun is in me left hand [*he is holding it in his right one*]; as sure as we're all poor, identified sinners; when I hot him for th' third time, I seen him changin' into a –

MICHAEL ⎫
         ⎬ [*together*]. What?
MAHAN   ⎭

SERGEANT [*whisperingly*]: What d'ye think?

MAHAN [*explosively*]: Oh, we're not thinkin'; we can't think; we're beyond thinkin'! We're waitin' for you to tell us!

SERGEANT: Th' soul well-nigh left me body when I seen th' unholy novelty happenin': th' thing that couldn't be, yet th' thing that was. If I never prayed before, I prayed then – for hope; for holy considheration in th' quandary; for power to be usual an' spry again when th' thing was gone.

MICHAEL: What thing, what thing, man?

MAHAN [*despairingly*]: Thry to tell us, Sergeant, what you said you said you seen.

SERGEANT: I'm comin' to it; since what I seen was seen by no man never before, it's not easy for a man to describe with evidential accuracy th' consequential thoughts fluttherin' through me amazed mind at what was, an' what couldn't be, demonstrated there, or there, or anywhere else, where mortals congregate in ones or twos or crowds astoundin'.

MICHAEL [*imploringly*]: Looka, Sergeant, we're languishin' for th' information that may keep us from spendin' th' rest of our lives in constant consternation.

SERGEANT: As I was tellin' you, there was th' crimson crest of th' Cock enhancin' th' head liftéd up to give a crow, an' when I riz th' gun to me shouldher, an' let bang, th' whole place went dead dark; a flash of red lightning near blinded me; an' when it got light again, a second afther, there was the demonized Cock changin' himself into a silken glossified tall-hat!

MICHAEL [*horrified*]: A silken tall-hat!

MAHAN: A glossified tall-hat!

MICHAEL [*to Mahan – viciously*]: Now you'll quit undher-estimatin' what th' holy Missioner said last night about th' desperate an' deranging thrickeries of evil things loose an' loungin' among us! Now can you see the significality of things?

MAHAN [*going away as far as he can from the tall-hat lying in the garden*]: Steer clear of it; get as far away from it as we can! Keep well abaft of it!

SERGEANT [*puzzled*]: Keep clear from what?

MAHAN [*pointing to the hat*]: Th' hat, man, th' hat!

SERGEANT [*seeing the hat beside him, and jumping away from it*]: I was near touchin' th' brim of it! Jasus! yous should have warned me!

MICHAEL [*close to the Sergeant – in a whisper*]: Does it look anything like th' thing you shot?

SERGEANT [*laying a shaking hand on Michael's arm*]: It's th' dead spit of what I seen him changin' into durin' th' flash of lightning! I just riz th' gun to me shouldher – like this [*he raises the gun to his shoulder*] to let bang.

    [*The garden is suddenly enveloped in darkness for a few moments. A fierce flash of lightning shoots through the darkness; the hat has disappeared, and where it stood now stands the* COCK. *While the lightning flashes, the* COCK *crows lustily. Then the light as suddenly comes back to the garden, and shows that the Cock and the hat have gone.*

    MICHAEL *and* MAHAN *are seen to be lying on the ground, and the* SERGEANT *is on his knees, as if in prayer.*]

SERGEANT: Holy St Custodius, pathron of th' police, protect me!

MICHAEL [*in a whisper*]: Are you there, Sailor Mahan?

MAHAN [*in a whisper*]: Are you there, Michael Marthraun?

MICHAEL: I'm done for.

MAHAN: We're both done for.

SERGEANT: We're all done for.

MAHAN: Th' smell of th' sulphur an' brimstone's burnin' me.

MICHAEL: Now you'll give up mockin' Shanaar, if it's not too late. You seen how Marion's head was ornamented, an' it'll not be long till Lorna has them too.

SERGEANT [*now sitting down, so that he is to the left of Michael, while* MAHAN *sits to the right of him, so frightened that he must blame someone*]: We'll have to curtail th' gallivantin' of th' women afther th' men. Th' house is their province, as th' clergy's tired tellin' them. They'll have to realize that th' home's their only proper place.

MICHAEL: An' demolish th' minds that babble about books.

SERGEANT [*raising his voice*]: Th' biggest curse of all!

Books no decent mortal should touch, should never even
see th' cover of one!

MICHAEL [*warningly*]: Hush! Don't speak so loud, or th'
lesser boyo'll hear you!

SERGEANT [*startled*]: Lesser boyo? What lesser boyo?

MAHAN [*whispering and pointing*]: Th' boyo in th' bottle
there.

SERGEANT [*noticing it for the first time*]: Why, what's in it?

MICHAEL: Th' best of whiskey was in it till some evil spirit
put a spell on it, desthroyin' its legitimate use.

SERGEANT [*unbelievingly*]: I don't believe it. Nothin' could
translate good dhrink into anything but what it was
made to be. We could do with a dhrink now. [*He
advances cautiously towards the table.*]

MICHAEL [*excitedly*]: Don't meddle with it, man; don't
stimulate him!

[*The* SERGEANT *tiptoes over to the table, stretches his hand
out, and touches the bottle. He immediately lets out a
yelp, and jumps back.*]

SERGEANT: Oh! Be God, it's red-hot!

MAHAN [*angrily*]: You were told not to touch it! You're
addin' to our dangers.

MICHAEL [*shouting*]: Good God, man, couldn't you do what
you're told! Now you've added anger to its imposi-
tional qualities!

SERGEANT [*nursing his hand*]: Aren't we in a nice quandary when an evil thing can insconce itself in a bottle!

MICHAEL: Th' whole place's seethin' with them. You,
Sergeant, watch th' road north; you, Sailor Mahan,
watch it south; an' I'll keep an eye on th' house.

[MAHAN *goes to one end of the wall, the* SERGEANT
*to the other, and both stretch over it to look different ways
along the road. During the next discussion, whenever
they leave where they are, they move cautiously, crouching a little, as if they were afraid to be seen; keeping as
low as possible for security.*] One of us'll have to take
th' risk, an' go for Father Domineer at once. [*He waits
for a few moments, but no one answers.*] Did yous hear
me, or are yous lettin' on to be deaf? I said one of us'll

have to go for Father Domineer. [*There is no reply.*]
Are you listenin' to me be any chance, Sailor Mahan?

MAHAN: I heard you, I heard you.

MICHAEL: An' why don't you go, then?

MAHAN [*coming down towards Michael – crouching low*]:
Nice thing if I met th' Cock barrin' me way? Why don't
you go yourself?

MICHAEL: What about th' possibility of me meetin' him?
I'm more conspicuous in this disthrict than you, an' th'
thing would take immediate recognisance of me.

SERGEANT [*coming down towards them – crouching too*]:
Me an' Sailor Mahan'll go together.

MICHAEL [*indignantly*]: An' leave me to grapple with
mysteriosa Daemones alone? [*He turns his face skywards.*]
Oh, in this disthrict there's not a sign of one willin' to do
unto another what another would do to him!

MAHAN [*fiercely*]: That's a lie: there isn't a one who isn't
eager to do to others what others would do to him!

[*The* BELLMAN, *dressed as a fireman, comes in, and
walks along on the path outside. He has a huge brass
fireman's helmet on his head, and is wearing a red shirt
and blue trousers. He has a bell in his hand which he
rings loudly before he shouts his orders. The three men
cease their discussion, and give him their full attention.*]

BELLMAN [*shouting*]: Into your houses all! Bar th' doors,
shut th' windows! Th' Cock's comin'! In the shape of a
woman! Gallus, Le Coq, an' Kyleloch, th' Cock's
comin' in th' shape of a woman! Into your houses, shut
to th' windows, bar th' doors!

[*He goes out in the opposite direction, shouting his
orders and ringing his bell, leaving the three men
agitated and more frightened than ever.*]

SERGEANT [*frantically*]: Into the house with us all – quick!

MICHAEL [*hindering him – ferociously*]: Not in there, you
fool! Th' house is full o' them. You seen what happened
to the whiskey? If he or she comes, th' thing to do is to
take no notice; if he or she talks, not to answer; and
take no notice of whatever questionable shape it takes.
Sit down, quiet, th' three of us.

[*The three men sit down on the ground –* MICHAEL *to the right, the* SERGEANT *to the left, and* MAHAN *in the centre.*]

MICHAEL [*trembling*]: Now, let th' two of yous pull yourselves together. An' you, Mahan, sing that favourite of yours, quietly, as if we were passing th' time pleasantly. [*As Mahan hesitates*] Go on, man, for God's sake!

MAHAN [*agitated*]: I can't see how I'll do it justice under these conditions. I'll thry. [*He sings, but his voice quavers occasionally*:]
Long time ago when men was men
An' ships not ships that sail'd just to an' fro-o-o,
We hoisted sail an' sail'd, an' then sail'd on an' on
  to Jericho-o-o;
With silks an' spice came back again because we'd
  nowhere else to go.

SERGEANT ⎱
MICHAEL ⎰ [*together*]. Go, go!

MAHAN [*singing*]:
Th' captain says, says he, we'll make
Th' pirates where th' palm trees wave an' grow-o-o,
Haul down their sable flag, an' pray, before we hang
    them all, heave yo-ho-ho;
Then fling their bodies in th' sea to feed th' fishes
    down below!

MICHAEL ⎱
SERGEANT ⎰ [*together*]: Low, low!

[*A golden shaft of light streams in from the left of the road, and, a moment afterwards,* LORELEEN *appears in the midst of it. She stands in the gateway staring at the three men squatted on the ground.*]

LORELEEN [*puzzled*]: What th' hell's wrong here?

MICHAEL [*in a whisper – motioning Mahan to continue*]: Go on, man.

MAHAN [*singing – with more quavers in his voice*]:
An' when we've swabb'd th' blood away,
We'll take their hundhred-ton gunn'd ship in tow-o-o;
Their precious jewels'll go to deck th' breasts of
    women, white as snow-o-o;

So hoist all sail an' make for home through waves
    that lash an' winds that blow!

MICHAEL   }
            } [*together*]: Blow, blow!
SERGEANT }

    [LORELEEN *comes into the garden, and approaches the
    men. The golden light follows her, and partly shines on
    the three singers.*]

LORELEEN [*brightly*]: Singin' is it the three of you are?
Practisin' for the fancy-dress ball tonight, eh? Ye do
well to bring a spray of light, now and again, into a dark
place. The Sergeant's eyes, too, whenever Lorna or me
passes by, are lit with a light that never was on sea or
land. An' th' bould Sailor Mahan is smiling too; only dad
is dour. [*She glances at the bottle on the table.*] The song
is heard, th' wine is seen, only th' women wanting. [*She
runs over to the porchway, and shouts into the house*]
Lorna, Marion, come on down, come out here, an' join
th' enthertainment!

    [LORNA *and* MARION *come trotting out of the house into
    the garden. They are both clad in what would be called
    fancy dress. Lorna is supposed to be a gypsy, and is
    wearing a short black skirt, low-cut green bodice, with a
    gay sash round her waist, sparkling with sequins. Her
    fair arms are bare. Her head is bound with a silver and
    black ornament, similar in shape to that already worn by
    Marion. Her legs are encased in black stockings, and
    dark-red shoes cover her feet. Marion is dressed as a
    Nippy, a gay one. She has on a short, bright-green skirt,
    below which a black petticoat peeps; a low-cut bodice of a
    darker green, and sports a tiny black apron to protect her
    costume. She wears light-brown silk stockings and brown
    shoes. Outside the white bandeau round her head she wears
    the ornament worn before. The two women stare at the
    three men.*]

LORNA [*vexatiously*]: Dhrunk is it? To get in that state
just when we were practisin' a few steps for tonight's
fancy-dress dance! [*She notices the bottle.*] Looka th'
dhrink left out in th' sun an' air to dhry! [*She whips up
the bottle, and places it inside on the floor of the porch.*]

An' even th' Sailor Mahan is moody too! [*She goes over
to the Sergeant, stands behind him, and lays a hand on his
head. She is now in the golden light which shines down on
the Sergeant too.*]
I saw a ship a-sailing, a-sailing on th' sea;
An' among its spicy cargo was a bonny lad for me!
[*The* SERGEANT *rises slowly, as if enchanted, with a fool-
look of devotion on his face, till he stands upright
beside Lorna, glancing at her face, now and again, very
shy and uncertain. While this has been happening,*
LORELEEN *has gone to Sailor Mahan, and now stands
behind him with a hand on his head.*]

LORELEEN [*down to Sailor Mahan*]:
I saw a man come running, come running o'er th' lea,
     sir,
And, lo, he carried silken gowns
That couldn't hide a knee
That he had bought in saucy towns;
An' jewels he'd bought beyond th' bounds
Of Asia's furthest sea.
And all were lovely, all were fine,
An' all were meant for me!
[SAILOR MAHAN *rises, as if enchanted, till he stands up-
right beside Loreleen, slyly looking at her now and again.*]

MARION: Aw, let's be sensible. [*She sees the gun.*] What's
th' gun doin'? Who owns th' gun?

SERGEANT: It's mine. I'm on pathrol lookin' to shoot
down th' demon-bird loose among innocent people.

MARION: Demon-bird loose among innocent people! Yous
must be mad.

SERGEANT [*indignantly*]: We're not mad! It's only that
we were startled when th' darkness came, th' lightning
flashed, an' we saw Mr Marthraun's tall-hat turnin'
itself into th' demon-bird!

LORNA [*mystified*]: Th' darkness came, th' lightning
flashed? A tall-hat changin' into a demon-bird!

MICHAEL [*springing to his feet*]: Ay, an' this isn't th' time
for gay disturbance! So go in, an' sthrip off them gaudy
things, an' bend your mind to silent prayer an' long

fastin'! Fall prostrate before God, admittin' your dire
disthress, an' you may be admitted to a new dispensation!

LORNA [*to Michael*]: Nonsense! Your new tall-hat was
delivered an hour ago, an' is upstairs now, waitin' for
you to put it on. [*To Marion*] Take that gun in, dear,
outa th' way, an' bring down th' tall-hat to show him
he's dhreamin'.

[MARION *takes up the gun, and goes into the house with
it, as* MICHAEL, *in a great rage, shoves Mahan aside to
face Lorna fiercely.*]

MICHAEL [*loudly*]: Who are you, you jade, to set yourself
up against th' inner sight an' outer sight of genuine
Christian men? [*He shouts*] We seen this thing, I tell
you! If you knew what you ought to know, you'd
acknowledge th' thrained tenacity of evil things. Betther
had I left you soakin' in poverty, with your rags coverin'
your thin legs, an' your cheeks hollow from mean feedin'.
Through our bulgin' eyes, didn't we see th' horrification
of me tall-hat turnin' into th' demonized cock? Me tall-
hat, you bitch, me own tall-hat is roamin' round th'
counthry, temptin' souls to desthroy themselves with
dancin' an' desultory pleasures!

MAHAN [*gripping Michael's arm*]: Aw, draw it mild, Mick!

MICHAEL [*flinging off Mahan's hold*]. Go in, an' take them
things, showy with sin, off you, an' dhress decent!
[*He points to Loreleen*] It's you who's brought this blast
from th' undherworld, England, with you! It's easy seen
what you learned while you worked there – a place
where no God is; where pride and lust an' money are the
brightest liveries of life! [*He advances as if to strike her,
but* MAHAN *bars his way.*] You painted slug! [MARION
*comes from the house, carrying a fresh, dignified tall-hat,
noble in its silken glossiness. She offers it to Michael who
jumps away from it.*] No, no, take it away; don't let it
touch me.

[MARION *puts the hat on the table, and the three men stare
at it, as if expecting something to happen.*]

LORNA [*darting into the porch, and returning with the bottle.*

It has gone back to its former colour]. Let's have a dhrink
to give us courage to fight our dangers. Fetch another
glass, Marion.

[MARION *goes in, and returns with a glass.* LORNA *un-
corks the bottle, and takes up a glass to fill it.*]

MICHAEL [*warningly*]: Don't meddle with that dhrink, or
harm may come to us all!

LORNA [*recklessly*]: If I can't wrap myself in th' arms of a
man, I'll wrap myself in a cordial. [*She fills the glass,
then she fills another, and gives it to Loreleen; then she
fills a third, and gives it to Marion.*] Here, Loreleen.
[LORELEEN *takes the glass.*] Here, Marion. [MARION *takes
the glass from her.*]

MAHAN [*doubtfully, and with some fear*]: I wouldn't, Lorna,
I wouldn't dhrink it – there's some kind of a spell on it.

LORNA: Is there, now? I hope to God it's a strong one!
[*Raising her glass*] Th' Cock-a-doodle Dandy!

MARION   } [*raising their glasses – together*]: Th' Cock-
LORELEEN } a-doodle Dandy!

[*The three women empty their glasses together.* LORNA *fills
her glass again, and goes over to the Sergeant.*]

LORNA [*offering the glass to the Sergeant*]: Dhrink, hearty
man, an' praise th' good things life can give. [*As he
hesitates*] Dhrink from th' glass touched by th' lips of a
very fair lady!

SERGEANT [*impulsively*]: Death an' bedamnit, ma'am, it's
a fair lady you are. [*He takes the glass from her.*] I'm not
th' one to be short in salutin' loveliness! [*He drinks, and
a look of delightful animation gradually comes on to his
face.*]

LORELEEN [*who has filled her glass again – going over to
Sailor Mahan, and offering him the drink*]: Here, Sailor
Mahan, man of th' wider waters, an' th' seven seas,
dhrink! [*As he hesitates*] Dhrink from th' glass touched
by th' lips of a very fair lady!

MAHAN [*taking the glass – impulsively*]: Here's a one who
always yelled ahoy to a lovely face an' charmin' figure
whenever they went sailin' by – *salud!* [*He drinks, and
the look of animation gradually comes on to his face too.*]

MARION [*who has filled her glass the second time – going over to Michael and offering him the drink*]: Dark man, let th' light come to you be dhrinkin' from a glass touched be th' red lips of a fair young maiden!

MICHAEL [*who has been watching the others enviously – taking the glass from her*]: Gimme it! I won't be one odd. Yous can't best me! [*He drinks it down greedily. A reckless look steals over his face.*]

[*During the last few moments,* LORNA *has been humming a tune, which has been taken up by an accordion, very softly. Then the* MESSENGER *appears on the pathway outside, and it can be seen that he is the player. He sits sideways on the wall, still playing softly a kind of a dance tune.*]

MICHAEL [*to Marion*]: In our heart of hearts, maid Marion, we care nothin' about th' world of men. Do we now, Sailor Mahan?

MAHAN [*cautiously – though a reckless gleam is appearing in his eyes too*]: We all have to think about th' world o' men at times.

MICHAEL: Not with our hearts, Sailor Mahan; oh, not with our hearts. You're thinkin' now of th' exthra money you want off me, Sailor Mahan. Take it, man, an' welcome! [*Enthusiastically*] An' more! You can have double what you're askin', without a whimper, without a grudge!

MAHAN [*enthusiastically*]: No, damnit, Michael, not a penny from you! We're as good as bein' brothers! Looka th' lilies of th' field, an' ask yourself what th' hell's money!

MICHAEL [*excitedly*]: Dhross, be God! Dhross, an' nothin' else! [*To Marion*] Gimme that hat there!

[*She gives it to him. He puts it on, puts an arm round her waist, and they begin to move with the beat of the music. As* MICHAEL *puts his arm around her waist, the ornament on her head rises into a graceful, curving horn, but he does not notice it.*

At the same time, the SERGEANT, *having put an arm round Lorna, moves in the dance, too. As he does so,*

*the ornament on her head, too, becomes a curving horn,
but he does not notice. Then* MAHAN *goes over stealthily
to* LORELEEN, *who is watching the others, and stabs her
shyly in the ribs with a finger. She turns, smiles, takes
hold of his arm, and puts it round her waist. Then the two
of them join the others in moving round to the beat of the
music, the cock-like crest in Loreleen's hat rising higher
as she begins to move in the dance.*

*After a few moments, the dance quickens, the excite-
ment grows, and the men stamp out the measure of the
music fiercely, while the three women begin to whirl
round them with ardour and abandon. While the excitement is at its height, a loud, long peal of thunder is heard,
and in the midst of it, with a sliding, rushing pace,*
FATHER DOMINEER *appears in the gateway, a green
glow enveloping him as he glares down at the swinging
dancers, and as a loud, lusty crow from the* COCK *rings
out through the garden.*

*The dancers, excepting Loreleen, suddenly stand
stock still, then fall on one knee, facing the priest, their
heads bent in shame and some dismay.* LORELEEN
*dances on for some few moments longer, the music
becoming softer, then she slowly ends her dance to face
forward towards the priest, the* MESSENGER *continuing
to play the tune very softly, very faintly now.*]

FATHER DOMINEER [*down to those in the garden – with
vicious intensity*]: Stop that devil's dance! How often
have yous been warned that th' avowed enemies of Christianity are on th' march everywhere! An' I find yous
dancin'! How often have yous been told that pagan
poison is floodin' th' world, an' that Ireland is dhrinkin'
in generous doses through films, plays, an' books! An'
yet I come here to find yous dancin'! Dancin', an' with
th' Kyleloch, Le Coq, Gallus, th' Cock rampant in th'
disthrict, desthroyin' desire for prayer, desire for work,
an' weakenin' th' authority of th' pastors an' masters of
your souls! Th' empire of Satan's pushin' out its founda-
tions everywhere, an' I find yous dancin', *ubique ululanti
cockalorum ochone, ululo!*

MESSENGER [*through his soft playing of the accordion*]: Th' devil was as often in th' street, an' as intimate in th' home when there was nor film nor play nor book.

FATHER DOMINEER: There was singin' then, an' there's singin' now; there was dancin' then, an' there's dancin' now, leadin' innocent souls to perjure their perfection. [*To Loreleen*] Kneel down, as th' others do, you proud an dartin' cheat, an' beg a pardon!

LORELEEN [*obstinately*]: I seek no pardon for th' dance that's done.

FATHER DOMINEER [*turning away from her*]: Seek for it then when pardon hides away.

MICHAEL: Oh, what have I done! I've bethrayed meself into a sudden misdoin'!

MAHAN: *Mea culpa*, me, too, Father!

FATHER DOMINEER: Oh, Michael Marthraun, an' you, Sailor Mahan, Knights of Columbanus, I come to help yous, an' I catch yous in th' act of prancin' about with shameless women, dhressed to stun th' virtue out of all beholdhers!

MICHAEL: It was them, right enough, Father, helped be th' wine, that done poor me an' poor Sailor Mahan in! I should have remembered that a Columbanian knight told me a brother Columbanian knight told him another brother has said that St Jerome told a brother once that woman was th' gate of hell! An' it's thrue – they stab a man with a knife wreathed with roses!

FATHER DOMINEER: Get up, get up, an' stand away from me; an' let ye never be loungers again in th' fight for good against evil. [*They all rise up humbly, the women to one side, the men to the other, and go back some way, as the Priest comes into the garden.* LORELEEN *strolls defiantly over to the table, and sits sideways upon it. To Mahan*] An' now, Sailor Mahan, a special word for you. On my way here, I passed that man of yours who's livin' in sin with a lost an' wretched woman. He dodged down a lane to give me th' slip. I warned you, if he didn't leave her, to dismiss him – did you do so? [*Mahan is silent.*] I have asked you, Mahan, if you've dismissed him?

MAHAN [*obstinately*]: I see no reason why I should dismiss me best lorry driver.

FATHER DOMINEER [*coldly*]: You don't see a reason? An' who are you to have any need of a reason in a question of this kind? [*Loudly*] I have a reason, an' that's enough for you!

MAHAN [*defensively*]: He's a fine worker, Father, an' th' nation needs such as him.

FATHER DOMINEER [*loudly*]: We're above all nations. Nationality is mystical, maundering nonsense! It's a heresy! I'm the custodian of higher interests. [*Shouting*] Do as you're told – get rid of him!

MICHAEL [*wheedling*]: It's all right, Father – he'll do what your reverence tells him. Sailor Mahan's a thrue Columbanian.

MAHAN [*angrily – to Michael*]: He won't do what his reverence tells him!

[*Down the path outside comes the* LORRY DRIVER, *a man of thirty years of age. He doesn't look a giant, but there is an air of independence and sturdiness about him. He is wearing a leather jacket, a pair of soldier's khaki trousers, and an oily-looking peaked cap. His face is tanned by the weather, and his upper lip is hidden by a well-trimmed moustache. He hesitates for a moment, when he sees Father Domineer; but, stiffening a little, he continues his walk to the gateway, into the garden. He stands a little way from Mahan, looking at him, evidently having something to say to him.*]

FATHER DOMINEER [*sneeringly*]: Ah, the gentleman himself has arrived. [*To the man*] We were just talking of you, my man. I have told Mr Mahan to dismiss you. You know why. You're a scandal to th' whole place; you're a shame to us all. Either leave this woman you're living with, or go to where that sort of thing's permitted. [*Loudly*] You heard me?

LORRY DRIVER [*surlily*]: I heard you.

FATHER DOMINEER [*impatiently*]: Well?

LORRY DRIVER: I come to speak with Mr Mahan, Father.

MAHAN [*quickly*]: Me, Jack! Oh, yes; what's the throuble now?

LORRY DRIVER: Plenty, sir. The turf-workers have left th' bog, an' we've no turf to load. Th' delegate says he sent a telegram to Mr Marthraun, sayin' th' men would leave th' bog, if no answer came within an hour.

MESSENGER: He did, an' I delivered it.

MICHAEL: Damnit, but I forgot about it! The tension here put it out of me mind!

FATHER DOMINEER [*catching the Lorry Driver by an arm*]: Never mind turf or tension now. Are you going to go from here?

LORRY DRIVER [*obstinately*]: I'll go, if Mr Mahan tells me to go.

FATHER DOMINEER [*in a fury*]: Isn't it a wondher God doesn't strike you dead! I tell you to give the wretched woman up, or go, an' that's enough for either Sailor Mahan or you. [*He shakes the Lorry Driver's arm.*] Will you give that wretched woman up; will you send that woman of yours away?

LORRY DRIVER [*resentfully*]: Eh, don't be pullin' th' arm outa me!

FATHER DOMINEER [*his fury growing*]: Did you send that woman away; are you going to do it?

LORRY DRIVER [*shaking his arm free, and stepping back*]: Aw, let go! I didn't an' I won't!

FATHER DOMINEER [*in an ungovernable burst of fury*]: You wretch, would you dare to outface your priest? Get out of me sight! [*He lunges forward, and strikes the Lorry Driver swiftly and savagely on the side of the head. The man falls heavily; lies still for a moment; tries feebly to rise; falls down again, and lies quite still.*]

MAHAN [*frightened*]: He's hurted, Father; you hot him far too hard.

FATHER DOMINEER [*frightened too – with a forced laugh*]: Nonsense! I just touched him. [*He touches the fallen man with his foot.*] Get up, get up – you're not that much hurt.

MAHAN [*bending over the Lorry Driver, and placing a hand*

on his breast]: I'm afraid he's either dyin' or dead, Father!

[*Father Domineer runs over agitatedly to the fallen man, kneels down beside him, and murmurs in his ear. Then he raises his head to face the others.*]

FATHER DOMINEER [*to the others*]: Yous all saw what happened. I just touched him, an' he fell. I'd no intention of hurting him – only to administer a rebuke.

SERGEANT [*consolingly*]: Sure, we know that, Father – it was a pure accident.

FATHER DOMINEER: I murmured an act of contrition into th' poor man's ear.

MESSENGER [*playing very softly*]: It would have been far fitther, Father, if you'd murmured one into your own.

END OF SCENE TWO

Scene Three

It is towards dusk in the garden now. The sun is setting, and the sky shows it. The rich blue of the sky has given place to a rich yellow, slashed with green and purple. The flag-pole stands black against the green and yellow of the sky, and the flag, now, has the same sombre hue.

The big sunflowers against the wall have turned into a solemn black, too; the house has a dark look, save where a falling shaft from the sun turns the window above the porch into a golden eye of light. Far away, in the depths of the sky, the evening star can be faintly seen.

In the distance, for some time, the sounds of drumming, occasionally pierced by the shrill notes of a fife, can be heard.

MAHAN is sitting at the table, busy totting up figures on papers spread out before him, his face knotted into creases of anxiety and doubt.

LORNA and MARION are leaning against the wall, away from the gateway, and near the house. Their gay garments are

*covered with dark hooded cloaks to temper the coolness of the
evening air.*

LORNA: They all seem to be out on th' hunt – police an'
soldiers, with th' bands to give them courage. Th' fools!

MARION: D'ye think they'll get him? Th' place'll lose its
brightness if th' Cock's killed.

LORNA: How can they desthroy a thing they say themselves is not of this world? [*She goes over to Mahan, and
stares at him for a moment.*] It's cooler. The sun's settin'.

MAHAN [*hardly noticing*]: Is it? I didn't notice. I'm busy.
Everything thrust through everything else, since that
damned Cock got loose. Th' drouth now dhryin' everything to dust; the turf-workers refusin' to work, th'
women thinkin' only of dancin' an' dhress. But we'll lay
him low, an' bury him deep enough to forget he ever
came here!

LORNA: Th' men on th' bog work hard; they should get
all you've got to give them.

MAHAN [*resentfully*]: An' why th' hell shouldn't they work
hard? Who'd keep th' fires of th' nation burning, if they
didn't?

LORNA: They work for you, too; an' for Michael. He's
got a pile in th' bank, an' rumour says you've got one
too.

MAHAN [*whining*]: Michael may; I never had, an' I'm
losin' th' little I had since I lost me best lorry dhriver –
blast th' hand that hot him! [*The* COCK *suddenly glides
in, weaving a way between Mahan at the table, and Lorna,
circling the garden, and finally disappearing round the
gable-end of the house; the dance tune softly keeps time
with his movements. Jumping to his feet*] What was that? I
thought I saw him prancin' by me!

LORNA [*startled too*]: What was what?

MAHAN: Th' Cock in his black plumage, yellow legs, an'
crimson crest!

MARION [*who has gone tense*]: You put th' heart across me!
I thought you meant th' poor dead man. [*She turns to
look along the road again.*]

LORNA [*to Mahan*]: There's little use worryin' over figures
till you settle with th' men.

MAHAN [*irritably*]: That's Mick's business, that's Mick's
business!

MARION [*running over to whisper excitedly to Lorna*]: Here
they are – Father Domineer an' Mr Marthraun comin'
along th' road!

MAHAN [*irascibly*]: Aw, what does that Father Domineer
want comin' here when we've so much to think about!
Delayin' things! I want to get away from here before it
gets dark.

LORNA: Didn't you know they're goin' to purge th' poor
house of its evil influences?

MAHAN [*irritably*]: Oh, can't they do first things first?

> [*Along the pathway outside come* FATHER DOMINEER
> *and* MICHAEL, *followed by a lad. The lad is* ONE-EYED
> LARRY. *His face is one alternately showing stupidity or
> cunning, according to whomsoever may be speaking to
> him. Where his left eye was is a black cavity, giving him
> a somewhat sinister look. He is lanky and rather
> awkward-looking. He is wearing a black cassock or
> soutane, piped with red braid, and is bare-headed. He is
> carrying a small bell, a book, and an unlighted candle.
> He shuffles along after the two men, and follows them into
> the garden.*]

FATHER DOMINEER: We'll banish them, never fear,
Michael, before I have to leave th' parish because of that
unhappy accident. I've faced worse. Be staunch. Th' bell
is powerful, so is th' book, an' th' blessed candle, too.
[*He glances at the women.*] Let yous women keep to th'
farther end of th' garden. [*He glances at Mahan.*] We
won't be long, Sailor Mahan. [*Suddenly, as he, Michael,
and One-eyed Larry reach the porch.*] Where's that other
one?

MICHAEL: Is it Loreleen, me daughter, Father?

FATHER DOMINEER: She's no daughter of yours, Michael.
[*Bending down to whisper warningly*] Get rid of her, get
rid of her – she's dangerous!

MICHAEL: How get rid of her, Father?

FATHER DOMINEER: Pack her off to America!

MICHAEL [*respectfully – as they are about to go into the house*]: I'll go first, Father.

FATHER DOMINEER [*setting him gently aside*]: No, no; mine th' gap of danger.

[*The three of them go in, the* PRIEST *first, then* MICHAEL, *and, lastly,* ONE-EYED LARRY. MARION *and* LORNA *move over to the farther side of the garden.*]

LORNA: It's all damn nonsense, though Michael has me nerves in such a way that I'm near ready to believe in anything.

MAHAN: Waste of time, too. It'll take a betther man than Father Domineer to dhrive evil things outa Eire.

MARION: Messenger says he's only addin' to their number, an' soon a noddin' daffodil, when it dies, 'll know its own way to hell. [*The roll of a drum is heard and a great booing. Marion runs to the wall to look over it, and up the road. Excitedly.*] A girl runnin' this way, hell for leather. My God, it's Loreleen!

[*After a few moments,* LORELEEN *runs along the pathway outside and dashes in through the gateway to* LORNA, *who catches her in her arms. Clumps of grass and sods of turf, and a few stones follow Loreleen in her rush along the road.*]

LORELEEN [*out of breath*]: God damn th' dastards of this vile disthrict! They pelted me with whatever they could lay hands on – th' women because they couldn't stand beside me; th' men because there was ne'er a hope of usin' me as they'd like to! Is it any wondher that th' girls are fleein' in their tens of thousands from this bewildhered land? Blast them! I'll still be gay an' good-lookin'. Let them draw me as I am not, an' sketch in a devil where a maiden stands!

LORNA [*soothingly*]: Be calm, child! We can't go in, for Father Domineer's inside puttin' things in ordher. [*Releasing Loreleen*] I'll run along th' road to them disturbers, an' give them a bit o' me mind! [*She catches hold of Marion's arm*] Come on, Marion! [*She and* MARION *rush out along the road, and pass out of sight.*]

LORELEEN [*staring at the house*]: He's inside, is he? That's not where th' evil is, th' gaum, if he wants to know.

MAHAN [*seriously*]: Come here, Loreleen; nearer, for I've something to say to you. [*As she does not stir, he grips her arm, and draws her farther from the house.*] We might be heard.

LORELEEN [*suspiciously*]: What do you want, Sailor Mahan? You're not of one mind with them who chased me?

MAHAN [*a little embarrassed*]: Aw, God, no! Me sails of love are reefed at last, an' I lie quiet, restin' in a lonely harbour now. I'm too old to be flusthered with that kinda folly. I just want to warn you to get outa this disthrict.

LORELEEN [*bitterly*]: Why must I go? Is it because I'm good-lookin' an' gay?

[*But the bold* MAHAN *isn't indifferent to the charms of Loreleen. So he goes on to show Loreleen the youthfulness of his old age; that his muscles are still strong, his fibres flexible. He becomes restless, and walks about, occasionally glancing at the house, nervous at what may be happening inside. When he comes to a chair, he nonchalantly swings a leg over the back of it, turning on the foot of the same leg to swing the other one back again. These actions, like the conversation, though not done in a hurry, are done quickly, as if he wanted to say all he had to say before any interruption.*]

MAHAN [*swinging a leg over a chair*]: Partly because you're good-lookin' an' partly because of th' reckless way you talk. Remember what happened to poor Jack. I'd clear out if I were you. [*He vaults on to the table, swings round it on his backside, and vaults from it on the opposite side, a little stiffly.*]

LORELEEN: How'm I to clear out? I've no money left. Th' forty pounds I had, Dad put into his bank for me, an' now won't give me a penny of it, because he says if I got it, I'd go to England; an' if I went to England, I'd lose me soul, th' shaky, venomous lout! An' I keep quiet because of Lorna. [*Hurriedly, as* MAHAN *is stiffly climbing*

a few feet up the flag-pole] Oh, don't be doin' th' monkey
on a stick! Maybe you could help me? Could you, would
you?

MAHAN [*sliddering from the pole, swinging a leg over a chair,
and coming closer to her*]: Now that's what I'd hoped
you'd say. This is th' first time I've caught you alone. I'll
give you what you need, an' you can weigh anchor, an'
be off outa this damned place. Listen, darlin': you steal
out tonight to th' Red Barn, west of th' Holy Cross, an'
I'll dhrive there with what'll get you as far as you want
to go. [*He suddenly puts an arm round her in a kind of
clutch.*] Jasus, you have lovely eyes!

LORELEEN [*trying to pull his arm away.*]: Oh Sailor Mahan,
don't do that! Let me go – someone may see us!

MAHAN [*recklessly*]: You deserve to be ruffled a bit! Well,
will you come to th' Red Barn, while th' rest are goin'
to th' dance, an' save yourself? Yes or no!

LORELEEN: Maybe, maybe; yes, yes, I'll go. Let go your
clutch!

[*The house shakes; a sound of things moving and
crockery breaking comes from it; several flashes of lightning spear out through the window over the porch; and
the flag-pole wags drunkenly from side to side.*

MARION and LORNA *appear on the pathway outside
the wall, and hurry along into the garden just as*
ONE-EYED LARRY *comes running out of the house, his
face beset with fear. His one eye takes in the picture of
Loreleen breaking away from Mahan.* LORELEEN *turns
aside from One-eyed Larry, while* MAHAN, *embarrassed,
turns to face him.*]

ONE-EYED LARRY [*excitedly*]: It's startin' in earnest!
There's a death-struggle goin' on in there! Poor Father
Domineer's got a bad black eye, an' Micky Marthraun's
coat is torn to tatthers!

LORNA [*hurrying into the garden*]: What's happened, what's
happenin'?

MAHAN [*with dignity – to One-eyed Larry*]: Misther Marthraun in your mouth, me lad.

LORELEEN [*mischievously*]: Let th' lad tell his funny story.

ONE-EYED LARRY [*turning on Loreleen*]: It's funny to you because you're in league with th' evil ones! [*To the others*] One o' Father Domineer's feet is all burned be a touch from one of them, an' one o' Mickey's is frozen stiff be a touch from another. [*To Mahan*] Maybe you'd ha' liked me to have lost me other eye while you were warmin' yourself in that one's arms! [*He points to Loreleen.*]

MAHAN [*furiously*]: You one-eyed gett, if you had two, I'd cyclonize you with a box!

LORELEEN [*unmoved – a little mockingly*]: An' how did th' poor lamb lose his eye?

MAHAN [*indifferently*]: Oh, when he was a kid, he was hammerin' a bottle, an' a flyin' piece cut it out of his head.

ONE-EYED LARRY [*venomously*]: You're a liar, that wasn't th' way! It was th' Demon Cock who done it to me. Only certain eyes can see him, an' I had one that could. He caught me once when I was spyin' on him, put a claw over me left eye, askin' if I could see him then; an' on me sayin' no, put th' claw over th' other one, an' when I said I could see him clear now, says he, that eye sees too well, an' on that, he pushed an' pushed till it was crushed into me head.

LORELEEN [*mockingly*]: What a sad thing to happen!
[*The house shakes worse than before, and seems to lurch over to one side. The flag-pole wags from side to side merrily; there is a rumble of thunder, and blue lightning flashes from the window. All, except LORELEEN, cower together at the far end of the garden. She stands over by the wall, partly framed by the sable sunflowers.*]

MARION [*full of fright*]: Sacred Heart! Th' house'll fall asundher!

LORELEEN [*gleefully*]: Let it! It's th' finest thing that could happen to it!

ONE-EYED LARRY [*trembling violently*]: It's now or never for them an' for us. They're powerful spirits. Knocked th' bell outa me hand, blew out th' candle, an' tore th' book to threads! Thousands of them there are, led be th'

bigger ones – Kissalass, Velvethighs, Reedabuck, Dance-
solong, an' Sameagain. Keep close. Don't run. They
might want help. [*Screeches like those of barn owls are
heard from the house, with the 'too-whit too-whoo' of other
kinds, the cackling of hens, and the loud cawing of crows.
Frantically pushing his way to the back of the others*]
Oooh! Let me get back, get back!

> [*The house shakes again; the flag-pole totters and falls
> flat; blue and red lightning flashes from the window, and
> a great peal of thunder drums through the garden. Then
> all becomes suddenly silent. They all hang on to each
> other, shivering with fear, except* LORELEEN, *who lights
> a cigarette, puts a foot on a chair, leans on its back, looks
> at the house, and smokes away serenely.*]

LORNA [*tremulously*]: Why has th' house gone so silent
suddenly?

ONE-EYED LARRY [*from the rear*]: They've either killed th'
demons, or th' demons has killed them.

MARION: God save us, they must be dead!

LORELEEN [*with quiet mockery*]: Welcome be th' will o'
God.

LORNA [*suddenly – with great agitation*]: Get back, get
back! Run! There's something comin' out!

> [*She,* MARION, *and* ONE-EYED LARRY *race for the gate-
> way, rush on to the sidewalk, and bend down, so that only
> their heads can be seen peeping over the wall.* MAHAN
> shrinks back to the far end of the garden, and* LORELEEN
> remains where she is.
>
> From the house, sideways, through the now lurching
> porch, come* FATHER DOMINEER *and* MICHAEL. *Both
> are limping, Father Domineer on his left foot, Michael
> on his right one. Domineer has a big black eye, his coat is
> awry on his back, and his hair is widely tossed. Michael's
> coat hangs in tatters on him. Father Domineer's face is
> begrimed with the smudges of smoke, and both look tired,
> but elated.*
>
> ONE-EYED LARRY *at once runs out, and takes his
> place reverently behind them, standing with his hands
> folded piously in front of his breast, his eyes bent towards*

the ground. MAHAN *straightens up, and* LORNA *and*
MARION *return to the garden.* LORELEEN *remains as she
was.*]

FATHER DOMINEER [*as he enters with Michael*]: Be assured,
good people, all's well, now. The house is safe for all. The
evil things have been banished from the dwelling. Most of
the myrmidons of Anticlericus, Secularius, an' Odeonius
have been destroyed. The Civic Guard and the soldiers
of Feehanna Fawl will see to the few who escaped. We can
think quietly again of our Irish sweep. Now I must get
to my car to go home, and have a wash an' brush up.
[*To Marion and Lorna*] Off you go into the house, good
women. Th' place, th' proper place, th' only place for th'
woman. Straighten it out, and take pride in doing it.
[*He shoves Marion towards the porch*] Go on, woman,
when you're told! [*To Michael*] You'll have to exert your
authority more as head of the house.

MICHAEL [*asserting it at once – to Lorna*]: You heard what
Father Domineer said. Go on; in you go, an' show yourself a decent, God-fearin' woman.

FATHER DOMINEER [*trying to be gracious – to Lorna*]: Th'
queen of th' household as th' husband is th' king.

[MARION *has gone into the house with a sour-looking
face, and* LORNA *now follows her example, looking anything but charmed.*]

FATHER DOMINEER [*turning to Loreleen*]: And you – aren't
you going in to help?

LORELEEN [*quietly*]: No, thanks; I prefer to stay on in the
garden.

FATHER DOMINEER [*thunderously*]: Then learn to stand on
the earth in a more modest and suitable way, woman!
[*Pointing to ornaments on crest of hat and breast of bodice*]
'An do you mind that th' ornaments ye have on of
brooch an' bangle were invented be th' fallen angels, now
condemned to everlastin' death for worshippin' beauty
that faded before it could be clearly seen? [*Angrily*]
Oh, woman, *de cultus feminarum malifico eradicum!*

MICHAEL: That one's mind is always mustherin' dangerous
thoughts plundered outa evil books!

FATHER DOMINEER [*startled*]: Books? What kinda books? Where are they?

MICHAEL: She has some o' them in th' house this minute.

FATHER DOMINEER [*roaring*]: Bring them out, bring them out! How often have I to warn you against books! Hell's bells tolling people away from th' thruth! Bring them out, *in annem fiat ecclesiam nonsensio*, before th' demoneens we've banished flood back into th' house again!

[MICHAEL *and* ONE-EYED LARRY *jostle together into the porch and into the house to do Father Domineer's bidding.*]

LORELEEN [*taking her leg down from the chair, and striding over to Father Domineer*]: You fool, d'ye know what you're thryin' to do? You're thryin' to keep God from talkin'!

FATHER DOMINEER: You're speakin' blasphemy, woman!

MAHAN: What do people want with books? I don't remember readin' a book in me life.

[MICHAEL *comes back carrying a book, followed by* ONE-EYED LARRY *carrying another.* FATHER DOMINEER *takes the book from Michael, and glances at the title-page.*]

FATHER DOMINEER [*explosively*]: A book about Voltaire! [*To Loreleen*] This book has been banned, woman.

LORELEEN [*innocently*]: Has it now? If so, I must read it over again.

FATHER DOMINEER [*to One-eyed Larry*]: What's th' name of that one?

ONE-EYED LARRY [*squinting at the title*]: Ullisississies, or something.

FATHER DOMINEER: Worse than th' other one. [*He hands his to One-eyed Larry*] Bring th' two o' them down to th' Presbytery, an' we'll desthroy them. [LORELEEN *snatches the two books from One-eyed Larry.* ONE-EYED LARRY *tries to prevent her, but a sharp push from her sends him toppling over.* LORELEEN, *with great speed, darts out of the gateway, runs along the pathway, and disappears. Standing as if stuck to the ground*] Afther her, afther her!

MICHAEL [*astonished*]: Me legs won't move!

MAHAN

ONE-EYED LARRY } [*together*]: Nor mine, neither.

[*As* LORELEEN *disappears, the* COCK *sudddenly springs over the wall, and pirouettes in and out between them as they stand stuck to the ground.*

Cute ears may hear the quick tune, played softly, of an accordion, as the COCK *weaves his way about. The* SERGEANT *appears running outside, stops when he sees the Cock, leans over the wall, and presents a gun at Michael.*]

MICHAEL [*frantically – to Sergeant*]: Not me, man, not me! [*Terribly excited, the Sergeant swings the gun till it is pointing at Mahan.*]

MAHAN [*frantically*]: Eh, not me, man!

[*After the* COCK *has pirouetted round for some moments, while they all remain transfixed, the scene suddenly goes dark, though the music continues to sound through it. Then two squib-like shots are heard, followed by a clash of thunder, and, when the garden enjoys the light of early dusk again, which comes immediately after the clap of thunder, the music as suddenly ceases.*

The returning light shows that FATHER DOMINEER *is not there; that* MICHAEL *and* MAHAN *are stretched out on the ground; and that* ONE-EYED LARRY *is half over the wall, his belly on it, his legs trailing into the garden, his head and shoulders protruding into the road.*]

MICHAEL [*moaning*]: Shot through the soft flesh an' th' hard bone!

MAHAN [*groaning*]: Shot through th' hard bone an' th' soft flesh!

ONE-EYED LARRY [*shouting*]: Mrs Marthraun, Marion, we're all killed be th' Cock an' the' Sergeant!

[LORNA *and* MARION *come running out of the house over to the two prostrate men.*]

LORNA: What's happened? Where's th' Sergeant?

ONE-EYED LARRY [*sliddering over the wall, frantic with fear*]: I seen him runnin' off when he'd shot us all! I'm goin' home, I'm goin' home! Father Domineer's been carried off be th' Demon Cock – I'm off! [*He runs swiftly down the road, and disappears.*]

LORNA [*bending over Michael*]: Where were you hit? D'ye think there's a chance of you dyin'?

MICHAEL [*despairingly*]: I'm riddled!

LORNA [*feeling his body over*]: I can't see a speck of damage on you anywhere, you fool.

MARION [*who has been examining Mahan*]: No, nor on this fella either.

MICHAEL: I tell you th' bullet careered through me breast an' came out be me back!

MAHAN: An' then tore through me back an' came out be me breast!

LORNA: What darkness was One-eyed Larry talkin' about? An' Father Domineer carried off be the Cock! Me nerves are all gettin' shatthered. It's all very thryin'. [*She pokes Michael roughly with her foot.*] Here, get up, th' both of yous. There isn't a thing wrong with either of you.

MAHAN [*sitting up cautiously, and feeling in his breast pocket*]: What th' hell's this? [*He pulls out a bullet bigger than a cigar.*] Looka, Michael Marthraun, th' size of th' bullet that went tearin' through you an' then through me! [*Very devoutly*] Good angels musta gone along with it, healin' all at th' same time that it tore our vitals.

MICHAEL [*as devoutly*]: Some higher an' special power musta been watchin' over us, Sailor Mahan. Sharin' a miracle, now, Sailor, we're more than brothers.

MAHAN [*fervently*]: We are that, now; we are indeed. I'll keep this bullet till th' day I die as a momento of a mementous occasion!

LORNA [*impatiently*]: Get up, get up. An' don't disturb us again while we're practisin' for the fancy-dhress dance tonight in th' hope of winning a spot prize.

MICHAEL [*furiously to her*]: You'll win no spot prize, an' there'll be no dance till that Demon Cock's laid low! [*To Mahan – piously*] Thrue men we are, workin' in a thruly brotherly way for th' good of th' entire community – aren't we, Sailor Mahan? That's what saved us!

MAHAN [*as piously*]: We are that, Michael; we are indeed; especially now that we've settled th' question finally so long disputed between us.

MICHAEL [*suspiciously, a note of sharpness in his voice*]: How settled it?

MAHAN: Be you arrangin' to give me, not only what I was askin', but twice as much.

MICHAEL [*sarcastically*]: Oh, did I now? That was damned good of me! [*Angrily*] No, nor what you were askin' either. D'ye want me to ruin meself to glorify you? An' didn't I hear a certain man promisin', nearly on his oath, he'd give his lorries for next to nothin' to serve th' community?

MAHAN [*shouting*]: When I was undher a spell, fosthered on me here! I'm goin', I'm goin'. I'll argue no more! [*He goes out by the gate and along the raod, pausing as he is about to disappear.*] For th' last time, Michael Marthraun, are you goin' to do th' decent for th' sake of th' nation, an' give me what I'm askin'?

MICHAEL [*with decision – quietly*]: No, Sailor Mahan, I'm not [*He shouts*] I'd see you in hell first!

MAHAN [*as he goes*]: A sweet goodbye to you, an' take a dhrug to keep from stayin' awake o' nights thinkin' of the nation's needs!

LORNA [*persuasively*]: Be reasonable, Michael. You're makin' enough now to be well able to give him all he asks.

MICHAEL [*savagely seizing her arm*]: Listen, you: even though you keep th' accounts for me, it's a law of nature an' a law of God that a wife must be silent about her husband's secrets! D'ye hear me, you costumed slut?

LORNA [*freeing herself with an effort*]: Don't tear th' arm out of me! If you want to embalm yourself in money, you won't get me to do it!

[*The sound of the wind rising is heard now – a long, sudden gust-like sound, causing Michael to do a sudden rush towards the gate, pressing himself back all the time, and gripping the wall when he gets to it. The two women do not notice the wind.*]

MICHAEL: Jasus! that was a sudden blast!

LORNA [*wondering*]: Blast? I felt no blast.

MARION [*shaking her head*]: He's undher a spell again.

> [ONE-EYED LARRY *comes running along the road out-
> side, excited and shouting. He is holding on tensely to the
> waist-band of his trousers.*]

ONE-EYED LARRY [*without the wall*]: A miracle, a miracle!
Father Domineer, outa th' darkness, was snatched from
th' claws of the Demon Cock, an' carried home safe on
th' back of a white duck!

LORNA [*amazed*]: On th' back of a white duck? When will
wondhers cease! They're all goin' mad!

MICHAEL [*clapping his hands*]: Grand news! Was it a wild
duck, now, or merely a domestic one?

ONE-EYED LARRY: Wild or tame, what does it matther? It
carried him cheerily through th' sky, an' deposited him
dacently down on his own doorstep!

MICHAEL [*with deep thought*]: It might well have been one
of me own sensible ducks that done it.

ONE-EYED LARRY [*coming to the gate*]: Wait till I tell yous.
Th' Demon Cock's furious at his escape, an' he's causin'
consthernation. He's raised a fierce wind be th' beat of
his wings, an' it's tossin' cattle on to their backs; whip-
pin' th' guns from th' hands of Civic Guard an' soldier,
so that th' guns go sailin' through th' sky like cranes;
an' th' wind's tearin' at the clothes of th' people. It's
only be hard holdin' that I can keep me own trousers
on!

MICHAEL [*eagerly*]: Th' wind near whipped me on to th'
road a minute ago.

> [*The* BELLMAN *enters on the pathway outside, and meets*
> ONE-EYED LARRY *at the gateway, so that the two of them
> stand there, the one on the left, the other to the right of it.*
>
> *The collar and one arm are all that are left of the Bell-
> man's coat, and his shirt has been blown outside of his
> trousers. He is still wearing the brass hat. His right hand
> is gripping his waist-band, and his left carries the bell
> that he is ringing.*]

BELLMAN [*shouting*]: Get out, get in! Th' Demon Cock's

scourin' th' skies again, mettlesome, menacin', molesti-
fyin' monsther! Fly to your houses, fall upon your knees,
shut th' doors, close th' windows! In a tearin' rage, he's
rippin' th' clouds outa th' sky, because Father Domineer
was snatched away from him, an' carried home, fit an'
well, on th' back of a speckled duck!

ONE-EYED LARRY [*startled into anger*]: You're a liar, it
wasn't a speckled duck! What are you sayin', fella? It
was a pure white duck that carried th' Father home!

BELLMAN [*angrily – to One-eyed Larry*]: Liar yourself, an'
you're wrong! It was a speckled duck that done it;
speckled in black, brown, an' green spots. I seen it with
me own two eyes doin' th' thrick.

ONE-EYED LARRY [*vehemently*]: I seen it with me one eye
in concentration, an' it was a duck white as th' dhriven
snow that brought him to his domiceel.

LORNA: I'd say white's a sensible colour, an' more apter
for th' job.

MICHAEL: I'd say a speckled duck would look more handsome landin' on a doorstep than a white fowl.

MARION [*thoughtfully*]: I wondher, now, could it have been
Mr McGilligan's tame barnacle goose?

MICHAEL [*explosively*]: No, it couldn't have been Mr
McGilligan's tame barnacle goose! Don't be thryin' to
scatther confusion over a miracle happenin' before our
very eyes!

[*The* SERGEANT *comes rushing in along the pathway outside the wall, and runs into the garden through the gateway, roughly shoving the Bellman and One-eyed Larry
out of his way. His cap is gone, a piece of rope is tied
round his chest to keep his coat on; and, when he reaches
the gate, all can see that he wears no trousers, leaving
him in a long shirt over short pants. He is excited, and
his face is almost convulsed with fear and shame.*]

SERGEANT [*shoving One-eyed Larry and Bellman aside*]:
Outa me way, you fools! [*Rushing into the garden – to
Michael*] Give me one of your oul' trousers, Mick, for
th' love o' God! Whipped off me be a blast of th' wind
me own were. When I seen them goin', me entire nature

was galvanized into alarmin' anxiety as to what might
happen next.

MICHAEL: A terrible experience! What's to come of us, at
all?

SERGEANT [*tearfully*]: Why isn't Father Domineer here
to help? He doesn't care a damn now, since he was
carried home, safe an' sound on th' back of a barnacle
goose!

ONE-EYED LARRY [*dumbfounded and angry*]: A barnacle
goose? What are you sayin', man? It was a dazzlin' white
duck that brought him home.

BELLMAN [*to One-eyed Larry*]: I'm tellin' you it was a
specially speckled duck that done it.

SERGEANT [*emphatically*]: It was a goose, I'm sayin'. Th'
Inspector seen it through a field-glass, an' identified it
as a goose, a goose!

LORNA [*amused – laying a hand on Marion's shoulder*]:
Look at him, Marion. All dollied up for th' fancy-dhress
dance!

MARION [*hilariously*]: It's lookin' like th' blue bonnets are
over th' bordher!

MICHAEL [*angrily – to the Sergeant*]: Get into th' house,
man, an' don't be standin' there in that style of half-
naked finality! You'll find some oul' trousers upstairs.
[*Turning on Lorna and Marion as the* SERGEANT *trots
timidly into the house*] You two hussies, have yous no
semblance of sense of things past an' things to come?
Here's a sweet miracle only afther happenin', an' there
yous are, gigglin' an' gloatin' at an aspect in a man that
should send th' two of yous screamin' away! Yous are
as bad as that one possessed, th' people call me daughter.
[*The sound of the wind now rises, swifter, shriller, and
stronger, carrying in it an occasional moan, as in a gale,
and with this stronger wind comes the* MESSENGER
*sauntering along outside the wall, sitting down on it
when he reaches the end farthest from the house. Nothing
in the garden is moved by the wind's whistling violence,
except Michael, the Bellman, and One-eyed Larry (who
have been suddenly hustled into the garden by the wind*).

*These three now grip their waist-bands, and begin to
make sudden movements to and fro, as if dragged by an
invisible force; each of them trying to hold back as the
wind pushes them forward. The* MESSENGER *is coaxing
a soft tune from his accordion; while* MARION *and*
LORNA *are unaffected by the wind, and stand staring at
the men, amused by their antics.*]

MICHAEL [*a little frantic*]: Listen to th' risin' evil of th'
wind! Oh, th' beat of it, oh, th' beat of it! We know
where it comes from – red wind on our backs, black
wind on our breasts, thryin' to blow us to hell!

BELLMAN [*gliding about, pushed by the wind; holding on to
his trousers with one hand, while he rings his bell with the
other one*]: Fly into th' houses, close th' windows, shut
th' doors!

ONE-EYED LARRY [*gliding in opposite direction*]: We can't,
we can't – we go where th' wind blows us!

MESSENGER: What ails yous? I feel only th' brisk breeze
carrying the smell of pinewoods, or th' softer one carryin'
th' scent of th' ripenin' apples.

MICHAEL [*to the women, while he holds fast to his waist-
band*]: Get in, an' sthrip off them coloured deccits,
smellin' of th' sly violet an' th' richer rose, sequestherin'
a lure in every petal! Off with them, I say, an' put on a
cautious grey, or th' stated humbleness of a coal-black
gown! [*The* SERGEANT *comes from the house wearing
Michael's best black Sunday trousers. He comes from the
porch shyly, but the moment he steps into the garden, his
face flashes into a grim look, and he grabs hold of the waist-
band, and glides about as the others do. Michael, seeing the
trousers – with a squeal of indignation*] Me best Sunday
black ones! Couldn't your damned plundherin' paws
pounce on something a little lowlier to wear?

BELLMAN: Get into th' houses, shut to th' doors, close th'
windows!

[FATHER DOMINEER *suddenly appears on the pathway
outside, and stands at the gateway looking into the
garden. A gust of wind, fierce and shrill, that preceded
him, declines in a sad wail, and ceases altogether,*

*leaving a sombre silence behind it. Father Domineer`s
hair is tossed about; he has a wild look in his eyes, and
he carries a walking-stick to help him surmount the
limp from the hurt he got when warring with the evil
spirits.*]

FATHER DOMINEER [*stormily*]: Stop wherė yous are! No
hidin' from the enemy! Back to hell with all bad books,
bad plays, bad pictures, and bad thoughts! Cock o' th'
north, or cock o' th' south, we'll down derry doh down
him yet. Shoulder to shoulder, an' step together against
th' onward rush of paganism! Boldly tread, firm each
foot, erect each head!

ONE-EYED LARRY⎫
MICHAEL   ⎬[*together – very feebly*]: Hurraah!
BELLMAN   ⎪
SERGEANT   ⎭

FATHER DOMINEER: Fixed in front be every glance, forward at th' word advance!

ONE-EYED LARRY⎫
MICHAEL   ⎬[*together – very feebly*]: Advance!
BELLMAN   ⎪
SERGEANT   ⎭

FATHER DOMINEER: We know where we're goin', an' we
know who's goin' with us.

MICHAEL: The minsthrel boy with th' dear harp of his
country, an' Brian O'Lynn.

BELLMAN: Danny Boy an' th' man who sthruck O'Hara.

ONE-EYED LARRY: Not forgettin' Mick McGilligan's
daughter, Maryann!

[*Sounds of fifing and drumming are heard, mingled with
the sound of booing, a little distance away.*]

FATHER DOMINEER [*jubilantly*]: Listen to th' band! We're
closin' in; we're winnin'! [*He puts a hand up to shade his
eyes, and peers forward.*] They've collared one of them!
Aha, a woman again! [*A pause.*] A fine, familiar one
too. [*He shouts*] Lead th' slut here, Shanaar, right here
in front of me! [*He goes through the gateway, and waits
in the garden for things to come.*]

[SHANAAR *appears on the pathway, followed by the two*

ROUGH FELLOWS *dragging Loreleen along. She is in a sad way. Her hair is tumbled about; her clothes are disarranged; her bodice unbuttoned, and her skirt reefed half-way up, showing a slim leg, with the nylon stocking torn. One of the Rough Fellows is carrying her hat with its cock-like crest in his hand. A blood-stained streak stretches from a corner of an eye half-way down a cheek. Her face is very pale, and intense fright is vividly mirrored in it. She is dragged by the arms along the ground by the men, led by Shanaar, to where the Priest is standing. When she is nicely placed before him, she hangs her head, ashamed of her dishevelled state, and of the way she has been pulled before him. Other men and women follow them in, but are checked from crowding the pathway by an order from the Priest. The* MESSENGER *rises from his seat on the wall, and comes near to where the men are holding Loreleen. He has placed the carrying straps of his accordion over his shoulders, and now bears the instrument on his back.* MICHAEL, *the* BELLMAN, *and* ONE-EYED LARRY *stand some way behind the Priest.* MARION *and* LORNA *have started to come to Loreleen's assistance, but have been imperiously waved back by* FATHER DOMINEER, *and have retreated back towards the house, where they stand to stare at what happens.* SHANAAR *stands at the gateway, gloating over the woeful condition of Loreleen.*]

FATHER DOMINEER [*to those following the men dragging in Loreleen*]: Go back; keep back there! Give th' honied harlot plenty of space to show herself off in.

SHANAAR [*down to Father Domineer*]: Tell her off, Father; speak to her in th' name of holy Ireland!

FATHER DOMINEER [*to Sergeant*]: You go, Sergeant, an' keep them from coming too close; [*to Shanaar*] an' you, Shanaar, stand at the opposite end to keep any others from pressing in on us. [*To the men holding Loreleen*] Bring her a little closer. [*The men drag her closer.*]

FATHER DOMINEER: Now, jerk her to her feet. [*The men jerk her upright.*] Well, me painted paramour, you're not looking quite so gay now; your impudent confidence has left you to yourself. Your jest with heaven is over, me lass! [*To the men*] How did you ketch her?

1ST ROUGH FELLOW [*with pride*]: We've been on her tail, Father, for some time. We ketched her in a grand car with a married man; with a married man, Father, an' he thryin' to put an arm round her.

2ND ROUGH FELLOW [*butting in to share the pride of capture*]: So we hauled her outa th' car, and hustled her here to you.

LORNA [*running over to the man nearest to her, and catching his arm*]: Let th' poor lass go, you cowardly lout! I know you: your whole nature's a tuft of villainies! Lust inflames your flimsy eyes whenever a skirt passes you by. If God had given you a tusk, you'd rend asundher every woman of th' disthrict!

FATHER DOMINEER [*angrily – to Lorna*]: Get back to your place, woman! [*Shouting, as she hesitates*] Get back when I tell you!

[LORNA *moves slowly away from Loreleen's side and goes into the house.*]

MARION [*as she follows Lorna into the house*]: Dastard Knights of Columbanus, do noble work, an' do it well!

LORELEEN [*to Father Domineer – appealingly*]: Make them let me go, Father, an' let me get into th' house! It was Sailor Mahan promised me enough to take me away from here that made me go to him. I shouldn't have gone, but I wanted to get away; [*brokenly*] get away, away! Five pounds he gave me, an' they took them off me, with th' last two pounds of me own I had left.

FATHER DOMINEER [*savagely*]: Sailor Mahan's a decent, honest soul, woman! A man fresh for th' faith, full of good works for clergy an' his neighbours. [*He bends down to hiss in her ears*] An' this is th' man, you sinful slut, this is th' man you would pet an' probe into a scarlet sin!

LORELEEN: I only wanted to get away. I wanted to get away from Sailor Mahan as much as I wanted to get away from all here.

FATHER DOMINEER [*to the two Rough Fellows*]: Where's Sailor Mahan?

1ST ROUGH FELLOW: Th' people pelted him back to his home an' proper wife, Father, an' he's there now, in bed, an' sorry for what he thried to do.

LORELEEN [*plaintively*]: Make them give me back th' last few pounds I had.

FATHER DOMINEER [*to the Rough Fellows*]: You shouldn't have handled Sailor Mahan so roughly. Where's the money?

2ND ROUGH FELLOW: We tore it up, Father, thinkin' it wasn't fit to be handled by anyone of decent discernment.

LORELEEN [*emphatically*]: They didn't; they kept it. [*Stifling a scream*] Oh, they're twisting me arms!

FATHER DOMINEER [*cynically*]: Don't be timid of a little twinge of pain, woman, for, afther th' life you've lived, you'll welther in it later. [*To the two Rough Fellows*] Yous should have kept th' money to be given to th' poor.

MESSENGER [*coming over to the Rough Fellow on Loreleen's right – calmly*]: Let that fair arm go, me man, for, if you don't, there's a live arm here'll twist your neck instead. [*With a shout*] Let it go! [*After a nod from the* PRIEST, *the* 1ST ROUGH FELLOW *lets Loreleen's arm go. The* MESSENGER *goes quietly round to the* 2nd *Rough Fellow.*] Let that fair arm go, me man, or another arm may twist your own neck! Let it go! [*The* 2ND ROUGH FELLOW *sullenly does so.*] Now stand a little away, an' give th' girl room to breathe. [*The two* ROUGH FELLOWS *move a little away from Loreleen.*] Thank you. [*To the Priest*] Now, Father, so full of pity an' loving-kindness, jet out your bitther blessin', an' let th' girl go. An' thry to mingle undherstandin' with your pride, so as to ease th' tangle God has suffered to be flung around us all.

FATHER DOMINEER [*fiercely – to the Messenger*]: Keep farther away, you, for th' crowd is angry and their arms are sthrong! We know you – enemy to th' glow of tradition's thruth, enemy to righteous reprobation, whose rowdy livery is but dyed in rust from th' gates of hell! [*To Loreleen*] An' you, you'd hook your unholy reputation to a decent man's life. A man, like Sailor Mahan, diligent in his duty, th' echo of whose last

prayer can ever be heard when another worshipper
enters th' church. You'd sentence him to stand beside
you, you shuttle-cock of sin!

LORELEEN [*roused to indignation*]: Oh, end it, will you!
You fail in honesty when you won't make them give me
back what they robbed from me. When you condemn a
fair face, you sneer at God's good handiwork. You are
layin' your curse, sir, not upon a sin, but on a joy. Take
care a divil doesn't climb up your own cassock into your
own belfry!

FATHER DOMINEER [*furiously*]: You'll dhribble th' black-
ness of sin no longer over our virtuous bordhers! [*He
hisses the words out*] Stipendium peccati mors est! Get
away from here quicker than you came, or it's in your
coffin you'll be – in your coffin, your coffin!

SHANAAR [*from the gateway*]: A merciful sentence, an aysey
one, for a one like her!

LORELEEN [*half defiantly*]: How am I to go where I'd like
to go, when they took all I had off me? How am I to
go for miles with me clothes near rent from me back,
an' frail shoes on me feet?

FATHER DOMINEER [*putting his face closer to hers*]:
Thrudge it; thrudge on your two feet; an' when these
burn an' blister, go on your knees; an' when your knees
are broken an' bruised, go on your belly; crawl in th'
dust, as did th' snake in th' Garden of Eden, for dust is
th' right cushion for th' like of you! [*He raises himself
erect, and commands in a loud voice*] Go now!

[LORELEEN *turns away, goes slowly through the gateway,
and along the road outside. As Loreleen reaches the gate,*
LORNA *runs out of the house. She is wearing a dark-red
cloak, and carries a green one over her arm. She has
a fairly large rucksack strapped on her back.*]

LORNA [*calling as she runs out of the house*]: Loreleen!
[LORELEEN *halts but does not turn her head.*] Loreleen, I
go with you! [LORNA *shoves Father Domineer aside at the
gateway, nearly knocks Shanaar over, and hurries to
Loreleen. Draping the green cloak over Loreleen's shoulders*]
I go with you, love. I've got a sthrong pair of shoes in the

sack you can put on when we're free from th' Priest an'
his rabble. Lift up your heart, lass: we go not towards
an evil, but leave an evil behind us! *[They go out slowly
together.]*

FATHER DOMINEER [*taking the Sergeant by the arm*]: Let
her go quietly to her own. We'll follow some of the way
to prevent anyone from harming her. [*Down to Michael*]
Be of good cheer, Michael; th' demon is conquered – you
can live peaceful an' happy in your own home now.

   [*He goes out with the Sergeant, followed by all who may
   be there, except Michael, the Messenger, and Shanaar.

   The* MESSENGER *goes back to the wall, sits on it sideways, takes the accordion from his back, and begins to
   play, very softly, the air of 'Oh, Woman Gracious'.
   Shanaar leans on the wall from the outside, looking down
   at Michael, who is now seated gloomily on a chair beside
   the table, an elbow resting on it, his head resting on the
   hand.*]

SHANAAR [*down to Michael*]: His reverence never spoke a
thruer word, Mick, than that of you'd have happiness
an' peace now. You were a long time without them, but
you have them now.

MICHAEL [*doubtfully*]: Maybe I have, Shanaar, an', God
knows, I need them. [*He pauses for a moment, thinking*]
I wondher will Lorna come back?

SHANAAR [*emphatically*]: Oh, devil a come back! You
need have no fear o' that, man. An' fortunate you are,
for a woman's always a menace to a man's soul. Woman
is th' passionate path to hell!

MESSENGER [*playing softly on his accordion and singing*]:

> Oh, woman gracious, in golden garments,
> Through life's dark places, all glintin' go;
> Bring man, in search of th' thruth tremendous,
> Th' joy that ev'ry young lad should know.
>
> Then come out, darlin', in reckless raiment,
> We'll dance along through Ireland gay,
> An' clip from life life's rich enjoyments,
> An' never want for a word to say.

[MARION *has come into the porch, and now stands at the door, watching the Messenger. She is covered to her knees by a bright-blue cloak.*]

> Cling close to youth with your arms enthrancin',
> For youth is restless, an' loth to stay;
> So take your share of th' kisses goin',
> Ere sly youth, tirin', can slink away!

[*Marion crosses the garden towards the gate, and is about to go through it when the* MESSENGER *catches her by the arm.*]
Would you leave me here, alone, without a lass to love me?

MARION [*gently removing the hold of his hand on her arm*]: Your voice is dear to me; your arm around me near seals me to you; an' I'd love to have —

MESSENGER [*quickly*]: Your lips on mine!

MARION: But not here, Robin Adair, oh, not here; for a whisper of love in this place bites away some of th' soul! [*She goes out by the gateway, and along the road taken by Lorna and Loreleen. The* MESSENGER *stays where he is, wistful and still. Just before she goes*] Come, if you want to, Robin Adair; stay, if you will.

SHANAAR [*to the Messenger*]: Stay, Messenger. Take a warnin' from a wise oul' man, a very wise oul' one, too. [*He turns his head to look peeringly to the left along the road.*] What's this I see comin'? If it isn't Julia, back from Lourdes, an' she on her stretcher still! I'd best be off, for I've no inclination to thry a chatter with a one who's come back as bad as she was when she went. [*He bends down nearly double, so as not to be seen, and slyly and quietly steals away.*]

[*After a pause,* JULIA *comes in on her stretcher, carried by the two* ROUGH FELLOWS *as before, her father, silent and stony-faced, walking beside her. The stretcher is laid down in the garden just inside the gate. Julia is covered with a rug, black as a winter's sky, and its sombre hue is enlivened only by the chalk-white face of the dying girl. The* MESSENGER *has gone from the gateway, and now stands in a half-to-attention, military way, a little distance from the stretcher, looking down at Julia. JULIA'S FATHER stands, as before, behind her head. MICHAEL sits, unnoticing, elbow on table, his head resting on his hand.*]

JULIA [*in a toneless voice – to no one in particular*]: Lorna, I want Lorna.

MESSENGER [*gently*]: She's gone, Julia.

JULIA: Gone? Gone where?

MESSENGER: To a place where life resembles life more than it does here.

JULIA: She's a long way to go, then. It's th' same everywhere. In Lourdes as here, with all its crowds an' all its candles. I want Loreleen.

MESSENGER: She's gone with Lorna, an' Marion's followed them both.

JULIA: Then there's no voice left to offer even th' taunting comfort of asking if I feel better.

MESSENGER: There's Michael Marthraun there.

JULIA [*after a long look at Michael*]: He, poor man, is dyin' too. No one left, an' th' stir there was when I was goin' – th' Mayor there, with all his accouthered helpers: th' band playin'; Father Domineer spoutin' his blessin'; an' oul' Shanaar busy sayin' somersaultin' prayers; because they all thought I would bring a sweet miracle back. [*She pauses.*] There was no miracle, Robin; she didn't cure me, she didn't cure me, Robin. I've come back, without even a gloamin' thought of hope. [*She pauses again; with a wan smile*] I can see your whole soul wishin' you could cure me. Touch me with your questionable blessin' before I go.

MESSENGER [*very softly*]: Be brave.

JULIA: Nothin' else, Robin Adair?

MESSENGER: Evermore be brave.

JULIA [*after a pause*]: Dad, take me home.

[*The ROUGH FELLOWS take up the stretcher and carry it out, the stony-faced father following in the rear without a word.*]

MICHAEL [*raising his head from his hand to look at the*

Messenger]: Maybe Lorna might come back. Maybe I mightn't have been so down on her fancy dhressin'.

MESSENGER [*tonelessly*]: Maybe she will; maybe you mightn't.

MICHAEL [*tonelessly too*]: It'll be very lonely for me now. All have left me. [*He takes a set of rosary beads from his pocket, and fingers them.*] I've no one left to me but th' Son o' God. [*He notices the* MESSENGER *settling the accordion comfortably on his back, and watches him going to the gate.*] Are you goin' too?

MESSENGER [*shortly*]: Ay.

MICHAEL: Where?

MESSENGER: To a place where life resembles life more than it does here.

MICHAEL [*after a pause*]: What, Messenger, would you advise me to do?

MESSENGER [*turning at the gate to reply*]: Die. There is little else left useful for the likes of you to do. [*He swings his accordion comfortably before him, and plays a few preliminary notes. Then he starts to sing softly as he goes away along the pathway outside; while Michael leans forward on to the table, and buries his head in his arms.*]

MESSENGER [*singing and accompanying himself on the accordion – as he is going off*]:

> She's just like a young star out taking the air –
> Let others be good or be clever –
>
> With Marion gay, a gay flower in her hair,
> Life becomes but a pleasant endeavour.
>
> When building a city or making the hay,
> I'll follow her close as night follows day,
>
> Or lads follow lasses out nutting in May,
> For ever and ever and ever!

THE END

STAR OF THE SEA

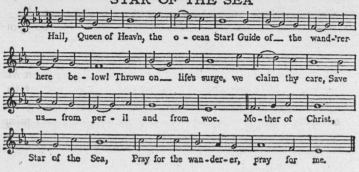

Hail, Queen of Heav'n, the o - cean Star! Guide of — the wand-'rer here be - low! Thrown on — life's surge, we claim thy care, Save us — from per - il and from woe. Mo - ther of Christ, Star of the Sea, Pray for the wan-der- er, pray for me.

WHEN MEN WAS MEN

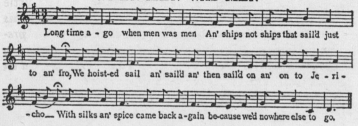

Long time a - go when men was men An' ships not ships that sail'd just to an' fro, We hoist-ed sail an' sail'd an' then sail'd on an' on to Je - ri - -cho — With silks an' spice came back a - gain be-cause we'd nowhere else to go.

LORELEEN'S SHANTY

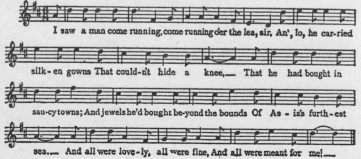

I saw a man come running, come running o'er the lea, sir, An', lo, he car-ried silk-en gowns That could-n't hide a knee, — That he had bought in sau-cy towns; And jewels he'd bought be-yond the bounds Of As - ia's furth-est sea, — And all were love-ly, all were fine, And all were meant for me! —

MUSIC FOR COCK'S DANCE

OH, WOMAN GRACIOUS

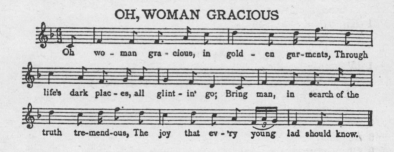

MARION

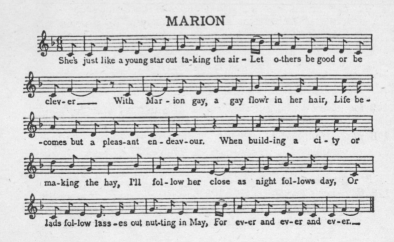

Notes

Scene One

147 *th' fair-haired boy*: the favourite.

150 *Deirdre come to life again*: Deirdre eloped with Naisi to Alba (Scotland), but King Conchubar, who loved her, persuaded them to return to Ulster and had Naisi murdered. Deirdre killed herself and Conchubar's treachery brought doom on his kingdom.

151 *Knights o' Columbanus*: a society of laymen dedicated to good works in honour of the Irish monk and saint, Columbanus (A.D. 543?–615).

151 *th' Rerum Novarum*: an encyclical letter published by Pope Leo XIII in 1891 on the condition of the working classes in which he rejects the idea of state ownership of the means of production.

153 *Shanaar*: in Gaelic 'Shan ahr' means 'old man'.

156 *Gehenna*: hell with a pun on 'hen'.

159 *Oh, rowelum . . . spam*: This is gibberish compounded of Latin words, like Shanaar's later invocations.

165 *Emer would have been jealous of you*: Emer, the beautiful wife of Cuchulain, was jealous of his infidelities with many other women, and particularly of his association with Fand, wife of the sea-god Manaan.

Scene Two

172 *tooral ooral . . . ay*: the refrain of a lullaby sung by Bing Crosby in the film called *The Bells of St Mary's*.

178 *places founded be Finian, Finnbarr*: St Finian (d. 579) established a monastery at Mooville, County Down; St Finbar (d. 633) founded a monastery round which grew the city of Cork.

173 *th' Seven Churches of Glendalough*: Glendalough, 'the valley of two lakes', in County Wicklow, contains the remains of two churches dedicated to St Kevin, Reefert Church,

St Mary's Church, St Kieran's Church, Trinity Church, and the Cathedral of SS Peter and Paul.

173 *Durrow of Offaly, founded be Columkille himself*: Columkille, i.e. St Columba (521?–597), founded a monastery at Durrow in County Offaly.

191 *ubique ululanti cockalorum ochone, ululo!*: dog Latin approximating to 'everywhere crying out "Cockalorum", alas, alas!'

Scene Three

203 *Feehanna Fawl*: i.e. Fianna Fáil, 'soldiers of destiny', the Irish political party founded in 1927 by Eamon de Valera.

203 *de cultus feminarum malifico eradicum*: dog Latin approximating to 'concerning women's dress I will root out evildoers'.

204 *in annem fiat ecclesiam nonsensio*: if this gibberish has any meaning it is 'for a year let the church be nonsense'.

204 *Ullisississies*: evidently James Joyce's novel, *Ulysses* (1922).

212 *the minsthrel boy . . . Mick McGilligan's daughter, Maryann*: these lines are compounded of the mythology of popular songs, including Thomas Moore's minstrel boy and the Danny Boy of the sentimental lyric set to the Londonderry air. Brian O'Lynn figures in some popular ballads as an Irish Casanova; in others as a labourer who always finds excuses for not working. In another ballad, Mick McGilligan's daughter has a face like a Connemara moon, feet like two battleships, and hair on her chest like a man's.

216 *Stipendium peccati mors est!*: 'the wages of sin is death'.